Sheldon Roningen

DEDICATION:

This book is dedicated to the diminishing number of honest but frustrated street reporters in the mainstream media who still have the courage to report the facts as they see them, while always knowing that most of the truth will never reach the public view.

—PAT SHANNAN, 2010

Everything They* Ever Told Me Was a Lie

VOLUME ONE

Everything They*
Ever Told Me Was a Lie

Volume One

ISBN 978-0-9823448-5-9

First U.S. Printing: August 2010

Published by: American Free Press
645 Pennsylvania Avenue SE
#100
Washington, D.C. 20003
1-888-699-6397
www.americanfreepress.net

ORDERING:
    Everything They* Ever Told Me Was a Lie (softcover, 280 pages, $30 plus $3 S&H inside the U.S.) can be ordered from AFP, 645 Pennsylvania Avenue SE, #100, Washington, D.C. 20003. To charge by phone call 1-888-699-NEWS toll free and use Visa, MasterCard, AmEx or Discover. See more books and videos from American Free Press at www.AmericanFreePress.net.

NOTE:
    This book reflects the opinions of the author and does not necessarily reflect the opinion of the publisher on every topic.

Everything They* Ever Told Me Was a Lie

VOLUME ONE

WRITTEN & RESEARCHED BY PAT SHANNAN

ACKNOWLEDGMENTS

No one can compile a work like this without lots of input from lots of people. This one took four years to complete, and during that time at least two of my longtime sources, Eustace Mullins and Ralph René, have passed on to that great "Truth-telling Rally in the Sky" and by now have had their much-maligned information forever confirmed as fact.

My further appreciation goes out to:

Jim Marrs of Texas, who always takes my calls and talks with me as long as I like about his favorite subject in the world—the JFK assassination;

Marty Miller of Mississippi, a retired English teacher with a discerning eye for grammar. She looked at the original draft so long ago that she may have forgotten, but what she will remember forever is the section on the "Moon Hoax" and saying, "You made a believer out of me!" Two other great editors and sticklers for meticulous detail were John Tiffany of West Virginia and John Voss of Colorado.

And one final accolade:

And nobody can throw enough flowers of appreciation toward unflappable and talented Paul Angel of Virginia, who wears so many different hats of wizardry every week as the layout artist and production manager for both AMERICAN FREE PRESS and THE BARNES REVIEW that his daily life is one of constantly spinning plates. Sometimes he "spins these plates" as much as 19 hours in a day. Yet he still managed, somehow, to get this book together for me and AMERICAN FREE PRESS. It will be my pleasure to work with him again soon, as we put together Volume Two.

—PAT SHANNAN, 2010

TABLE OF CONTENTS

The author of this volume, Pat Shannan, has been investigating crime and conspiracy in America for the past 45 years.

EVERYTHING THEY*
EVER TOLD ME WAS A LIE

*Of course, the "everything" part is a slight exaggeration, but not nearly as big as one might be likely to believe. And just who are "they" anyway? The answer often varies, as in "Ya' know, *they* say. . ." yet nobody ever defines who "they" are; but in this report we'll limit it to the *elected politicians* and *bureaucrats* (who are actually *paid* to deceive the citizenry), their parrots in the mainstream news media (yes, even the "conservatives" at the beloved Fox-TV—the likes of which have unbalanced America's collective mind into believing that theirs is the "balanced news") and uninformed parents and teachers, who good-heartedly perform every day out of sheer ignorance and deception.

About 180 years ago, a French nobleman by the name of Alexis de Tocqueville came to America with the sole purpose of investigating the success of this young country and writing a book about it. He spent months traveling throughout the land, visiting with the people and the nation's politicians in Washington, studying the government functions, seeing the farms and the fisheries, and learning America from top to bottom and inside & out as nobody ever had.

When he returned to France and began to write, his book became the immensely popular but misnamed *Democracy in America*[1] and from it came one of the most famous quotes of the 19th century; that being the author's conclusion that *"America is great because America is good; and when America ceases to be good, she will cease to be great."*

Just over a century later Will Durant wrote in *Caesar and Christ*, "A great civilization is not conquered from without until it has destroyed itself within. The essential causes of the Roman decline lay in her people, her morals, her class struggles and failing trade, her bureaucratic despotism, her stifling taxes and consuming wars."

We would add to Mr. Durant's insight , ". . . and constant, repeated lies to the people."

Tocqueville wrote of the Americans, "Americans are so enamored of equality that they would rather be equal in slavery than unequal in freedom."

Failing to heed the warnings, America has ceased to be good.

—PAT SHANNAN
SEPTEMBER 11, 2010

ENDNOTE:
1 The title was deceiving because it implied that de Tocqueville was endorsing democracy when he was actually pointing out its pitfalls, as we will do in the following pages, and declaring its dangers to be as tyrannical as a rule of aristocracy. He analyzed the influence of political parties and the press on the government, the effect of democracy on the social, political and economic life of the American people; and offered some startling predictions about world politics, which history has now borne out.

UNDERMINING TRUTH

A couple of decades ago, there was a popular book on the best seller list entitled *All I Really Need to Know I Learned in Kindergarten*. The information was a helpful reminder to those of all ages—"share everything, play fair, don't hit people"—and the tie-in to adulthood made it a cute and entertaining read. I must confess that the title of that book had some influence on my choice for this one, even if it was in a negative sort of way, with apologies to Robert Fulghum.

Not to fault the author, because he told the truth, but the fact is that it was not very long after kindergarten in my life that somebody or some faction began to apply the brakes to our truths, and everything began to change.

In elementary school we received *The Weekly Reader* every mid-week, a seemingly great little 4- to 6-page publication aimed at our age group with anecdotes about other kids around the country and a little bit of low-level political update. I vividly remember reading almost every week about the importance of the United Nations and our great "democracy."

In high school it was more of the same with larger doses. We had to memorize and recite the Preamble to the Constitution, but it went no further. We never studied a word of the context or the very important Bill of Rights. I was nearly 40 years old before I got around to reading and understanding Article IV, Section 4, which guaranteed the people "a republican form of government." Now just what did *that* mean? I can tell you, I found that answer the same week I found out about the sham of democracy.

Subsequent to this revelation, I found with just a little bit of reading in *The Federalist Papers* an easy understanding of the real value of a constitutional republic, how much the founders *abhorred* a democratic form of government, and how little time they spent even considering molding America into a system of democracy. Founder James Madison put their opinion of democracies into perspective early on, in the 10th essay of the more than 80 essays written which comprise *The Federalist Papers,* when he wrote: "Hence it is that such democracies have ever been spectacles of turbulence and contention; have ever been found incompatible with personal security or the rights of property; and have in general been as short in their lives as they have been violent in their deaths."

The words, "democratic" or "democracy" cannot be found anywhere in any of the founding documents.

So where did my schoolteachers get the idea of telling us about the great "American democracy"?[2]

College was worse. Almost every class on any subject had some socialistic slants. My personal collegiate *coup de grace* came when my Kansas University freshman English Lit teacher, who just happened to be a Brit, "flagged" my paper which was explaining the future folly of forced integration of the races in America. (I wonder how she feels now, in her old age, about what the same folly has done to her mother country of crime-ridden dear ol' England.) The frustration of this violation of my First Amendment right of free speech coupled with my deep-seated wonder of *what the hell am I doing here anyway?* cemented my decision to depart the area of formal academics. Except for intermittent automobile drives past Notre Dame's hallowed football stadium in South Bend and Harvard's ivy walls in Cambridge decades later, I have never returned and have realized more than ever what a waste of time and money the endeavor was in the first place.

As a lifelong truth-seeker, I never returned to the college classroom because much of what I found there was at the very least based upon a lie and sometimes a total fabrication from its outset. The whole education industry is designed not to inspire learning and instill wisdom but to program young men and women to conform to government regulation and conventional "wisdom." (If "Big Brother" said it, it is true.)

DEMOCRACY DEFINED

Democracy prevails when the majority are convinced that evil is good and that all who resist evil shall be ridiculed and punished by a jury *not* of their advertised peers. In other countries, we call democracy "Communism." The Greek roots of "democracy" translate to: "rule by man."

Real estate, income and inheritance taxes fill the first three planks of Karl Marx's *Communist Manifesto*. Resist governments claims on one of these and you can win an all-expense-paid federal vacation *behind bars*, before finding your property confiscated and auctioned away as called for in plank #4.

Plank #5 gave an exclusive monopoly in the creation of money to a few foreign bankers spuriously known as the "Federal Reserve." (Remember we mentioned that Nobel Laureate Paul Samuelson referred to the Fed as an "omnipotent counterfeiter" in his *Economics, Fourth Edition*.) Plank #6 called for the centralization of control of communications and transportation. Have you ever heard of the Federal Communications Commission? How about the Department of Transportation?

ERA, when finally ratified, filled #8's "Equal liability of all to labor" and gave women the same right to avoid the draft that men have. All 10 planks were fully or partly enforced in America by bankers, lawyers, judges, journalists, juries, jerks and fools prior to the sacrifice of 110,000 Americans in Asia under the pretext of "halting the expansion of Communism." Why did they do that? Almost no one knew what they had done, and they were paid with the life blood of Communism which is paper money. Plank #10 gave us free indoctrination in public schools in order to make all of the above easier to sell to future generations.

God forbids democracy (Exodus 23:2) and the Constitution precludes democracy (Art. 4, Sec. 4). In all places, democratic or communistic, the people are controlled with legal tender, credit, fear, lies, illusions, disease and amusements that inhibit serious thinking. Nevertheless, every Bush- or Obama-deceived, Sunday attendee of the "Judeo/Christian" corporations we call churches is programmed to chirp on and on about "our wonderful democracy" and have not a clue about the constitutional republic our founders gave us.

This is a nation of jet-propelled, air-conditioned, beer-swilling, hamburger-eating slaves who are abused, amused, confused, defused, diseased, divided and conquered as well as aborted, indoctrinated, intimidated, regulated, "aluminated" (forgive me for coining that one), alienated, chlorinated, fluoridated, intoxicated, interrogated, incarcerated, hallucinated, vaccinated, "mercuryated" and decimated.

We cannot be independent, self governing and free until all in public office are dependent on being paid with something that workers produce, be it gold, silver, corn, coal or anything of substance. Our now-dead Constitution limited their payment to gold and silver coins, but we must be aware of non-thinking slaves who insist there is not enough gold and silver when in actuality it is the scarcity that makes these an ideal means of payment. Lead coins would work also, as substance with intrinsic worth, but we'd need a wheelbarrow to haul enough of them just to buy groceries.

Where the federal government was contracted (via the U.S. Constitution) to accept limited power for the overall good of both states and people, it has become a monster of gargantuan proportions, claiming authority over virtually every liberty and right known to man. And in the process, it decided it didn't need God, either.

How foolish. No nation in world history has ever been able to get away with turning its back on God Almighty. Mark my words—He will not tolerate this modern Sodom and Gomorrah much longer either.

To restore Constitutional government, we must stop our ridicule and punishment of those who want God's law upheld. (See Exodus 23:1, 2; Deut. 25:13-15.) To file tax returns is to waive your rights that millions bled and died to preserve for us, and all returns are false that report an income of "dollars" if you received no substance measured in dollars. With the 1792 Coinage Act, our founders saw to it that nothing but gold and silver is so measured.

Neither the IRS, nor your congressman, nor your CPA can produce a statute making (most of) us subject to the income tax, and everything they ever told us was a lie. This was proved over and over during the past two decades, yet Americans continue to parade along in the dum-dum line without question. An amusing question that I have always enjoyed asking of those who have succumbed to the government lie of the income tax has been: do you file each year because you want to support the government and "pay your fair share," or because you fear the reprisals if you don't? Even though some are completely honest and supply the only correct answer that would pass a polygraph, it is amusing to watch the squirming reactions and multiple excuses from those who wish to avoid the issue.

So far, we have sketched but a smattering of the prevarications we have been fed by the professional deceivers, but with the expansion of only a few basic deceptions, *everything else that follows* becomes a lie too. This is the world in which we live.

Now it is revealed that not only do we not live in a democracy, which has always been a lie, but rather under a similar word, about which almost no one has ever heard: dulocracy, literally rule by privilege (or license):

> 1. *Black's Law Dictionary* 4th Ed: "dulocracy: A government where servants and slaves have so much license and privilege that they domineer." [". . . have so many privileges that they essentially rule." 8th Ed.]

J.D. Sweeney did some research and informed us of this (mostly unknown) word and definition.

The true intent behind the New Deal legislation of President Franklin Delano Roosevelt was legal destruction of the constitutional freedoms through privilege. One of the best ways to define this to the layman is to point out the so-called "drivers license" that he carries in his wallet.

Everything in these driver licensing laws applies to transportation, be it described in terms of vehicle or motor vehicle, driver, operator, all of which are terms of a commercial nature—that is, being used to describe the public hire of hauling goods or persons from place to place.

However, by changing the terminology of one who is behind the wheel of his conveyance from "traveler" to "driver," and terming the conveyance a "vehicle," the state has circumvented the right to travel and forced the licensing of such travel. It has unlawfully forced private citizens into a status of "commerce" in order to further regulate them.

Sweeney shows what traditions, what precedents, what events forced the Supreme Court of the United States to expand its interpretation of the interstate commerce clause, in an attempt to bring all business activity under the clause's jurisdictional umbrella. The story is one of subterfuge and apostasy. It illustrates how the opportunists in government are working diligently to create a scheme using Congress' exclusive control over interstate commerce, to relieve the citizenry of the federal union of their inherent and constitutionally secured rights.

Sweeney reveals how, during the 1930s, the people themselves, by clearly abandoning their individual responsibilities to God, themselves, their posterity and ancestors, aided in the transformation of this nation from a constitutional republic to a cleverly cloaked socialistic/communistic dulocracy.

What was conceived as a nation of confederated sovereign states united by and under the national Constitution, metamorphosed into a collective endeavor pointed to the management of a large population under principles legally associated with mass peonage—both the labor and persons of the citizenry being converted into little more than commodities or "human" resources, to be consumed and controlled for the purpose of promoting a socialistic concept of utopia founded on a hopelessly insolvent welfare state.

Sweeney clearly explains how virtually all of the statutes passed by Congress since the mid-1930s hinge upon the interstate commerce clause and the "necessary and proper" clause of the federal Constitution. As is evidenced in this work, the citizenry at large have effectively connected themselves with congressionally controlled privileges in exchange for what they perceived as promises of security in their individual lives. Clearly and easily, Sweeney ties up the whole economic and social history of the country and reveals how the Social Security number when introduced in 1936 became a federal license to engage in interstate commerce. He explains how, by the use of the number, the holder is presumed to be a "person" who is engaged in congressionally controlled and regulated interstate business. Volumes II & III will reveal how the Social Security number in 1939 was expanded from a simple license, into a pledge by the citizenry to exchange their future performance as surety for a non-existent federal debt. Through the use of this number the federal government controls and regulates all your activities, "for your own protection."

The understanding of this might lead American citizens to see our greatest single domestic issue since the "Civil War" clearly and without bias, rather than through a hazy mass of accumulated prejudice.

—PAT SHANNAN

ENDNOTE:

1 They were innocent victims of "Bravo Sierra." If you don't comprehend the meaning of this, ask any airplane pilot—private or commercial or military—and he/she will explain such phonetics to you.

MEDIA DECEPTION & 'RACISM'

Lee Oswald did not shoot at—not even once—John F. Kennedy in Dallas, Texas on November 22, 1963. James Earl Ray did not shoot at Martin Luther King on April 4, 1968. And while Sirhan Bishara Sirhan *certainly did attempt to shoot at* Robert F. Kennedy in the early morning hours of June 5, 1968, it is already a long ago proven fact that he *did not* kill Sen. Kennedy and did not wound him even once. Tim McVeigh did not kill 169 people with an ANFO bomb in Oklahoma City, nineteen Saudi terrorists did not fly any planes into the World Trade Center and Pentagon on 9-11, and those three (not just the twin towers, but the 47-story Building 7) skyscrapers did not collapse without pre-wired demolition help. All of these murders were committed by someone other than those we have been led to believe were the actual culprits. If you have never questioned these things before, we know this sounds absurd, challenging your ingrained belief, but if we may have your attention, we can prove it.

On the other hand, if you are an emotional victim of cognitive dissonance (C.D.),[1] your mind has already been involuntarily shut down, you will be unable to receive the information that follows, and you are almost ready to shut the covers of this book. Too bad, because in that case you are doomed to wallow in the same lies that have plagued you all of your life. We're sorry but there was no money-back guarantee offered here, so you could best recover some of your loss by finding some bargain-minded friend—preferably a "conspiracy theorist"[2]—to whom you could sell this book at half-price before reading any further.

Oh! And we've got one more, at least for now; not for you but now for your friend that you "suckered" into buying this: Armstrong and Aldrin never walked on the Moon in 1969. Now that oughta finish off all the doubters for sure.

Good! Now that we are left with only open-minded thinkers capable of operating "outside of the (propaganda) box," we can move on.

In light of the present financial crisis, it's interesting to read what Thomas Jefferson said in 1802:

> I believe that banking institutions are more dangerous to our liberties than standing armies. If the American people ever allow private banks to control the issue of their currency, first by inflation, then by deflation, the banks and corporations that will grow up around the banks will deprive the people of all property until their children wake up homeless on the continent their fathers conquered.

And I believe that more Americans understand and appreciate that in 2010 than ever before.

And of course, because we all suffer from the above-mentioned malady to one degree or another, one's ability to receive and accept the truth is often in direct proportion to the severity of his/her C.D. crippling, which was inflicted over the past 40 years or so by our newspapers in the morning and the TV nightly news in the evenings. They are the real enemies of liberty, and the biggest deceiver of all is the one that conservative-thinking Americans trust the most—Fox News.

You need to know that these "news" sources are not your trusted friend and informer but your adversary and deceiver. They work for the current presidential administration, be it Republican or Democrat. They make a big deal out of liberal vs. conservative, right vs. left, black vs. white, separation of church and state, and how great it is to live in a "free country"; but none of these is nearly as important to them as the displacement of your freedom-protecting constitution with a world government privately referred to as a "New World Order." It is a cloud of deception over your life everyday of the year.

Maybe as it likely did for you, it all began for me with Santa Claus, who brought toys down the chimney (even somehow, bicycles, washing machines and televisions, while his team of flying reindeer waited on the roof), the Easter Bunny, who must have stolen dozens of chicken eggs from some unsuspecting farmer and painted them in a variety of colors before hiding them in the yard and house (we always found a few rotten ones in the fall after the grass had died or under the mattress at the end of summer when it was time to flip it), and the Tooth Fairy, who put a dime under my pillow (when a dime was still good for a coupla' packs of gum or even a Saturday afternoon trip to the Johnny Mack Brown double feature, mind you) in exchange for a used-up and spent baby tooth extracted by an over-zealous bite from an apple.

So, no, we're not going to spend a lot of time on these deceptions, which our parents passed off as a little fun and entertaining diversions from their own drab, postwar lives; never realizing what effects such lies might have on our believing the important things later—such as the birth, life, death and resurrection of Jesus Christ.

Holy Jerusalem! They program us from the earliest childhood to believe elementary chicanery that we are bound to discover to be horse puckey before the age of puberty, then they expect us to believe the wildest one of all—which is the only one we should have paid attention to in the first place—but it's the one that's lost to so many because of a pre-programming that has already been dictated by our battered disbelief, "I ain't gonna' fall for that again!"

PATRIOTISM OR RED, WHITE & BLUE FEVER?

Where do we get our beliefs, anyway? **Answer:** From the people and books we love and respect.

In my day this began at home with the parents, soon to be followed by teachers and preachers (1950s and 1960s). The ones we liked better than the others were the ones to whom we paid more attention and, therefore, were the ones who influenced us the most. Those of us blessed with God-fearing parents also had that biblical filter through which we naturally processed all incoming information.

Consequently, by the time we became teenagers, the temptation of premarital sex was far easier to overcome (especially for the girls) than, say, inhaling that first cigarette or sipping on a singular bottle of beer with the party group. And the fear of committing the sin of fornication (for which one could be forgiven) was probably secondary in most cases to the fear of becoming pregnant (for which one could not—at least not by the local gentry)!

And while this was always the theory in my teenage years—one of those things that everybody *knew* to be true without evidence—it was proved beyond a reasonable doubt with the advent of "the pill" in the early 1960s.

And there can be no doubt today that nothing neutralized the sin of fornication so much as the ability to commit it without fear of reprisal. Television would probably rank second on Satan's list of assets in this department. The network sitcoms talk about "having sex" today as readily as having dessert or whether or not one wishes to "have fries with that"!

I remember the first time I heard the expression "having sex." I was well into my adulthood and thought the term was pretty stupid. I said to myself, *of course we have sex. I have male and she has female. We were born with it.* Soon, though, I did begin to understand that this was a new expression developed by the planners to more easily move the act of sexual intercourse into the everyday conversation of the masses—especially the teenagers—with the more passive expression soon to be readily acceptable in mixed company. For some reason, "sexual intercourse" was not as comfortable as simply "having sex" to insert into casual conversation.

Television can sell us anything and exchange falsehoods for truth. Josef Stalin was ecstatic when he saw it for the first time in the 1940s and realized what a powerful tool of propaganda it could become. And it did. His Marxist predecessor, Karl Marx himself, may have been best remembered for his philosophical quote "Religion is the opiate of the people." Both powerful men knew what truths had to be supplanted with which lies.

The electronic media is the enemy's most powerful tool and freedom's fearful adversary. Television doesn't tell people what to do. It shows them. How long can the young and fertile minds absorb filth without becoming filthy? How many times must humans, professing to be Christians, hear "Oh, my God," from the image box before they begin to repeat it in everyday conversation without ever realizing that with each repetition they are violating God's Third Commandment by using his name "in vain."[3]

Images sell, and images can kill, too. But if viewers see something happening over and over, month after month, if they see the same values approvingly portrayed, they will adopt both behavior and values. Sometimes it takes years, but it works. (How many millions did the Marlboro Man murder over the 50 years of his macho image appearing on horseback with a cigarette dangling from his lips?) To be sure, it works. We put our children in front of the screen from infancy. While stupid people would not watch intelligent television very long, intelligent people *will* watch stupid television for hours on end.

Only the generation that has lived as long as I have has observed the total transformation (or maybe we should say *degradation)* of the everyday language. Today, I hear women—and I don't mean just barflies and street sluts, but "ladies" of supposed class—use gutter language that at one time would have earned me a mouth-washing with soap and later when I was older, a good whuppin', had I dared to utter some of these words around anyone in mixed company. Now, so-called society ladies use four-letter words at the country club luncheons and local bridge clubs that would have repelled them and me in general conversation only a generation ago. The feminist movement's war on conservatism in America has killed chivalry and trained too many women to think and act like men. As a result, many young conservative women do not know anymore what it means to be a lady.

A lady does not tell dirty jokes along with men, and she does not tolerate men telling dirty jokes in her presence. She does not swear, and she is not considered "one of the guys." She is respected instinctively because her demeanor demands it. In spite of new fashion trends, a lady always dresses appropriately, leaving a lot to the imagination. When at a social gathering, a lady does not do things she will regret the next day. Above all, a lady is well-mannered, dignified, gracious and kind.

What has caused this twisting of morals and culture and style?

In a word: television. In a few words, the cable channels and movies, which some moron naively supposed (and proposed and got into policy) could be locked out from innocent ears; and the forced elevation of the ignorant Negro in American society, whose language has always been at this level; and by way of the false hero creation in sports and movies of such inferior-cultured people.

This is not to denigrate the percentage of the decent and upstanding citizens from the African communities around the country, whose children obey the law and attempt to emulate their parents by pursuing an education followed by a respectable and honorable lifestyle. They are no more likely to spend a night in jail than anyone else's children. These people raised themselves higher in society by striving and running away from the sub-culture into which they were born. They are as horrified as any of us by the degenerate "N-words" who desecrate the name "African-American" and populate the true crime shows on television by 9 to 1 over Whites. On the other hand, according to the Pew Research Center (PRC), 72% of all black babies born in 2008 were out of wedlock. For all intents and purposes, the black community is now overwhelmingly a matriarchal society. Is it any wonder that the crime rate is so high among young black males?

Recently, when Obama chastised FOX-TV for not showcasing enough blacks and Hispanics within its programming, one comic said FOX should start showing "America's Most Wanted" twice a week.

These derelicts were ridiculed publicly in 2004 by one of their own who had risen above it—Bill Cosby—but it seems that even he realizes that he is fighting what may be a hopeless cause.

The athletes and screen stars, who earn so much money before they are capable of handling it, so often seem to slide into drugs and immorality and are never able to become responsible citizens. Their financial successes become their lifetime failures when their innate irresponsibility surfaces.

Cosby aimed his vitriolic attack at these "successes" as well as the irresponsible teenagers who were dropping out of school and hanging around the streets—potential criminals waiting for their careers to be launched. Yet even this type of character is sanitized by the TV sitcoms into something special for the youth of America to emulate.

In actuality, these are anti-heroes and are no less deified by a very slanted and unfair news media that covers little of the outrageous violent crime committed by these people against whites, such as in Wichita, Kansas and Knoxville, Tennessee in recent years.[4]

When multiple black kids attack a single white boy on a school bus and beat him into unconsciousness and hospitalize him, the incident goes unnoticed. But when one white man says "nigger" and walks away without striking a blow, it is a prosecutable offense that often sends him to jail.

The disgusting details of all of these repulsive crimes—hate crimes—

indicate an innate hatred for whites,[5] but the national media totally ignore them and who the real racists are. During the beginning days of the Knoxville case, when the bodies were being found and the assailants captured, America learned nothing and instead heard night after night, *ad nauseam*, the boring and repetitive details of where the remains of Anna Nicole Smith, another anti-heroine, might be buried. Predictably, the same was true at trial time, just as it was in Wichita, where five white people—three men and two women, all in their 20s—were attacked in the residence of one, kidnapped, raped, brutalized and murdered. However, one, who is certainly mentally scarred for the rest of her life, survived to identify the killers of her friends.

What America must face is the fact that the Civil Rights Act, put in place for nearly a half century now, and the *forced* integration that followed, has proven to be a dismal failure. And of course it was doomed from the start because it attempted to realign God's natural order of things. The Knoxville and Wichita cases are not isolated incidents. Blacks have been taught to "hate whitey." These crimes are going unreported by the mainstream media (MSM) all over the country. Even the FBI, in a suppressed report, admitted a decade ago that 87% of the crime in America is committed by 13% of the population. Even with the continual failure of the MSM to identify the race of the assailants in the various cases, do most of us of average intelligence have any problem readily figuring out exactly which 13% that is?

FACT: 90% of all inter-racial crime is committed BY blacks AGAINST whites.

FACT: There are 20,000 black-on-white rapes every year in the U.S., but fewer than 100 white-on-black rapes.

FACT: The majority of hate crimes are committed by blacks, in spite of the fact that blacks make up only 12% of the population, and in spite of the great reluctance of authorities to report hate crimes when they are committed by blacks. (That means that blacks commit VASTLY MORE hate crimes in proportion to their numbers than whites.)

FACT: Blacks commit NINE TIMES the crimes of whites. This means that if there were equal numbers of blacks and whites in our population, *nine of every 10 criminals would be black.*

FACT: The average white IQ is 100; the average American black IQ is

85; the average African black IQ is 70 (borderline retarded). There has never been a civilization worthy of the name founded by blacks, and blacks have not even been able to retain the civilizations which have been created for them by whites ("white colonialism").

John "Birdman" Bryant provided the above figures and more in a recent article after pointing out the following:

> Over the time period in which the essay below has been posted, the "anti-racists" and other liberal types who have read it have basically offered two objections (or "objections"): First, they claim that the cited facts are not true; second, they claim these facts constitute "hate"; and third, they claim that the unpleasant facts, particularly those relating to blacks—are not really due to any fault in blacks, but are rather due to the fault of "racist" whites and their "racist" system.
>
> As to the first objection, I can assure you that the facts cited here are truly facts, and that they may be verified by checking the very large collection of articles in the Articles of Others section (accessible from the Home Page). These articles are arranged by subject matter and are carefully titled according to content—conditions which should make it easy to verify any particular fact, usually with several sources.
>
> As to the second objection, I will say just two things: (1) Ask not whether I am a hater; ask only whether I am RIGHT; and (2) There is nothing the matter with hate, provided only that it is directed against hateful things.
>
> As to the third objection, this is not really an objection to the content of the essay, but rather an objection to the obvious conclusions which derive from the cited facts. The thrust of the objection is the claim that blacks' problems are due to "social conditions" (presumably those caused by whites, such as "racism"), and that "if only this, that or some other condition is brought about, then blacks would prove "equal" to whites." But if this claim had any credibility in times past, it has none now; for liberals have been playing the "if only . . ." game for half a century, and blacks are still just as much losers as they ever were—just as criminal, just as low-IQ, just as poor, just as violent, just as unmotivated, and all the rest. In the last 50 years, blacks went from being discriminated AGAINST to being discriminated FOR (affirmative action, set-asides, quotas, etc), and now they are actually WORSE OFF than they were in the 50s: Although some have "made it" by affirmative action or living off white guilt (like Jesse Jackson and Al Sharpton), the special

privileges and deferences granted to blacks have merely served to increase their dependency, their lack of motivation, their drug taking, their crime, and all the other bad things for which they are so well known, including especially their demands for yet MORE special privileges (reparations, anyone?).

If you are like a lot of people, you believe that racism is wrong.

So let me tell you a couple of things I believe will surprise you.

FIRST, the "racists" are RIGHT.

And SECOND, I can PROVE IT IN JUST ONE SENTENCE.

But first, allow me to introduce myself. My name is John "Birdman" Bryant. I am the author of 40 books, a member of the legendary high-IQ society Mensa, have had my works praised by many of the world's most distinguished men including Nobel prizewinners, and am listed in many of the standard biographical references, including *Who's Who in America* and *Who's Who in the World*. I also run a website (the one you are on) which is devoted, among other things, to breaking the embargo on information about race and related matters which the Establishment media have sought to suppress.

I said earlier that I could prove that the "racists" are right in one single sentence. My proof stems from the fact that racial matters are never genuinely debated today, because the only thing you ever see in the major media is the politically-correct "anti-racist" viewpoint. The "other side" is never allowed to make its case, ie, THE "RACIST" SIDE IS SUPPRESSED. And you sure as hell can't have a debate about race if one of the sides is never allowed to speak. So here is the one-sentence proof that the 'racists' are right: *There is no reason to suppress a viewpoint unless it is true*, because a false viewpoint can easily be combated with facts and logic, while truth cannot be combated except by lies which are vulnerable to refutation. Or to put it another way, the "racist" view HAS to be suppressed, because if it weren't, *most people would become "racists"*!

So what is the "racist" view? Very simply, it is one that takes the facts I cite—along with a lot of others—into account.

And now that I perceive that I have hit your pre-programmed "racist" button, this may be a good place for me to defer to another voice of experience—that of Star Parker, a black Los Angeles woman writer who is intelligent enough not to be enamored with a president just because he is (half) black.

Ms. Parker says:

Six years ago I wrote a book called *Uncle Sam's Plantation*. I wrote the book to tell my own story of what I saw living inside the welfare state and my own transformation out of it. I said in that book that indeed there are two Americas—a poor America on socialism and a wealthy America on capitalism.

I talked about government programs like Temporary Assistance for Needy Families (TANF), Job Opportunities and Basic Skills Training (JOBS), Emergency Assistance to Needy Families with Children (EANF), Section 8 Housing and Food Stamps.

A vast sea of perhaps well-intentioned government programs, all initially set into motion in the 1960s by Democrats that were going to lift the nation's poor out of poverty.

A benevolent Uncle Sam welcomed mostly poor black Americans onto the government plantation. Those who accepted the invitation switched mindsets from "How do I take care of myself?" to "What do I have to do to stay on the plantation?"

Instead of solving economic problems, government welfare socialism created monstrous moral and spiritual problems—the kind of problems that are inevitable when individuals turn responsibility for their lives over to others.

The legacy of American socialism is our blighted inner cities, dysfunctional inner city schools, and broken black families. Through God's grace, I found my way out. It was then that I understood what freedom meant and how great this country is.

I had the privilege of working on welfare reform in 1996, which was passed by a Republican-controlled Congress. I thought we were on the road to moving socialism out of our poor black communities and replacing it with wealth-producing American capitalism.

But, incredibly, we are now going in the opposite direction.

Instead of poor America on socialism becoming more like rich America on capitalism, rich America on capitalism is becoming like poor America on socialism.

Uncle Sam has welcomed our banks onto the plantation, and they have said, "Thank you, Suh."

Now, instead of thinking about what creative things need to be done to serve customers, they are thinking about what they have to tell Massah in order to get their cash.

Worse, socialism seems to be the element of our new young president. And maybe even more troubling, our corporate executives seem happy to move onto the plantation.

In an op-ed on the opinion page of the *Washington Post*, Mr. Obama is clear that the goal of his trillion-dollar spending plan is much more than short-term economic stimulus:

"This plan is more than a prescription for short-term spending—it's a strategy for America's long-term growth and opportunity in areas such as renewable energy, healthcare and education."

Perhaps more incredibly, Obama seems to think that government taking over an economy is a new idea. Or that massive growth in government can take place "with unprecedented transparency and accountability."

Yes, sir, we heard it from Jimmy Carter when he created the Department of Energy, the Synfuels Corporation and the Department of Education. Or how about the Economic Opportunity Act of 1964—the War on Poverty—which President Johnson said ". . . does not merely expand old programs or improve what is already being done. It charts a new course. It strikes at the causes, not just the consequences, of poverty."

Trillions of dollars later, black poverty is the same. But black families are not, with triple the incidence of single-parent homes and out-of-wedlock births.

It's not complicated. Americans can accept Barack Obama's invitation to move onto the plantation. Or they can choose personal responsibility and freedom.

Does anyone really need to think about what the choice should be?

It appears that at a very young age Ms. Parker was smart enough to see through this race-baiting, stirred by the news media, recognized the inability of most of her race to desire any more than "something-for-nothing" (even though she was one who did) and is now zeroing in on government and citing blame there for its giveaway programs that motivate no one to achieve anything.

Kathleen Willey's inside report (9-21-09) from the Washington offices of the Cash-for-Clunkers program is illustrative of the accuracy of Parker's premise:

"When I asked if I needed to take any kind of test, the answer was, 'No,'" Willey said. "She told me to report for work the next day at 4:30 p.m. When I asked if I had to pass a background check before I started, she said, 'No.'"

I was the only one dressed for a job interview. Everyone else had on jeans and T-shirts. Most women wore flip-flops. One woman was barefoot. The women were dressed extremely unprofessionally, in jeans and very revealing tops. A lot of them wore T-shirts that barely covered their stomachs. What I noticed most were the foul mouths of everyone around me.

The next day, Willey reported that as many as 300 new employees attended orientation for new positions with Vangent.

She said she knew of only two professional trainers who had been brought in by the Department of Transportation to train everyone—supervisors, managers and employees. The supervisors and managers frequently contradicted one another and talked to the employees as if they were "in the first grade." The recruits were told they would soon receive photo identification badges.

A PAYCHECK TO DO 'ABSOLUTELY NOTHING'

The following day, on Sept. 2, employees waited outside from 4:30 p.m. until 6 p.m. to get into the building.

"Once inside, we waited another 30 minutes to sign in 'so we would get paid,' Willey recalled. "I noted that it was written on the piece of paper that our work day started at 4:30. We then waited in line at the 'badge table' to get our badges. When I got there, I had no badge. I finally got to my desk at about 6:45 p.m., where I sat with nothing to do until 10 p.m."

The employees waited for their user IDs and passwords to access the Car Allowance Rebate System, or CARS. Meanwhile, they were being paid $14.71 an hour "to do absolutely nothing," Willey said.

Willey, a Level 2 reviewer who examined Cash for Clunkers vouchers after they had been checked once by a Level 1 reviewer, said the vouchers were being returned to "irate" dealers as many as seven times.

She said the vouchers are "rife with idiotic mistakes by Level 1 reviewers who are rejecting them for no reason at all, mostly because [the reviewers] are not paying attention."

"I am amazed at the number of vouchers that have been rejected in the last six weeks," Willey said. "Many have been rejected and returned to dealers three to seven times! And for no good reason. What is happening here is that the Level 1 examiners are so inept and lazy that, rather than take the time to closely examine and review these vouchers the way that they should, they just hit the reject or approve button without a second thought. That, of course, slows down the whole process and the dealers aren't getting paid by the Department of Transportation. The dealers are frustrated and irate, and make no bones about it when they return their documents that are correct and don't need to be revised. When their documents are returned for revision, they have no number to call or person to e-mail."

While Ms. Willey is too much of a lady to define these people in the manner that most of us would, can we have any doubt as from which culture the very large majority of these people she describes have come?

During a 37.5-hour work week, Willey reported actually working only 14 hours—but she was paid for more than 37 hours of work.

"Two of those nights, I had no work at all," she said. "On those two evenings, when I left, I complained to two different supervisors, and I got two different responses: 'Milk it, baby!' and, 'Free money!'"

What Kathleen Willey describes here is the corruptive result of two poisons: legal tender and political favoritism (the second of which is provided through the nearly unlimited power of the first). But who can blame the poor and ignorant Negro who is seeking a free ride? He/she has found it. The pay is steadier than house-breaking and street mugging, and the risk of jail is non-existent—at least until he/she becomes too greedy.

If there is "hate" here, then it has to be hate for the system—hate that has forced decent, law-abiding Americans to muddle beneath their abilities, talents and social status, and to sacrifice their daily desires in order to satisfy a government edict that can never be satisfied.

I grieve when I hear the race-stirring lies and remember the wonderful and, yes, even loving relationship we had with some of the Southern Negroes[6] when I was growing up in the 1940s and 50s. My dear "Liza" whipped my butt when I needed it and played second base when we needed her, and we loved her. Contrary to the deceiving literature of today, we didn't ever refer to her as our "nigger" but rather as our "help," our "maid," our "housekeeper" (in which she took pride, incidentally), and a woman so pertinent to the day-to-day operations that she had full control when my parents left town for a weekend. She was the major domo—in total charge and with total respect. Liza was our surrogate Mama on the scene.

Liza cooked for me and my parents and brothers, washed clothes and rode herd. But as I look back, I realize that the love we had for her was "arm's length," and could never be any more. Even the Bible dictated it. We are to remain separated. God's law abhorred homogenization of anything in his world, most of all His races of people.[7] Even as children, we knew this instinctively. Don't these liberal CEOs behind the Sunday corporate pulpits (known as preachers) know anything about God's laws regarding miscegenation? Of course, they do, but their governing corporate charter forbids their speaking out of these and other truths.

But hate between the races at that time? Maybe in Chicago and Detroit. But in the Mississippi Delta such a projection is ridiculous and is just one more example of everything they ever told us about the subject being a lie. The real hate has emerged since the forced integration of the races during recent decades and has been further ignited by the fiction, imagination and inflammatory headlines of various MSM reporters. The real separation and hate is far more magnified today from the black to the white than it ever was from white to black during the days of my youth in the Deep South.

Even when the miniscule[8] Ku Klux Klan reorganized in an attempt to ward off the oncoming Civil Rights Movement, its motivation was not hate for the Negro race but rather hate for the system that was forcing the integration of the races.

In both 1862 and 1962 (and not much has changed since within the heritage), the Southern people were law-abiding, Bible-believing separatists, who had no hate for the Negro race but feared the mingling of the cultures. As it turned out, the South was right. It was not the black skin to be feared but the amalgamation of the African culture. And as it has now evolved, the forced integration of the two races in America has destroyed, to a considerable point, both cultures.

Who really thinks that the blacks *want* to be integrated with the whites? Really? You do? Then take a minute and explain to me the existence and pride the blacks take in the exclusively black *Jet* magazine, the Black Entertainment Television network, the United Negro Fund, Miss Black America and Mr. and Miss Black University of Whatever. If you think birds of a feather do not flock together, just walk into any public high school cafeteria at lunchtime and see who is sitting with whom.

When Martin Luther (birth name—Michael) King told the world that he dreamt of the day when the little black child would be judged not by the color of his skin but the *content of his character,* many people viewed it as fair advice and took him up on it, and quickly found it to reveal the other side of the coin that King had not intended.

And the rejection, from both sides of the contention, has never been the skin color but the accompanying culture. The African descendants are incapable of stretching and growing to the more civilized culture into which they were pushed (and most didn't want to go anyway), and the European descendants certainly take no pleasure in sending their children to the public, government-controlled schools where the whole system is deliberately dumbed-down to meet the lesser abilities of the interlopers.

Now I already hear the uproar of your accusations, so instead of rambling any further, I want to quote the words of that renowned "racist" (add a "sic"—as I am only making fun of Al Sharpton and Jesse Jackson before they can do it to me) Albert Schweitzer, the humanitarian who spent a whole adult lifetime in Africa trying to raise these people to a standard somewhere above "animal" and finally realizing he was dealing with an inferior human. Nobody in the history of the world tried harder for a lifetime before being forced to admit his failure.

Everything they ever told us about these people being "equal" was a lie—and there were two inaccurate sides of this distortion.

If they are "equal," then how come so few white boys can compete with them athletically? Have you noticed over past few decades how many (let's make that *few*) white boys make the USA Olympic sprint relay teams?[9] Have you taken a look at the NBA or the NFL rosters lately? The blacks are not inferior but *superior* athletically. Who won't admit that? And while we are on this subject, let us not fail to notice how few (zero until the last Olympics) Negroes make the swimming team of *any* country. The African nations don't even bother sending a team.

But, as the expert on the subject, Schweitzer said that the African is not equal emotionally, mentally and socially, and never will be. Give a listen to Dr. Schweitzer reflecting upon a whole lifetime of experience:

> I have given my life to alleviate the sufferings of Africa. There is something that all white men who have lived here like I have must learn and know: that these individuals are a sub-race. They have neither the mental or emotional abilities to equate or share equally with

white men in any functions of our civilization. I have given my life to try to bring unto them the advantages which our civilization must offer, but I have become well aware that we must retain this status: white the superior, and they the inferior. For whenever a white man seeks to live among them as their equals, they will destroy and devour him, and they will destroy all his work. And so for any existing relationship or any benefit to this people, let white men, from anywhere in the world, who would come to help Africa, remember that you must maintain this status: you the master and they the inferior, like children whom you would help or teach. Never fraternize with them as equals. Never accept them as your social equals, or they will devour you. They will destroy you.

Try for another 50 years, deluded American, if you think it is idealistic and egalitarian, but you will reach the same dead-end street that Schweitzer did after a lifetime of sincerely trying to better a group of humans that really don't want to be anything more than what they are right now. And by that time we will be a nation of mulattoes, because you were brainwashed into believing that multi-cultures, intermarrying and miscegenation were the route to "peaceful coexistence."

Are you being "destroyed and devoured"? Think not? Have a look at Detroit, Michigan or South Central Los Angeles or Leroy Brown's "South Side of Chicago" or Washington, D.C., or Montgomery or Birmingham, Alabama or Jackson, Mississippi, or Atlanta, Georgia today and see where the black "majority rule" has dragged society down to destructive levels while devouring it with confiscatory taxes.

It is not true that all people are equal and the same. The Constitution asserts that everybody has equal rights, which the founding fathers guaranteed, but these rights have nothing to do with abilities, character, background, breeding, wants and desires. People are all different. Some are born criminals, lacking any sense of responsibility, integrity and self-guidance. This most certainly is true of the non-English-speaking immigrants, many of them illegal, who have nothing in common with the language and culture of the United States.

It is also true of anyone, black or white, who is raised in a home without a rule book, such as the Holy Bible.

Andy Rooney, certainly not one who could ever wear the label of "racist"—even through the distorted eyes of the most prejudiced liberal—wrote a quarter century ago, "We are all warned that prejudice is a bad thing, but it is very hard to separate prejudice from experience. If the same experience produces the same result for you time after time, you get so you know what to expect. You prejudge what the result will be." (This pretty accurately sums up the previous few dozen paragraphs here.)

An anti-hero is a main character in a dramatic or narrative work, characterized by a *lack* of traditional heroic qualities, such as idealism or courage. Webster's further describes an anti-hero as one who "lacks the virtues and estimable traits of a traditional hero." His effect upon his audience is one of deceit. He is a liar.

Can anyone imagine a more accurate description of an anti-hero than the aforementioned cast, along with Paris Hilton, Madonna, Dennis Rodman, O.J. Simpson, Robert Blake, Tiger Woods and so many others in the news today who tend to make almost every "news" paper and TV report appear to be no more than another issue of a supermarket tabloid?

The news media are weavers of opinion, which usually makes the whole conglomerate a weaver of deceit. Consequently, it qualifies as another consummate liar.

We find it interesting that just as the Obama administration and the Democratic-controlled Congress were trying to reinitiate the Fairness Doctrine, the latest Rush Limbaugh media attack took place. (Many would argue that liberals define fairness as removing all access to conservative ideas and ideals from public broadcasting networks.) Stemming from an incident that took place in 2003, the media typewriters began to clatter and the talking heads began to scream "racist" all over again because "Rush Limbaugh is trying to acquire ownership in the National Football League."

Actually, Rush was not trying to get into the NFL. The NFL was inviting him in, which was just a slight detail that everyone left out at the time. Sportswriter Bob Lee, a close personal friend to Limbaugh, told the truth in his column a week later and explained that David Checketts, director of JetBlue Airlines, former boss at New York's Madison Square Garden and longtime professional sports executive, approached Rush on a Palm Beach golf course in June and finagled a lunch meeting with him at his oceanside compound. Checketts currently runs the St. Louis Blues National Hockey League team. He offered Rush a minority investor share in an ownership group he was assembling to buy controlling interest in the St. Louis Rams of the NFL.

When the truth was out, it was learned that the very first question Rush had asked Checketts was, "Do you understand who I am and the firestorm that erupts whenever my name is associated with anything?" "Not a problem," Checketts said. "I already cleared you thoroughly with top executives in the NFL before I came to you." Rush believed him.

"Of all the groups and all the names of the proposed investors only *one* was leaked like bloody raw meat to a mob of slobbering media zombies— yep, El Rushbo," said one sportswriter.

Let me digress here a moment and explain that I am not much of a Rush Limbaugh radio show listener, but not for the same reasons as the liberal, truth-hating socialists. Actually, I don't believe that there exists anyone who can do that particular job as well as he. Rush Limbaugh makes listeners think with logic and common sense.[10] He has shown the media to clearly be the hypocrites they pretend they are not. However, there are a certain few subjects he will not touch or even get near, several of which are covered in this book.

The liberal media writers and reporters like to think of themselves as non-racist, when their very actions prove them to be among the most rabid racists in the world, and this is what Rush proved back in 2003 when be made some very accurate observations about a subject that the MSM viewed as "insensitive" and "racist."

Those who wielded the microphones in the world of sports in 2003 were reporting Limbaugh to be a racist because of on-air comments he made suggesting that the Philadelphia Eagles' black quarterback, Donovan McNabb, was, in his opinion, being given unearned kudos by some members of the media who are using him to create a black quarterback hero. His negative comments were addressed to the media, not the quarterback.

Limbaugh said—very accurately—that some members of the dominant establishment press are too race-conscious. He said some sports reporters wanted a black quarterback to succeed so badly, they were willing to overstate McNabb's achievements.

"If McNabb is playing like a superstar, he deserves all of the positive press he gets. If he is not, and if the media is singing his praises as if he were, then the media is guilty of reverse racism."

Telling this simple truth cost him his short-lived job as a Monday Night Football commentator.

However, the statistical data proved what Limbaugh said was precisely accurate. His comments had nothing to do with racism. His words represented truth. No wonder the MSM had no problem ridiculing it.

Was Rush being a racist? Or, was he merely telling the truth? Here's the mathematical—not opinion-based, but mathematically accurate—answer to that question and what it fairly reported:

The following statistics come from the web site of the Philadelphia Eagles. For those who are not football fans, indulge me for a moment and digest these statistics. Shortly after the explosive media incident, former sportswriter and current political columnist Marilyn Barnewall explored some of the data current at the time and discovered just how accurate Limbaugh had been with his speculation.

She gathered statistics for each quarterback who placed first in each category, and the quarterback who placed 12th in each category. She picked No. 12 because it represented average performance.

According to statistics from the American Football Conference (AFC), the highest rated passing quarterback at the midseason moment was Tommy Maddox of Pittsburgh with 1,304 yards. David Carr of Houston ranked 12th with 880 yards.

National Football Conference (NFC) statistics placed Patrick Ramsey of Washington in the #1 slot with 1,307 passing yards. The 12th ranked quarterback was Marc Bulger of St. Louis with 734 yards. *Donovan McNabb was in 14th place with 664 yards passing.*

"As a passing quarterback, McNabb is below average. The statistics say so," she wrote.

"Donovan McNabb is first in rushing in the NFL. He has rushed 25 times for 174 yards resulting in 7.0 yards per carry. He has fumbled the ball four times while rushing but scored four rushing touchdowns.

"By comparison, Jake Plummer of Denver—with less time on the field for the Bronco game against Pittsburgh—has rushed 18 times for 119 yards (or 6.6 yards per carry). He fumbled twice and scored five rushing touchdowns. When it came to passing touchdowns, the comparison stats were much the same.

"In the AFC, Peyton Manning of Indianapolis is first with nine touchdown passes, and Tommy Maddox of Pittsburgh is 12th with 5 touchdown passes.

"In the NFC, Brett Favre is #1. He has passed for nine touchdowns. Joey Harrington of Detroit is second. He has passed for seven touchdowns. *Donovan McNabb is ranked 18th with one touchdown pass.*

"When it came to AFC overall ranking, a computerized compilation of performance, the quarterback points ranked Tony Banks of Houston No.1 with 104.7 points. Jon Kitna of Cincinnati was ranked 12th with 78.4 points.

"NFC quarterback rankings placed Todd Bouman of the New Orleans Saints first at the time with 126.0 points and Patrick Ramsey 12th with 80.9 points. *Philadelphia Eagles quarterback Donovan McNabb was in 22nd place with 51.3 points.*"

Marilyn informed us, "Looking at McNabb's statistics at the time, if he was praised by the media as an outstanding quarterback, Rush Limbaugh was correct. The media was trying to make a quarterback hero out of a less-than-average quarterback.

"Limbaugh's comments do not appear to be racially motivated—not even racially insensitive. People who are paid to tell the truth about the performance of others are, as long as they tell the truth, not racists. Nor are they responsible for the overly sensitive reactions of others," Barnewell concluded.

If people are going to accuse Rush Limbaugh of something, at least let them be accurate. Limbaugh did not make racist remarks about McNabb. He told the truth, which is never racist. It merely is fact. Of course this is a hard concept for liberals to grasp. It removes their snivel, holier-than-thou rights.

For once, Rush showed the media mouths to clearly be the hypocrites they pretend they are not.

Another deceiving group that has managed to gain a foothold with the MSM is this misnamed Southern Poverty Law Center (SPLC), which, along with the ADL, is responsible for all of the recent "hate speech" aimed at constitutionally concerned American citizens opposed to bankruptcy-by-Communism in America.

In 2007, SPLC identified 888 separate "active hate groups" in the

United States. Despite the (perceived) events of 9-11 and an ongoing threat of additional terror strikes here and abroad, not one of the 888 "active hate groups" identified was Islamic, which was acceptable, since no Arabs had anything to do with 9-11 crime anyway. Detroit, Michigan had more violent killings than Iraq and Afghanistan combined, but none of the (nearly all black) groups responsible for those killings made the list of 888.

According to the SPLC, black on white crime is not "hate." Black on black crime is not "hate." Muslim on Christian crime is not "hate." Only white, capitalist, constitutionist,[11] Christian, pro-freedom, in other words, "right-wing extremists" made the list. According to the SPLC, only white, Christian capitalists opposed to Marxism and attending town hall meetings are guilty of "hate." That's what their report says, and everyone from Obama's DHS and FBI to England's press has bought that report hook, line and sinker.

The talking TV heads resort to the SPLC as their "source" for all kinds of news distortion, most of which, when not creating a false guilt in the minds of those who are better off than the poor blacks, is designed to stir fear and hate between the races.

The SPLC's 2010 list of the 40 new "terrorists" is the most ridiculous of all. Chief deceiver Mark Potok, who certainly must possess a masters degree in public deception from somewhere like the Martin Luther King School of Perverse Prevarication, has come up with a list of Christian, patriotic Americans that most of whom would have been on the side of the Founding Fathers 230 years ago—and would have been labeled for execution on sight by King George III.

With this new list of All-American Patriots being disparaged as "terrorists" by SPLC, Potok has displayed just how desperate he and the other deceivers really are, as they attempt to execute the most American of Americans. However, as he and Obama and his czars et al. grasp at these straws, the illuminating result is that the American people are not quite stupid enough to buy it.

It has been said that lawyers, by nature and training, are the greatest single group of liars in the nation. If this is true of the whole, then I would say from experience that that single part could be pared down even more specifically to prosecutors and judges, who get to lie with impunity and all of whom come from the legal profession today. In any case, as Jay Leno reported with authority, "99 percent of the lawyers give all the others a bad name."

Once we come to the conclusion that the media are intentionally deceiving us, we can apply the principles of problem-reaction-solution. This formula takes a problem by either creating it or allowing it to happen and presenting that to the population. It could be terrorism, molestation, extraterrestrials. These topics create fear, and no one in his right mind would support terrorism or crime. Therefore, it is fine to blast over the television, the papers and radio "the problem" that must be addressed. The natural reaction from the people is a request for more control to ensure more safety. Most will let their fear and emotional sides control their decisions and usually translate it into something like "The government needs more power over our lives to make us safer and freer from tyranny. I believe what the media tells me, so I will support whatever decisions they make."

Did these people never read *The Protocols of the Learned Elders of Zion?* What's happening today is all there, written a century ago.

Today's corporate MSM corporate program discourages dissent of the war and paints activists with the hint of treason. At the same time, the so-called journalists are cogs in a much larger machine who know that if they report a story that paints the government in a dark light, their story is likely to remain off the front page and maybe not even be published at all.

The end of the world as we know it is being sold to us, and we are buying it because of the power of the MSM. Local and network news are designing their editorials about despair and fear because the owners, producers and editors now understand that fear sells. The masters of modern spin understand that we like to be terrified. Just look at the success in the action/suspense/terror genres that have been plopped onto the conveyor belt and packaged for our zombie consumption.

When the editors in charge found out that simply plastering a terror alert chart didn't scare the people the same way it used to, they began to kick up the campaign of terror a few notches with new and creative ways to sell the police state.

When we get to the other side of the terror alerts of all shapes and sizes, we find another nightmare masquerading as the savior. The "Ministry of Truth" will protect us. The mother government is here to rescue us and squash this brown terrorist bug, this swine flu and every other nightmare that the nightly news brought us.

The finest public relations specialists take the science of worshiping our kings down to a frame by frame level. Barack Obama (aka Barry Soetoro) is pictured in numerous poses with a halo around his head. In other news shots, he stands tall with dozens of American flags blowing in the wind behind him. A more blasphemous display features him speaking in front of the cross of Jesus Christ. The message sent couldn't be more clearly presented: our current leaders are of the messiah status and only through them will we reach the gates of safety. The lie that has been accepted by so many as truth is that this is a religious war. If the American people accept the fact that the crusades are here, that first George Bush and now B.H. Obama report directly to God, and that the end times are here, then the enemy has won the war for our minds.

ENDNOTES:

[1] Psychologists use the term "cognitive dissonance" to apply to the inability of one to accept the viability of evidence beyond that of which he/she has been pre-programmed to believe, regardless of how convincing that evidence might be. For instance, even after Magellan circumnavigated the world, the notion that the Earth was flat prevailed amongst the majority of the world's populace for decades following.

[2] It is only the "coincidence theorists" at the mainstream media who cannot recognize conspiracy facts and who then must falsely label them as "theory."

[3] One need not say "God damn" to be guilty of this Biblical offense. The word "vain" means "uselessly." Now apply this to "Omigod" and ask yourself if there is really any difference. The enemies of truth have developed many other subtle and surreptitious ways of causing us to incriminate ourselves under our own worshipful laws without even our even knowing it. To further strengthen this premise, I have just learned from inadvertent research that the "F-word" was used 246 times in the gangster movie *Good Fellas*. How could such a multiple insertion in dialog not turn such a formerly vile expression into common and everyday usage, when the near-same is true of most of the other productions as well? Didn't our teachers teach that repetition is the best teacher?

[4] See *The Wichita Horror* by Denise Noe. In Knoxville in early 2007, Christopher Newsome and girlfriend Channon Christian were carjacked by a group of five Negroes, one a woman, then kidnapped, brutalized, raped, mutilated, murdered and burned. See: http://thugreport.com/

[5] Not surprising. The government schools have programmed these people for the past two generations to believe the lie that "Whitey" enslaved and mistreated their ancestors. Falling for the distorted history, most Whites have bought into the lie, too, and are on a guilt trip. See: http://thugreport.com/

[6] To call one "black" was a slight and "African" a total insult.

[7] Many Bible scholars today believe, define and refer to "adultery" not only as a breach of marriage but as an adulteration of the blood through the miscegenation of races.

[8] More crimes and racial incidents in the decade of the 1960s were instigated by FBI informants who had infiltrated the Klan than by organized planning of the Klan itself. It was a way to gain national sympathy for the black people, and it worked. See *War at Home* by Brian Glick; also Google for "COINTELPRO."

[9] I'm an old track man from the 1960s. While I was not nearly good enough to make the Olympic team in 1964, I had several old "runnin' buddies" who were, so I went to Tokyo on the chartered AAU flight and hung around the Olympic Village with them most every day. That year the 400 meter relay team was made up of one white and three blacks and set the world record at 39 seconds flat, thanks to (black) Bob Hayes, a man a generation ahead of his colleagues who always ran as fast as he had to and brought the U.S. team from 8th place to first with the fastest final 100 meter leg ever. He was unofficially timed, as reported in the AAU's monthly magazine, at 8.6 seconds (that is no misprint—eight point six). White men and women seldom, if ever, can even make the hundred meter final or the sprint relay teams anymore.

[10] Limbaugh lost me way back in the mid-'90s when I deduced him to be a mere cheerleader for the Republican Party, pretending that Bob Dole and George Bush, Sr. would have made any difference at the time. When he began to toot the same horn in 2001 for George Jr., while ignoring the "inside job" aspect of 9-11 and its cover-up, the non-existent weapons of mass destruction in Iraq, and later the stolen election of 2004 etc, it became obvious that Rush was also the very best tool for the enemy to use as "controlled opposition." As they continue to be deceived into believing that FOX News is different and embrace Glenn Beck as their new darling of conservatism, the very large majority of naïve Americans will never understand how effective this weapon can be in the war for their minds.

[11] Contrary to popular belief, this is the correct term for one who believes in and adheres to the U.S. Constitution. The popular but absurd term of "constitutionalist" could only define one who believes in a constitutional, which your grandpa referred to as a "good ol' country crap."

*"We hang the petty thieves
and appoint the great ones
to public office."*

—AESOP

"Give me control of a nation's money and I care not who makes her laws."

—MEYER AMSCHEL ROTHSCHILD

THE FORGOTTEN HISTORY OF MONEY

Liars are rampant in our lives, and I say that it wasn't always that way in my life and that it all started with the destruction of lawful money. Now since most of the reading audience doesn't have a clue about this, following a lifetime of delusion carried on by both the government schools and the news media, we shall go back to the beginning of this claim, which explains how "Big Government" became big and the root of the problem. ("Ya' know, Vern, that's pretty bad when a nation's people have become so deceived that they don't even know what hit 'em.")

We all know we've been done in, but I am certain that almost *everyone* who reads this book does not know the root of how it happened—its enablers—so we'll cover that first.

POLITICIANS AND OTHER DECEIVERS . . .

For years we have referred to it as "hiding in plain sight."

Yet it was the greatest financial heist in the history of the world! How can this be? How were the American people so blinded?

> I am a most unhappy man. I have unwittingly ruined my country. A great industrial nation is controlled by its system of credit. Our system of credit is concentrated. The growth of the nation, therefore, and all our activities are in the hands of a few men. We have come to be one of the worst ruled, one of the most completely controlled and dominated governments in the world—no longer a government of free opinion, no longer a government by

> conviction and vote of the majority, but a government by the opinion and duress of small groups of dominant men.
> —Woodrow Wilson, 28th U.S. president, regretting his decision to assist in the creation of the Federal Reserve System

In 1975, renowned Harvard economics professor John Kenneth Galbraith wrote *MONEY: Whence It Came, Where It Went.* In it he uttered the statement, *"The study of money, above all other fields in economics, is one in which complexity is used to disguise truth or to evade truth, not to reveal it. The process by which banks create money is so simple the mind is repelled."*

Galbraith's revealing statement that complexity is used by modern economics to confuse the truth about money is a fact. Simply put, bankers replaced money with credit and debt in order to profit by the indebting of others. It's why bankers are now so rich. It is also why others are now so poor.

Understanding money is not rocket science. Modern currencies are a fraud, a fraud that has escaped detection much as did Bernard Madoff's ponzi-scheme. Madoff's scheme was based on the fraud that investors' money was, in fact, invested. The fraud of modern economics, however, is that "money" isn't actually money—and "they" don't want you to know it isn't.

The last sentence you just read is the defining moment of this whole segment. It seems to me that the generation born since 1970 has been brainwashed into dealing with gold and silver as a "commodity," because they never knew that gold and silver not only performed "as money," but actually was the money.

When the Colonists broke away from England and began to form a confederation in the 1780s, one of the first problems to be faced and solved was that of the hyper-inflating currencies of the various colonies. Each had its own, and none was backed by anything of value—thereby rendering it less and less valuable each week or so by the constant printing of more.

How was the perpetuating dilemma solved? With something which was to become known as "lawful money." Connecticut founder Roger Sherman inserted the powerful 17 words within Article I, Section 10: *No state shall make any **thing** except gold and silver coin a tender in payment of debt."*

Now when the 1960s heist was pulled, just what part of "any *thing*" did the American people not understand? It went on right before our eyes. There was not a general outcry, so the number then could not have been very large. A score of years went by, until an awakening of many, and several efforts were made by concerned groups during the 1980s and 1990s to restore lawful money. Most recently, however, the number finally grasping the heist has multiplied many times, thanks in part to Ron Paul's 2008 (very educational) presidential campaign.

It actually began with the dark night of December 23, 1913, when Congress surreptitiously passed the Federal Reserve Act. The official records have long since been "deep sixed," but we do know that nearly all of the bureaucracy had gone home for Christmas by that time and but a scant few (hand-picked) Congressmen remained to vote for the birth of the greatest theft in world history.

Since the founding of the nation, particularly with the 1792 Coinage Act, "lawful money" has been defined by statute as a particular measurement of gold or silver coin. Ask a man today to show you a "dollar," and he will likely open his wallet and pull out a green piece of paper and flash a Federal Reserve note, which is not a dollar at all but a bogus facsimile.

(Did you forget already? Everything they ever told us was a lie!)

Originally, a "dollar" had nothing to do with paper at all and was precisely a measurement of gold or silver—25.8 grains of gold or 412.5 grains of silver (note the 16:1 ratio). So if at that time you were to ask a store clerk how your bill totaled, he would likely reply at the time something like, "Eight dollars of silver," or "Eight dollars of gold."

Just as liquid was measured in ounces, pints, quarts and gallons; or distance was measured in inches, feet, yards and miles; gold and silver were measured in "dollars." Got it? A dollar was not a piece of paper but a measurement of something of value. The Federal Reserve "note" in your possession that purports to be a dollar or dollars is actually a counterfeit. Those in charge, those entrusted to look after your financial freedom, lied and cheated and stole from you before you were born. They changed the receipt into the entity.

At one time, we Americans had a receipt for the gold and silver coin that was deposited in the warehouses, later known as banks. After 1913, we had no proof of possession of any lawful money on deposit, and after

1964, it all had disappeared anyway.

Okay, now we need to ask ourselves and our historians, "Why gold and silver? Why not something else?" This is a reasonable question in these confusing times.

History has shown that just about everything you can imagine has been used as a medium of exchange through the years. Leaves, bark, tallies, tokens, beads, livestock, produce and precious metals have been used as money at one time or another. However, gold and silver have proved to be the best for various reasons, including 1] a proven storehouse of value because of scarcity; 2] storability of product—shrinkage is non-existent, even if buried in the ground; and 3] easily tradable for goods and services in small quantities because of features 1 and 2.

When the constitution was written by the founders and ratified by the states and the federal nation was officially founded between 1787 and 1791, nothing bound the people to liberty more tightly than the 17 magic words in Article I, Section 10: No State shall make any *thing* except gold and silver coin a tender in payment of debts."

It would take the enemies of monetary freedom 125 years to sever those bonds, and this was the beginning of the downhill slide for the American people.

AND NOW A BRIEF FLASH FORWARD TO 2010

It is the month of August; a resort town sits next to the shores of a lake. It is raining, and the little town looks totally deserted. It is in the toughest times since 1934, everybody is in debt, and everybody lives on credit; mostly from each other.

Suddenly, a rich tourist comes to town. "*Whooo, boy!*" Everyone says to themselves when they spot his limousine. "*How long can we keep this rich guy in town?*"

The limo stops, the back door opens and the bigshot enters the only hotel. He drops a 100-dollar bill on the reception counter, and asks to inspect the rooms upstairs in order to pick one he might like.

The moment the elevator closes taking the new customer upstairs, the hotel proprietor takes the 100-dollar bill and sprints four doors down the sidewalk to pay his debt to the butcher. The butcher takes the 100-dollar bill, and runs out back to pay his debt to the pig farmer. The pig farmer takes the 100-dollar bill, and hurries to pay his debt to the supplier of his feed and fuel. The supplier of feed and fuel takes the 100-dollar bill and hurries to pay his debt to the town's prostitute that in these hard times, gave her services on credit. The hooker runs to the hotel, and pays off her debt with the 100-dollar bill to the hotel proprietor to pay for the rooms that she rented when she brought her clients there.

It all happened in less than 10 minutes, and the hotel proprietor promptly placed the 100-dollar bill back on the counter so that the rich tourist would not suspect anything.

And it was just in time, too, because only a moment later, the rich tourist came down after inspecting the rooms, picked up his 100-dollar bill, remarked that he did not like any of the rooms, and left town.

No one earned anything. However, the whole town was suddenly without debt, and was looking to the future with a lot of optimism.

And now you have seen a quick snapshot of how the federal government (don't blame just Obama, it's been going on for nearly a century), via the handy Federal Reserve credit machine, operates in our society.

UPDATE:

A fiat money system of the sort we are now painfully watching collapse creates a false world of false feelings of well-being and elevated lifestyles. During the expansion phase of such a system, those living under it spend or borrow more than they should, have more children than they can afford, nationally, come to believe they can afford to allow a score of millions of illegals to come here for educations, welfare payments, medical care, etc. They reject the immutable and universal economic realities and embrace what my old friend, the late Tupper Saussy, labeled "the IDEASPHERE."

Dave Wilber of St. Louis has spent most of his adult life as a monetary realist, and his mentor was the great Merrill Jenkins. Wilber says:

> A Federal Reserve note is a paper token that the first users get for nothing, and a United States note is a paper token that the first

users get for nothing. A solution to the world's problems cannot include paper tokens that the first users get for nothing. We will either have a barter system or a slave system.

There is no other option. In a barter system, you will not see paper tokens that the first users get for nothing. When producers accept paper tokens that the first users get for nothing, the ratio of production to consumption must be ruthlessly regulated lest consumption exceed production and the worthless paper become useless paper. Can there be a better way to enhance the ratio of production to eliminate non-productive consumers such as babies, retirees, cripples and military? You think water is fluoridated to protect your teeth and that abortion was legalized because of women's rights and that the 110,000 Americans lost in Asia were "halting Communist expansion"? If you believe this, then I have a bridge for you!

Now that the inevitable economic catastrophe is upon us, it would be much fun to watch the idiots in Congress who triggered this thing scramble for cover by blaming everyone else, if it were not so tragic and troubling.

About the only folks who feel good now are the international banksters of the world who are in the process of conducting what may prove to be one of the largest raids on the real wealth of this nation—our labor and real property—ever witnessed.

HOW THE THEFT TRANSPIRED

Here we have the fascinating story, in their own words, of the efforts by certain of the Founding Fathers to prevent the economic distress we find all around us today. It is also a sad story on the basis that modern, "sophisticated" Americans have abandoned the corrective institutional mechanism that remains in place to this day.

As you read the opening statement, bear in mind that this is from a very worried George Washington *prior to the Constitutional Convention in Philadelphia* and was not written in 2010.

As you proceed, think about a world with many fewer S&Ls, banking scandals, political corruption and economic problems that now have so blinded us to God's laws for His world.

A FEW FAMOUS QUOTES

"Blood running in the streets. Mobs of rioters and demonstrators threatening banks and legislatures. Looting of shop and home. Strikes and unemployment. Trade and distribution paralyzed. Shortages of food. Bankruptcies everywhere. Court dockets overloaded. Kidnappings for heavy ransom. Sexual perversion, drunkenness, lawlessness rampant. The wheels of government are clogged, and we are descending into the vale of confusion and darkness. No day was ever more clouded than the present. We are fast verging on anarchy and confusion."

—GEORGE WASHINGTON in a 1786 letter to James Madison, describing the effects of *fiat* paper money inflation then ravaging America in the pre-constitutional period.

"The annihilation (of the paper economy) was so complete that barbershops were papered in jest with the bills; and sailors, on returning from cruises, being paid off in bundles of this worthless money, had suits made of it, and and with characteristic lightheartedness, turned their loss into frolic by parading through the streets in decayed finery which in its better days had passed for thousands of dollars."

—Contemporary writer, HENRY BRECK, 1786

"Paper money polluted the equity of our laws, turned them into engines of oppression, corrupted the justice of our public administration, destroyed the fortunes of thousands who had confidence in it, enervated the trade and husbandry and the manufactures of our country and went far to destroy the morality of our people."

—PELETIAH WEBSTER, 1786

THE POWER TO COIN MONEY

At the drafting of the U.S. Constitution, there were many "friends of paper money" present. On August 16, 1787, when the discussion arose on Article 1, Section 8, the proposed wording was this: "The Legislature of the United States shall have the power to coin money and emit bills of credit of the United States."

A hot argument ensued on the power to emit bills of credit, which is another way of saying "printing paper money."

Here are the actual words James Madison wrote describing the debate in his diary:

> Mr. G. Morris moved to strike out "and emit bills of credit." If the United States had credit, such bills would be unnecessary; if they had not, unjust and useless.
>
> MADISON: Will it not be sufficient to prohibit the making them a tender? This will remove the temptation to emit them with unjust views. And promissory notes in that shape may in some emergencies be best.
>
> MORRIS: Striking out the words will leave room still for notes of a responsible minister which will do the good without the mischief. The monied interest will oppose the plan of the government, if paper emissions be not prohibited.
>
> COL. MASON: Though he had a mortal hatred to paper money, yet as he could not foresee all emergencies, he was unwilling to tie the hands of the legislature [Congress].
>
> MR. MERCER (A friend to paper money): It was impolitic—to excite the opposition of all those who were friends to paper money.
>
> MR. ELLSWORTH thought this was a favorable moment to shut and bar the door against paper money. The mischiefs of the various experiments which had been made, were now fresh in the public mind and had excited the disgust of all the respectable part of America. By withholding the power from the new government, more friends of influence would be gained to it than by almost anything else. . . . Give the government credit, and other resources will offer. The power may do harm, never good.
>
> MR. WILSON: It will have a most salutary influence on the credit of the United States to remove the possibility of paper money. This expedient can never succeed whilst its mischiefs are remembered, and as long as it can be resorted to, it will be a bar to other resources.
>
> MR. READ thought the words, if not struck out, would be as alarming as the mark of the Beast in Revelation.
>
> MR. LANGDON had rather reject the whole plan than retain the three words ("and emit bills"). The motion for striking out carried.

Historian George Bancroft later wrote: "James Madison left his testimony that 'the pretext for a paper currency,' and 'particularly for making the bills a tender, either for public or private debts,' was cut off. This is the interpretation of the clause, made at the time of its adoption by all the statesmen of that age, not open to dispute because too clear for argument, and never disputed so long as any one man who took part in framing the constitution remained alive."

(Bancroft—founder of the U.S. Naval Academy at Annapolis among other accomplishments—wrote a book on this very subject entitled *A Plea for the Constitution of the United States: Wounded in the House of Its Guardians.* During WWII, FDR—a serious friend of paper money—ostensibly to supply the war effort, ordered the printing plates for many historical books smelted. The plates for Bancroft's book were among them.)

ROGER SHERMAN (1721-1793) should be a name familiar to every American—as familiar (or more) as Washington, Jefferson, Madison and Adams. He is the only man to have signed all four documents surrounding the formation of the United States of America: the Continental Association of 1774; the Declaration of Independence; the Articles of Confederation; and the United States Constitution. None of the others did that. Did you ever read about Roger Sherman in school? Most of us cannot remember him at all.

Sherman was a judge of the Superior Court in New Haven, Connecticut, serving that office with distinction from 1766 until 1788. He served as treasurer of Yale University from 1765 to 1776. He was renowned for his high intelligence and unswerving honesty and was described by John Adams "as honest as an angel and as firm in the cause of American independence as Mount Atlas." He served in the U.S. Senate from 1791 until his death in 1793.

So why is Roger Sherman's name so unfamiliar? I submit that it was because he was an outspoken enemy of paper money. In 1751, as a young businessman in Connecticut, Roger Sherman and his brother William sued James Battle of Rhode Island for paying a debt to their shop in New Milford, Connecticut, in depreciating paper currency. Over a period of 15 months, Battle had charged "divers wares and merchandizes" amounting to 129 pounds of what Sherman assumed were pounds of Connecticut "Old Tenor," a stable currency whose value was well preserved by taxation taking it out of circulation. But Battle assumed the debt was denominated in pounds of ever depreciating Rhode Island currency, tendered in same, and the Shermans took a beating in the payment and sued for recovery of loss by depreciation. The Shermans lost when Battle argued that he was merely following the accepted custom of the day.

In 1752, Sherman wrote his pamphlet *A Caveat Against Injustice, or An Inquiry into the Evils of a Fluctuating Medium of Exchange* indicting unbacked paper money.

It was this experience that Judge Sherman brought to the Constitutional Convention and prompted him to rise on August 28, 1787 and propose a new, more restrictive wording to Article 1, Section 10. The standing version under consideration was worded this way: "No state shall coin money; nor grant letters of marque and reprisal; nor enter into any Treaty, alliance, or confederation; nor grant any title of Nobility." (From Madison's *Notes of the Convention*) "Judge Sherman and Mr. [James] Wilson moved to insert after the words 'coin money,' the words 'nor emit bills of credit, nor make any *thing* but gold and silver coin a tender in payment of debts,' making these prohibitions absolute; instead of making the measures allowable with the consent of the legislature of the U.S. Mr. Sherman thought this a *favorable crisis for crushing paper money*. If the consent of the legislature could authorize emissions of it, the friends of paper money would make every exertion to get into the Legislature in order to license it." Mr. Sherman's and Mr. Wilson's motion was quickly agreed to and became the supreme law of the land.

MORE PERTINENT QUOTES

Here are some additional quotations to ponder. While we are inundated today with false and deceptive monetary advice from those who have helped enslave us economically, the founders followed the Godly wisdom of Deut. 25:13-16. Without inserting "religion" per se, they were able to utilize the Old Testament laws provided by the Almighty as the right ones to follow on the Earth. History has shown that when His people followed these laws, they were blessed. When they did not, they were cursed. Not much has changed in the 21st century.

The following quotes are from the letters and spoken words of the most erudite personages of the 18th century founding days.

* * *

"All the perplexities, confusion and distress in America arise not from defects in the constitution or confederation, nor from a want of honor or virtue so much as from downright ignorance of the nature of coin, credit and circulation."

—JOHN ADAMS, in a letter to Thomas Jefferson, 1787

* * *

"I deny the power of the general government to making paper money, or anything else, a legal tender." —THOMAS JEFFERSON

* * *

"You have doubtless been informed, from time to time, of the happy progress of our affairs. The principal difficulties seem in great measure to have been surmounted. Our revenues have been considerably more productive than it was imagined they would be. I mention this to show the spirit of enterprise that prevails."

—GEORGE WASHINGTON in a letter to the Marquis de LaFayette, June 3, 1790 *after* the United States Constitution prohibited unbacked paper money at Article 1, Section 10

* * *

"Since the federal constitution has removed all danger of our having a paper tender, our trade is advanced 50 percent. Our monied people can trust their cash abroad, and have brought their coin into circulation."

—December 16, 1789 edition of *The Pennsylvania Gazette*

* * *

"Our country, my dear sir, is fast progressing in its political importance and social happiness."

—GEORGE WASHINGTON in a letter to LaFayette, March 19, 1791, the prosperity already being realized from circulating gold and silver coin

* * *

"The United States enjoys a sense of prosperity and tranquility under the new government that could hardly have been hoped for."

—GEORGE WASHINGTON, in a letter to Catherine Macaulay Graham, July 19, 1791

* * *

"Tranquility reigns among the people with that disposition toward the general government which is likely to preserve it. Our public credit stands on that high ground which three years ago would have been considered as a species of madness to have foretold."

—GEORGE WASHINGTON, in a letter to David Humphreys, July 20, 1791)

* * *

"It is apparent from the whole context of the Constitution as well as the times which gave birth to it, that it was the purpose of the convention to establish a currency consisting of the precious metals. These were adopted by a permanent rule excluding the use of a perishable medium of exchange, such as certain agricultural commodities recognized by the statutes of some states as tender for debts, or the still more pernicious expedient of *paper currency*."

—ANDREW JACKSON, 8th Annual Message to Congress
December 5, 1836

* * *

Despite what you were taught in school, the historical record is crystal clear: America was to have been spared the destructive effects of an unbacked paper money system. Most of the problems we face today can be traced to what Andrew Jackson called "the pernicious expedient of paper money."

History teaches that "artificial money" creates an artificial world where the price for some items—even our most popular welfare program—can be deferred to future generations (our $11 trillion national "debt") or paid with "money" created out of thin air which dilutes the value from the "money" we might have in our pockets at that moment. A "dollar" of legal tender (a Federal Reserve note) is a piece of paper that the first user gets for nothing and for which the last user will get nothing.

When Roger Sherman and the other founders in 1789 declared Article I, Section 10 to be the governing law of the land, it and the other supreme laws should have been set in concrete forever. However, Mankind being as depraved as it is, an attack was certainly inevitable. It came in the early days of the 20th century and culminated on December 23, 1913, when Congress, with only a few present because most had already gone to their respective homes for Christmas, passed the Federal Reserve Act, which created the dreaded central bank that Jefferson, Jackson and every other honorable American interested in the liberty of the people had fought against their whole political lives.

With the birth of the Fed came the control of the people and their governments at all levels through the power of legal tender. With the ability to create "money" out of thin air came the control of the total population. The federal government was suddenly able to fund all kinds of alphabet agencies that it formerly had no ability to fund without the consent of the states.

After 125 years, the central government in Washington, D.C. finally had the ability to capture the 48 (later to be fifty) states, and nobody— or should we say, *very few*—even realized that the power that had been theirs had now been usurped by the feds from the states. It was hiding in plain sight.

The nation was born with the states being all-powerful and with the federal government operating as an inferior and subservient lackey who needed to go to the states with hat in hand whenever it needed money for a proposed project. If the states agreed, then they taxed themselves equally by apportionment to fund the new federal project. The U.S. Constitution mandates this system, and it was installed to keep the strength of government within the states and out of the hands of a central government.

In such a system, the money floated upward from the states to Washington, and the federal government's hands were tied with this "binding down with the chains of the constitution," as Thomas Jefferson once termed it. However, when the Federal Reserve was enacted in 1913, the lawful deal was off and the deceitful deal was in. Another lie. America had begun to operate on imaginary money.

In the same year, 1913—certainly the darkest single year for liberty in our nation's history—two other blistering acts took place within the halls of Congress with the culmination of two constitutional amendments, the 16th and the 17th, both of which were never properly ratified by the states. Our nation had lost its way.

An income tax has no functional purpose in a barter system of gold and silver coin. However, it is very important in the Communistic drift of imaginary money we are experiencing in America.

Our founders in 1792 were so concerned about counterfeiting that in passage of the Coinage Act, they fixed the dollar as a measure of silver and provided a *penalty of death* for officers of the Mint who might participate in counterfeiting. A later Congress in 1913 with a quorum of just three, with passage of the Federal Reserve Act, provided presses, paper ink and labor for the counterfeiters and in 1965, as we are about to see, provided the copper and zinc to the Mint in order to counterfeit the coin as well.

Amusingly enough, the crime of counterfeiting originally pertained to and was defined (1792) as the "counterfeiting of gold and silver coin." The #1 dictionary definition of the word is "to make a copy of, to feign, imitate, to make a spurious semblance of," which has been the mission of the Federal Reserve for nigh now a century. As mentioned earlier, the crime was so serious that it carried the death penalty, because the founders were already aware from previous experience of the seeds of national destruction being planted with the corruption of a nation's money system. Nevertheless, the banksters managed to not only pull off the crime but actually legalize it. But here is the amusing and educational part: the federal statutes no longer prohibit "counterfeiting" but rather "illegal counterfeiting." Should you be caught running Federal Reserve notes on your copy machine, you will be prosecuted under the federal law prohibiting "illegal counterfeiting." In other words, the counterfeiting carried on by the Fed since 1914 is overlooked, but should you do the same thing, you will not be prosecuted for "counterfeiting" but for "illegal counterfeiting." It was one of the cleverest pieces of wool-over-the-eyes subterfuge ever pulled on the American people. Everything they ever told us was a lie!

Nobel Laureate Paul Samuelson, in his *Economics, Fourth Edition,* said the Federal Reserve is an "omnipotent counterfeiter," and its own publications tell us that their system "works only with credit" that would keep its value "if there were fewer people bidding against each other."(booklet, "Keeping Our Money [their credit] Healthy," Library of Congress catalogue No. 60-14368, revised Jan. 1979.)

(Question for round table discussion: If the money controllers understand that the money will "keep its value" when there are "fewer people bidding against each other," do they not have the incentive to keep fewer people alive?)

In 1920, Economist, John Maynard Keynes wrote: "If governments should refrain from regulation (taxation), the worthlessness of the money becomes apparent and the fraud upon the public can be concealed no longer." (*The Economic Consequences of the Peace*)

In this satanic system that works us only with credit, taxes are illusions that help regulate the ratio of production to consumption. There can be no better way to enhance the ratio of production to consumption than to eliminate non productive consumers such as babies, retirees, cripples and military. Do you see why abortion was legalized under the false pretense of women's rights? Do you see why our extermination by fluoridation continues unabated 11 years after the professionals at the EPA began telling the world that fluoride is killing people? Search: fluoride. Do you see why those omnipotent foreign bankers tell their FDA, EPA and USPHS to ignore aspartame, sugar, milk, canola, MSG and other toxins in our food and drinks? Can you understand why a cancer cure has been suppressed for nearly 80 years? This not a theory; it is history. And if you don't call it "conspiratorial," because your college professor told you that such a thing was ridiculous folly, then what do you call it?

Thomas Jefferson said in 1802:*"I believe that banking institutions are more dangerous to our liberties than standing armies. If the American people ever allow private banks to control the issue of their currency, first by inflation, then by deflation, the banks and corporations that will grow up around the banks will deprive the people of all property until their children wake up homeless on the continent their fathers conquered."*

(I know, I already done tol' ya. But listen ag'in. Does this sound remotely prophetic in 2010, with home foreclosures at an all-time high? And now to the coinage fraud.)

AN EYEWITNESS TO COUNTERFEITING

In every nation in the history of the world, has it not always ended up a war between the ruling class and the people? The king wants more and more, and the people continually settle for less and less. In 20th-century America, the bureaucracy reversed the roles of master and servant by absconding with the wealth—lawful money—and silently became that ruling class. The currency switch was one chimerical sleight-of-hand, but the installation of slug coins was another that was not so easy. Nevertheless, they pulled it off—climaxing in 1965—and here is how it was done.

In late 1959, National Rejectors of St. Louis, Missouri—the manufacturer of 97 percent of the coin acceptance devices in the United States—received an unannounced visit from several agents of the U.S. Treasury Department and the St. Louis branch of the Federal Reserve Bank officiously flashing their badges and credentials. The company's top inventor-designer was a brilliant New Yorker from Brooklyn by the name of Merrill Jenkins. The officers desired an interview with Mr. Jenkins regarding a subject that was normally kept under tight corporate security.

"What techniques," the government agents posing as anti-counterfeiters asked him, "might a counterfeiter use to deceive state-of-the-art coin acceptance machines?"

Believing that he was helping to protect the interests of the United States Treasury and, therewith, the American people, Jenkins revealed over the course of the interview that the counterfeiter who could manufacture a copper slug sandwiched between two faces of nickel would have himself a coin costing between one and two cents (depending upon its size). The mechanical acceptors would then mistakenly read the coin as being made of the silver the machines were designed to receive.

"But don't worry about it," Jenkins assured the officials. "We are talking about a complicated process. Only a very sophisticated syndicate with unlimited resources could turn out these coins in quantity."

Little did he realize that he was revealing secrets of national security to that very syndicate, the actual one with its eye on discovering the method of creating from those unlimited resources. "The counterfeiter the Treasury was pretending to guard against," he later constantly told lecture audiences for the rest of his life, "was the Treasury Department itself."

When the Coinage Act of 1965 began turning those coins out in dime, quarter, half-dollar and dollar denominations, the middle-aged inventor was shocked. Merrill Jenkins felt his confidence had been betrayed. Eventually, he quit the firm and began exploring the historical relationship of governments to money, and he spent the rest of his life writing books and speaking publicly in an attempt to help ordinary mortals comprehend the gravity of the situation. Strange to him at the time, no major publishing house would touch his writings, and he had to self-publish each piece as he could afford it. After his death in 1979, a handful of followers picked up his torch.

At the time of Mr. Jenkins' death, America had endured more than a decade of the infusion of *fiat* money. Both the coins and currency in circulation were irredeemable in gold or silver for the first time since the "not worth a continental" days of the 1780s. Predictably, the once great nation had plunged itself into the very kind of economic chaos the Constitution had been written to cure and prevent. Inflation began to creep like never before in our lifetimes, but the people swallowed all the economic propaganda without question.

And the television news and sideshows were programming the citizenry to believe whatever government spokesmen said.

The American people had been so cleverly lulled to sleep that they had no idea it had happened.

The enemy is very patient. The paper currency had been undergoing a slow but continuous capture since the establishment of the first Federal Reserve Bank in 1914. In 1965, the enemy of the people had finally designed a method by which to capture the silver coin, too, and the formerly valuable silver coins had morphed into nothing more than counterfeit slugs. And the people made not a peep.

The final result would be seen in 1968.

THE JFK RUMOR

In 1981, a rumor was circulated that President Kennedy had been assassinated by agents of the hidden money powers because he had signed Executive Order #11110 instructing the Treasury to print $4.3 billion in United States Notes—paper bills without gold or silver backing issued by the government, instead of the Federal Reserve. According to the rumor, the bankers were furious because they would lose interest payments on the money supply. In actuality, the order was not for United States notes but ". . . to issue silver certificates against any silver bullion, silver or standard silver dollars in the Treasury not then held for redemption of any outstanding silver certificates. . . ."

Others later said that the very first presidential act by Lyndon Johnson was the rescinding of that Kennedy order on Saturday morning, November 23, 1963. However, there is no existing record of such action in the law library. Considering the apparent devious removal of other documents, as well as the surreptitious insertion of even more, this void of available data does not mean the subterfuge did not take place, but we suspect it was another ungrounded rumor.

Some researchers have attempted to obtain a copy of Executive Order #11110 and have been told it does not exist. We have found it but without any mention of the amount—$4.3 billion or any other figure. Was it "deep-sixed," as apparently was the original Thirteenth Amendment? Can anyone produce a certified copy of either the Kennedy order or the Johnson rescission? The one copy we have seen of the Kennedy order contained the (rumored) wording, the date, the amounts etc., but no signature or seal. Except for these discrepancies, it appeared to have been copied from an original. However, we could not prove its authenticity with anything found in the law books. There we found only the executive order for the silver certificates with no specific amount mentioned.

Longtime researcher and author G. Edward Griffin offers a tasty piece of logic. From page 570 of his *The Creature from Jekyll Island*, we find: "Kennedy had been a life-long socialist and internationalist. He had attended the Fabian London School of Economics; became a political scientist who cooperated with the monetary scientists in the destruction of the American money supply; and, as president, enthusiastically participated in the transfer of American wealth to foreign nations. There is little reason to believe he had suddenly 'seen the light' and was preparing to reverse his life-long beliefs and commitments."

The erudite Griffin goes on to say, "The persistent rumor regarding the bankers' role in JFK's death was reinforced by several books circulated in conservative circles." He's right! Yours truly is one of those mistaken authors. And while I have for now satisfied myself to the contrary of certain long-held suspicions, it still bothers some of us that those Fed notes would have been released so soon after Kennedy's assassination. To assume that the machinations went into motion on Friday afternoon—the designers, the engravers, the printers—and a new note was produced the following Monday or Tuesday is ludicrous. Was Kennedy part of the new money plot or was he totally in the dark about the whole operation?

A few things are certain. John F. Kennedy was killed on Friday and buried the following Monday, November 25th. The 1963 series of irredeemable (and patently counterfeit) Federal Reserve "notes" was released that week, and the news was buried in the back pages of the nation's newspapers at a convenient time when nobody cared anyway. Johnson ascended to the presidency and buried the assassination facts beneath the shield of his own hand-picked Warren Commission. In 1965, cupronickel coins began to replace the silver ones and worked perfectly in the vending machines. On June 24, 1968, the bankers' windows of redemption slammed shut and the U.S. government reneged on its obligation to exchange lawful money for the millions of outstanding notes in circulation among the people. The fraud was complete, and the perpetrators silently slipped away from the American people with impunity.

For years we have been warned by those who have been there: "Don't try to explain the money issue to a jury. They just can't get it in one short lesson." Agreed. But if the "paper money" scheme seems tough to sort out, believe it that the clad coinage fraud is even tougher.

Merrill Jenkins understood it better than anyone. After all, he lived the deception first hand. From his masterpiece, *Money - The Greatest Hoax on Earth*, from which there is an education on every page, we glean a tidbit: "If it were possible to educate the people, and if it were possible to go back to wealth media, the extraction of wealth would cease and our nation would resume its progress toward ever greater individual standards of living. That is why they outlawed gold and silver coins. This was our wealth media. That is why they melted our silver coins and sold our silver at auction. They don't want us to use wealth media. If we use our wealth media, we own our wealth and the elected officials become servants of the people. The public would regain the power to direct the policies of their government."

"IT'S THE ECONOMY, STUPID!"

In 1992, political advisor James Carville launched Bill Clinton toward the White House with that slogan posted on the walls of every campaign office. He was on the target but missed the bull's-eye. In reality, "It's the legal tender, Stupid."

A friend wrote that when his first great-grandchild arrived a few weeks ago, he thought, "Gotta start a little education fund for the tyke," just as he had done with all his grandchildren. Then he reminded himself that the Federal Reserve has just promised to turn up the money-inflating machine, making any conventional savings program a waste of time—not to mention the money.

The weakness of the dollar makes any saving of paper assets pointless. Why would any rational person, unless totally ignorant of what is happening, save a dollar in an account that pays less than 3 percent a year when the rate of inflation is 10 percent or more? Disregarding the "official" annual rates that are continual, boring lies, just reach back in your own mind to only one year ago. How much did you pay for eggs? Bread? Gasoline? Steak? And if you can buy any of those today for less than a 10% increase from 12 months ago, please tell me where to do it, because I can't. These are the true inflation indicators—at your lunch counters, gasoline stations and supermarkets—not some figures from a government-funded, bureaucratic deceiver.

Speaking of lunch counters, on my first sales job in the 1960s, I was traveling 11 states throughout the southeast, and my daily lunch always cost between 65 and 75 cents of lawful money (silver coin), depending upon where I was and how much I wanted to splurge that day. (Oh, how wonderful it was to blow an extra dime and sit in a first class joint.) And I filled the tank of my old Chevy for four bucks.

A few years ago, when your average plate lunch of an entrée and two or three veggies, with iced tea included, went to exactly 10 times the 60's figures, I began to talk and write about it, remembering that nothing had changed about the meal except the price. The buildings were just as modern, the floors and tables were just as clean, the restrooms still needed attention and the waitresses were just as sassy. Only the price had gone up.

But then I remembered my independent education with lawful money and realized that the price of lunch and everything else was actually still the same, too. A dollar of lawful money required 10 Fed notes to obtain. So anyone with knowledge of lawful money realized that the plate lunch was still costing the same as in the 60's. It was just that the banksters had hoodwinked us into using their paper scrip. Now put the same yardstick to today's price of lunch and you will find that it matches the real cost of 40 years ago. A $1,000 bag of pre-65 silver coin now goes for $16,000 in fed notes.

(This means that anyone who earned $100 a week in 1964 (I did) needs to earn $1,600 today (I don't) in counterfeit "dollars" just to be even.)

How much did you pay for lunch today? I paid $10.40, with no dessert. Divide that by 16 and see what you get. (65 cents.) It should help you realize that nothing has increased in cost during your whole life, but what you have been using to make purchases has continually decreased in value, thereby requiring more of it. The nation's founders had the same problem in the 1780s and solved it with hard money. That lasted for 125 years until the wicked banksters schemed a way around the constitutional mandate (never been amended and still on the books), "No State shall make any *thing* but gold and silver coin a tender in payment of debts."

George Bush, wallowing in a fool's paradise, said that he'd "perk up the economy this summer" (2008) by sending $158 billion back to the people. Should that happen, take whatever paltry part is yours and 1] pay off some debt or 2] buy some silver or gold coins. Do not spend this "rebate" on a vacation trip or anything that you don't absolutely need. Of course, if you use this to extinguish debt, it won't have the desired effect of stimulating the economy, but that is only a politician's way of temporarily staving off the inevitable hyperinflation anyway. It will prove in the long run to be the financial equivalent of dumping gasoline on a forest fire. After all, the $158 billion Band-aid will be created out of nothing, and you know the rest of that story.

Remember, every economic boom, fueled chiefly by debt, always implodes into a deflationary spiral. Buying stocks and real estate with other people's money when inflation is roaring is almost a guaranteed winner, but it is lethal with the turnaround into deflation, a situation already evident in real estate foreclosures in Florida and elsewhere. Bear Stearns had a market value of $20 billion only a year ago. Last week it sold out for $236 million—two bucks a share.

The current housing crisis and all that flows from it come from two main sources, both deriving from Washington.

In 1977, Congress passed the "Community Reinvestment Act" compelling financial institutions to make loans to people with lower incomes. These regulations were then amended in 1995 and 2005 to create different rules for institutions of different sizes, so that various kinds of institutions would be better able to meet the government's goal of fostering home ownership in lower-income communities.

Next, the Federal Reserve started making loans available to the banking system at extremely low interest rates. Then, the lenders combined to make cheap housing loans available to people who previously could not have afforded or qualified for them. This caused an increased demand for housing that sent home prices spiraling upward.

Now mortgage lenders began managing the risk involved in making these loans by selling their mortgages to other companies, believing that they were accomplishing this with a wide variety of mortgages in their portfolio. However, these decisions were all in error, because the Fed's policy of easy money had falsely inflated the value of all homes. This meant that good mortgages could not be used to manage the risk involved in questionable mortgages, because the value of all homes was falsely inflated.

Finally, as with all inflationary booms, increases in home prices absorbed the increased purchasing power provided by the Fed, leading to a slowdown in home purchases. When this moment arrived everyone realized that the homes they had purchased weren't really worth what they had paid for them. The defaults and foreclosures then began, along with the collapse of the financial institutions that owned these unsound mortgages.

Now the complicated, multi-part scenario described above has been simplified in popular reporting to just two words: sub-prime loans. These two words, combined with the idea that lenders took advantage of poor unsuspecting customers, are supposed to explain everything.

Perhaps this will explain it better. On Labor Day of 1984, my longtime friend Martin "Red" Beckman sat in a seminar in Orlando, Florida, squirming in his seat as many of the highly publicized and oft-quoted hard money advocates spoke of the soon-to-come $3,700 an ounce price of gold. Finally, the meeting was opened to questions, and Red began to speak from the floor.

He gently chided the "experts" about their predictions before launching into an explanation of why they were wrong. Yet when he finished, not one could disagree.

Red said to them, "The problem is you are asking the wrong questions. What you need to ask is who is buying all this gold.

"The Federal Reserve Bank buys gold at 10 cents an ounce, so why would they want to push the price to $3,700?" Gold was at $400 at the time, and the cost of production was $187 to the mining companies. By keeping the price reasonable, Red explained that it also kept the mining companies operating.

Hearing the mumblings of disbelief in the audience, Red said, "Oh, you didn't know that the Fed bought gold for 10 cents an ounce? Well, let me tell you how they do it."

He then reminded them of something that everyone in that audience already knew but had not put into the equation: that the Fed printed paper bills—from $1 to $100 denominations, the price of ink and paper was the same—at a cost of 2.5 cents each. So four one-hundred-dollar bills were created at a cost to the Fed of 10 cents, and these could then be traded for one ounce of gold.

"Now, if you had control of this printing press," Red said, "and could purchase anything you wanted, what could you want more than the gold? Wouldn't you go after that first?"

A quarter century later we would add, "And why would you stop?"

(And let us remember that the Fed also creates the paper necessary to pay its bills, such as the 10 cents for paper and ink in the above illustration, so the net cost is zero. A Federal Reserve note is something that the first user gets for nothing and for which the last user will get nothing.)

A BRIEF FLASHBACK

How Illegals & Multiculturalism Destroyed Detroit

Michigan State grad and author Frosty Wooldridge lived and worked in Detroit for 15 years, from the mid 1970s to 1990, and watched it descend into the abyss of crime, debauchery, gunplay, drugs, school truancy, car-jacking, gangs and human depravity. He writes that he watched entire city blocks burned out.

"I watched graffiti explode on buildings, cars, trucks, buses and school yards," he says. "Trash everywhere! Detroiters walked through it, tossed more into it and ignored it. (At the risk of sounding anti-something or 'nother once more, I ask for a pause and a brief consideration here as to which racial group does the reader believe Wooldridge is referring here. Aha! You said it. I didn't, and neither did Frosty. *You* must be the racist here.)

"Tens of thousands and then hundreds of thousands today exist on welfare, free housing and food stamps! With Aid to Dependent Children, minority women birthed eight to 10 and in one case, one woman birthed 24 kids as reported by the *Detroit Free Press—all* on American taxpayer dollars. A new child meant a new car payment, new TV and whatever mom wanted. I saw Lyndon Baines Johnson's 'Great Society' flourish in Detroit. If you give money for doing nothing, you will get more hands out taking money for doing nothing.

"Mayor Coleman Young," says Wooldridge, "perhaps the most corrupt mayor in America, outside of Richard Daley in Chicago, rode Detroit down to its knees. He set the benchmark for cronyism, incompetence and arrogance. Detroit became a majority black city with 67 percent African-Americans."

Wooldridge was a schoolteacher in those days, and during the summers he worked as a United Van Lines truck driver and mover. He moved hundreds of American families toward a new life in another city or state and watched as the city's population halved from 1.8 million to 912,000 today. Yet at the same time, legal and illegal immigrants so much converged on the city that the Muslims now number over 300,000 and Mexicans over 400,000.

"As the Muslims moved in, the whites moved out," he writes. "As the crimes became more violent, the whites fled. Finally, unlawful Mexicans moved in at a torrid pace. You could cut the racial tension in the air with a knife! Detroit may be one of our best examples of multiculturalism: pure dislike and total separation from America."

Detroit high school flunk-out rates reached 76 percent last June according to NBC's Brian Williams. Classrooms resemble foreign countries more than America. English? Few speak it. The city features a 50 percent illiteracy rate and growing. Unemployment hit 28.9 percent in 2009 as the auto industry vacated the city.

In *Time* magazine of October 4, 2009, "The Tragedy of Detroit: How a great city fell and how it can rise again," the establishment (MSM) writer missed the target, as usual, of how it actually fell.

"If Detroit had been savaged by a hurricane and submerged by a ravenous flood, we'd know a lot more about it," wrote Daniel Okrent. "If drought and carelessness had spread brush fires across the city, we'd see it on the evening news every night. Earthquake, tornadoes, you name it— if natural disaster had devastated the city that was once the living proof

Many parts of Detroit and its suburbs today look like they have been hit by bombs.

of American prosperity, the rest of the country might take notice."

"But Detroit, once our fourth largest city, now 11th and slipping rapidly, has had no such luck. Its disaster has long been a slow unwinding that seemed to remove it from the rest of the country. Even the death rattle that in the past year emanated from its signature industry brought more attention to the auto executives than to the people of the city, who had for so long been victimized by their dreadful decision making.

"By any quantifiable standard, the city is on life support. Detroit's treasury is $300 million short of the funds needed to provide the barest municipal services," Okrent said. "The school system, which six years ago was compelled by the teachers' union to reject a philanthropist's offer of $200 million to build 15 small, independent charter high schools, is in receivership. The murder rate is soaring, and 7 out of 10 remain unsolved. Three years after Katrina devastated New Orleans, unemployment in that city hit a peak of 11%. In Detroit, the unemployment rate is 28.9%. That's worth spelling out: twenty-eight point nine percent.

At the end of Okrent's report, he said, "That's because the story of Detroit is not simply one of a great city's collapse. It's also about the erosion of the industries that helped build the country we know today. The ultimate fate of Detroit will reveal much about the character of America in the 21st century. If what was once the most prosperous manufacturing city in the nation has been brought to its knees, what does that say about our recent past? And if it can't find a way to get up, what does that say about our future?"

But Wooldridge counters with logic. "The auto industry won't come back—not in Detroit, not even in this country, in our lifetimes. Immigration will keep pouring more and more uneducated third world immigrants from the Middle East into Detroit—thus creating a beachhead for Islamic hegemony in America. If 50 percent illiteracy continues, we will see more homegrown terrorists spawned out of the Muslim ghettos of Detroit. Illiteracy plus Islam equals walking human bombs. We have already seen it in Madrid, London and Paris, with train bombings, subway bombings and riots. As their numbers grow, so will their power to enact their barbaric Sharia law that subjugates women to the lowest rungs on the human ladder and negates republican forms of government. Detroit will soon see more honor killings by upset husbands, fathers and brothers that demand subjugation by their daughters, sisters and wives. Muslims prefer beheadings of women to scare the hell out of any other members of their sect from straying."

Multiculturalism: what a perfect method to kill our language, culture, country and way of life.

Ahh, yes, and indeed it already had, but when will someone uncover the elephant in the living room? Does anyone understand that without the power of legal tender—creation of money at will—this sort of problem would never have surfaced in the first place? Where could Coleman Young have gotten these funds to further weaken the ambitions of those of his race without a government (via the Fed) to create and hand money to him? Had he done the same on his own, he would have spent a lengthy stretch for something called "illegal counterfeiting."

And where would Obama have gotten the multiple trillions he created to further destroy the economy?

This is why we inserted this particular story in this particular segment—to portray the omnipotent power of legal tender. It was not "taxpayer's money," as we were told, it was government money, created out of thin air. Everything they ever told us about it was a lie.

While history is written by the winners, these writers are by no means necessarily the righteous. When America emerges from the social and financial wreckage of this current economic situation, it is important that it be understood how it all came to end up in this sorry state.

> "The supply of gold is governed by nature; it is not, like the supply of paper money, subject merely to the schemes of demagogues or the whims of politicians. Nobody ever thinks he has quite enough money. Once the idea is accepted that money is something whose supply is determined simply by the printing press, it becomes impossible for the politicians in power to resist the constant demands for further inflation. Gold may not be a theoretically perfect basis for money; but it has the merit of making the money supply, and therefore the value of the monetary unit, independent of governmental manipulation and political pressure."
>
> —HENRY HAZLITT,
>
> *Man vs. the Welfare State* (1969)

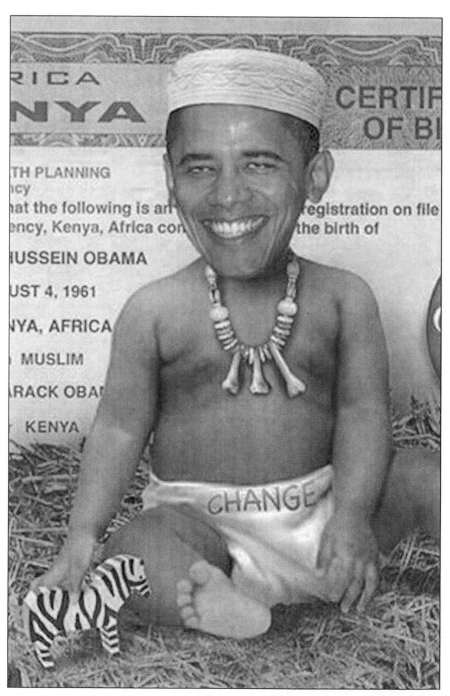

OBAMA THE USURPER

This ongoing debate about Barack Obama being born in Kenya and therefore not eligible to be president of the United States goes back further than we thought. When Obama was making his run for the U.S. Senate in Illinois in 2004, the Sunday edition of the *East African Standard* newspaper boasted with its headline, "Kenyan-born Obama All Set for U.S. Senate." Of course, his place of birth was not vitally important at the time because "natural born" is not a constitutional requirement to be a United States senator.

The power to control the people was achieved with the founding of the Fed and the creation of legal tender. With it, they can control anything and everything. This includes elections and control of the news—such as when an unlawful candidate not only slips through the state primaries, but gets his party's nomination, and is elected president of the United States.

Barack Obama has "spent" over $2 million in legal fees in avoiding the simple task of publicly displaying his birth certificate to show that he was really born in Hawaii on August 4, 1961, as he claims. The U.S. Constitution requires that a president be "natural born," that is, born within the boundaries of the United States.

About half of the people in the United States believe that this whole argument is ludicrous because in June of 2008, Obama "proved" his Hawaiian birth with "evidence." This "evidence," provided by his backers, was a forged document purporting to be a Certificate of Live Birth from the state of Hawaii. We'll have a look at it in this section on page 73.

Do you see anything fishy here? I have to admit that I missed the most obvious one initially but probably caught the one that almost nobody else spots at first glance. That being the "Race of the Father" halfway down on the left. It says, as you can see, "African."

You see, in 1961, I was 21 years old and living in the Deep South. And that time, it would have been insulting to refer to any black man or woman as "African." This would have been more disparaging at the time than the term "nigger," matter of fact, which was the slang of the day and really was not offensive at the time, believe it or not.[1] Today, the politically correct term for these people is "African-American," and that is what made the document suspect in my eyes at first glance. "African" is no more a race of mankind than is "American." But there it is, Barack Obama's father's race is listed on an "official" document as being "African."

No one had screamed "foul" yet, and when they did, their evidence would be much more solid than what I had just spotted, but I was already onto an adjunct to the obvious. As Edward R. Murrow said: "The obscure we see eventually. The completely obvious takes a little longer."

Yup, Mr. Murrow got that one right on. The "obvious" was what any astute investigator should have caught first—the fact that this document had been created with a laser printer. How stupid for the perpetrators to think that they could get by with such an anachronism. I didn't know precisely what year the laser printer went on the market—sometime in the early '90s I saw my first one—but I knew it was a long time after B.O. was born in 1961.

Then even a more obvious fact was revealed, hiding, once again, in plain sight. In the bottom left-hand corner of the document, requiring a magnifying glass on the computer but plainly visible to the naked eye in an 8x11 hard copy printout, are the words visible on every government document advising of the current status of that document. This one says, "Revised 11/01."

Because it would be even more ridiculous to assume that this form was revised in 1901 than it is to imagine that it was used in 1961, we have to know without debate that the revision date was in 2001, when Obama was age 40.

What obviously happened is that some B.O. supporter, a black man or woman around 30 years old, took it upon him or herself to quash the rumors that their hero was not lawfully eligible to occupy the White House.

So he/she created the "proof" that he was. It was such a cheap imitation that the whole Obama staff of lawyers must have shuddered at the sight, but it being all they had, they had to defend it. They passed it on to their friends in the propagandizing press but must have instructed them to not publish it and just defend it.

It was not only a forgery but a very poor one, but it was also the only thing that the MSM had to lean on, so it became the basis of every story refuting the Obama challenges over the next year. The phony document was seldom displayed but was always referred to as the "proof that this birth certificate thing has long ago been proven" and that Obama was born in Hawaii.

Those millions (literally) of challengers, who began to demand to see the proof, eventually became disparagingly known in the press as the "birthers," but a full year would pass before the issue would make it to the MSM headlines. These flames were fanned by a few web sites and only *American Free Press* with a scant 100,000 readers in the print media, but our screams were heard.

During that year, the MSM had all it could do to suppress the news of the court cases being filed all over the country, while Joseph Farah at WorldNetDaily.com and we at AFP were screaming to the rooftops.

Farah sent his investigator, Dr. Jerome Corsi, to Kenya to get interviews, and we at AFP began to report his results as well as the cases in both state and federal courts across the nation. Dr. Corsi secured an affidavit from Obama's paternal grandmother swearing that she was at the birth of little Barack at a Kenyan hospital on August 4, 1961.

Dozens of court cases, beginning with the former assistant attorney general of Pennsylvania in August of 2008, demanding that Obama prove his natural birth by simply producing his Hawaiian birth certificate, were dismissed by the various courts claiming the plaintiff lacked "standing" to be filing such a suit. Meanwhile, Obama prevailed upon the governor of Hawaii to seal his records from any public scrutiny.

The *St. Petersburg Times* claims that its fact-checking web site politiFact.com has examined the "birthers" issue several times over the past year and has "found a mountain of evidence that proves Obama was born in Hawaii." This "mountain" includes in total the contrived, laser-printed certificate (non-existent in 1961), birth announcements in two Honolulu newspapers, and remarks from the director of Hawaii's Department of Health, who released a statement saying he had "seen the original vital records maintained on file verifying BHO was born in Hawaii and is a natural-born American citizen." The newspaper concludes that this "plentiful" evidence should settle the dispute.

Not if an imposter was going to be commander-in-chief of the armed forces, said a few military men, also without a final resolution. Retired Naval Lt. Commander Walter Fitzpatrick took a stand in March of 2009 by filing criminal charges of treason against Obama in federal court in Knoxville but is yet to have the court address it. Instead, the U.S. attorney in Tennessee reported to his Washington superiors at the DOJ that Fitzpatrick may be a "terrorist." This earned Fitzpatrick a visit from the Secret Service but little else.

Then the question of Barack Obama's birth status and challenges thereof reached a new level in July when U.S. Army Reserve Maj. Stefan Frederick Cook, set to deploy to Afghanistan from Fort Benning, Georgia, decided he shouldn't have to go until his alleged commander-in-chief proves the legitimacy of occupation of the White House. This began yet another bizarre chain of events that resulted once more in the government's continued refusal to address the issue at any level.

First, the Columbus (Georgia) *Ledger-Enquirer* reported that Maj. Cook was refusing his deployment orders to report for duty because Barack Obama is not the lawful commander-in-chief. The newspaper then parroted the party line assertion that Obama was actually born in Hawaii in 1961, two years after it became a state, thereby implying that Maj. Cook's charges were ridiculous. However, the newspaper, in typical MSM fashion, neglected to mention that Obama has never answered the numerous legal cases demanding he prove his claim is a fact.

A hearing in federal court was booked for Thursday, July 16th, 2009 but then canceled on the day before when the Army backtracked and declared that Maj. Cook would not be deployed to Afghanistan after all, displaying once again the government's reluctance to face the facts of the case. However, Cook learned later the same day that someone from the Department of Defense had pressured his civilian boss into firing him.

California-based attorney Orley Taitz, who has handled various other suits against Obama, filed a 20-page document with the U.S. District

Court for the Middle District of Georgia asking the court to consider granting his client's request based upon Maj. Cook's belief that Obama is not a natural-born citizen of the United States.

Cook further stated in his brief that he "would be acting in violation of international law by engaging in military actions outside the United States under this President's command . . . simultaneously subjecting himself to possible prosecution as a war criminal by the faithful execution of these duties."

Cook, a reservist, received the orders mobilizing him to active duty on June 9, and a hearing to discuss Cook's requests was to take place in federal court in Columbus on Thursday, July 16th, but when the Army rescinded his orders, the hearing was rendered moot.

"We won! We won before we even arrived," attorney Orley Taitz said with excitement. "It means that the military has nothing to show for Obama. It means that the military has directly responded by saying Obama is illegitimate—and they cannot fight it. Therefore, they are revoking the order. No explanation, no reasons, just revoked."

Cook added, "[If Obama is not there lawfully] any order coming out of the presidency or his chain of command is illegal. Should I deploy, I would essentially be following an illegal order. If I happened to be captured by the enemy in a foreign land, I would not be privy to the Geneva Convention protections," he said.

"That and the fact the individual who is occupying the White House has not been entirely truthful with anybody," he said. "Every time anyone has made an inquiry, it has been either cast aside, it has been maligned, it has been laughed at or just dismissed summarily without further investigation."

He said he would be prepared for a backlash against him as a military officer, since members of the military swear to uphold and follow their orders. However, he noted that following an illegal order would be just as bad as failing to follow a legal order. Meanwhile, retired Maj. Gen. Carol Dean Childers and active U.S. Air Force reservist Lt. Col. David Earl Graeff have joined the suit "because it is a matter of unparalleled public interest and importance and because it is clearly a matter arising from issues of a recurring nature that will escape review unless the court exercises its discretionary jurisdiction."

Before news of the order being revoked was reported, MSNBC anchor Keith Olbermann called Cook a "jackass" and Taitz a "conwoman," as he labeled both of them the "worst persons in the world." He verbally flogged the soldier with the cheap shot that he was "an embarrassment to all those who have served without cowardice," as if bravery were the issue.

Over the past year, when reporters from the major media weren't ignoring this birth issue totally, they were belittling it with attempted character assassination, such as with Olbermann, while turning a blind eye to the most important factor, the law.

Upon receipt of the revocation order from the military, Cook called his civilian boss, the CEO of Simtech, Inc. The company does DOD contracting in the general field of information technology/ systems integration, at which Cook was employed as a senior systems engineer and architect until taking a military leave of absence on July 10, 2009, in preparation for his deployment to Afghanistan.

The purpose of his call was to inform his boss that he would not require the military leave of absence after all and could return to work. Instead, according to sources, Larry Grice, the CEO of Simtech, Inc., informed Mr. Cook that his services were no longer required. The Department of the Army had wasted no time in pressuring Simtech into creating a repercussion for Maj. Cook, who was only attempting to behave lawfully and force his superiors to do the same.

Why are these Barack Hussein Obama documents off-limits?
1. Certified copy of original birth certificate
2. Columbia University transcripts
3. Columbia thesis paper
4. Campaign donor analysis requested by seven watchdog groups
5. Harvard University transcripts
6. Illinois State Senate records
7. Illinois State Senate schedule
8. Law practice client list and billing records/summary
9. Locations and names of all half-siblings and step-mothers
10. Medical records (only the one page summary released so far)
11. Occidental College transcripts
12. Parents' marriage certificate

13. Record of baptism
14. Selective Service registration records
15. Schedules for trips outside of the United States before 2007
16. Scholarly articles
17. List of all campaign workers that are lobbyists
18. Punahou, Hawaii grade school records

And, we must ask, where might the passport used by Stanley Ann Durham Obama (rebellious mother of Barack Jr.) in 1961 be found? If a private investigation could produce this, it would reflect exactly where she was on August 4th. Because computers were not in use at the time, the passport itself, with its visa stamps and date of entry and exit from the various countries, would be the only accurate record.

TIP OF THE ICEBERG

Just who has been sending "the message" to discredit anyone who dares question B.H.O.'s eligibility to be president? And how did it permeate not only the media, but also the once-respected U.S. Congress and the courts of our land, including the once-incorruptible Supreme Court?[2] And what menacing forces made the once-courageous conservative media abandon their mission to stand on truth and expose rank corruption and collusion?

Two words: Money talks!

Who in the naïve public can imagine what happens to a media mogul that gets word from the FCC that the company's license will be pulled immediately and irrevocably if his reporters/talking-heads mention the three words "Obama's birth certificate"? Poof! A disappearing act is immediately performed, and one of three things is about to evaporate immediately, and it is never No. 1, the company. The boss sends the message to the employees and tells them that their mega-salaries and even their very employment are on the line. No. 2 is the employee who stepped over the boundary, and only on very seldom occasions does he/she happen to be one with strong enough principles to walk away from the money and prestige in exchange for telling the truth. That leaves only No. 3, and it is the one to go nearly every time: the story, and it merely disappears from

Young Barack Obama and the grandmother who swears he was born in Kenya.

the airwaves and print without further comment, and something like the birth certificate question becomes a non-issue because it is no longer mentioned. Out of sight, out of mind. It's the Communist way.

Lou Dobbs of CNN felt this exact heat in July of '09 for simply saying on-air that he believed that Obama was truly born in Hawaii but that in order to bring all the hoopla to a halt, "he should show his birth certificate." The resulting action from above tended to prove Dobbs was wrong on both counts. Dobbs' resignation a few months later was thought by many to have been tied to this and other muzzling attempts, although he never said so.

If you're a conservative talk-show host and you get your boss's directive not to dare mention forbidden words, you are handcuffed. Period. Lips sealed; curiosity zero! If the money thing doesn't work, there's always the threat thing, i.e., "going public" about tax records, health status or family secrets. Or be audited by the IRS. Or be investigated by any number of regulatory agencies, such as the DEA, as in Rush Limbaugh's case.

And if these methods don't work, how about being reminded of all those "accidents" and "unfortunate incidents," broken kneecaps, missing children, "falls" from buildings and punctured tires resulting not in joblessness or embarrassment but in death?[3]

We know that's how the Mafia works. It's also how political machines work. It's also how community organizers work. It was Obama himself who in 2008 said: "If they bring a knife . . . we bring a gun," and in 2009 advised his followers to "Get in their faces!"

So determined are Obama's handlers to keep the facts of his parentage and place of birth out of the public domain that, as so many writers, unrestricted of corporate control, have scrupulously documented, the Federal Elections Commission shows Obama's campaign has made regular payments to Perkins Coie since Jan. 1, 2007, the month he formed a presidential exploratory committee and only weeks before he formally announced his candidacy for president and [up to the present] has paid Perkins Coie, a single law firm, $2.5 million to crush eligibility lawsuits, according to reports citing Federal Election Commission records.

But paying lawyers to quash the dozens of lawsuits that have challenged Obama's eligibility still doesn't answer the question of who exactly is behind the blanket blackout of the media, Congress and courts when it comes to Obama's origins, parentage, credentials, indeed identity.

We seem to have slipped much further down the road to world government (democracy=socialism=Communism=world government) than anyone had suspected. It appears that Obama was protected and knew that he was protected even before he announced his run for the presidency. With the capture and control of the black box voting computers, the news media and apparently now even the judiciary, the "anointed one" had nothing to worry about, and the legal fees were undoubtedly paid from the mysterious millions that came into his campaign fund from "persons unknown overseas" to aid his election.

The world is witnessing a fundamental transformation of America while Americans sit idly by and say, "Duh."

When Obama wrote a book and said he was mentored as a youth by Frank Marshall Davis, an avowed Communist, and that his grandparents sent his mother to a socialist school, people said that didn't matter and were not bothered either by the fact that he was raised a Muslim from early childhood. After all, these people wanted "change," and most anything would be a refreshing change after the eight deceptive years of George Bush.

But after he took office and so many other shocking truths began to surface, why is there no uproar? Does no one care that the president of the United States is not only sitting unlawfully but he has said that should the political winds ever shift in an ugly direction he will "stand with the Muslims"?

When he admitted in his book that he chose Marxist friends and professors in college and then sought the endorsement of the Marxist Party in 1996 as he ran for the Illinois Senate, so-called "American" people voted for him anyway.

When Obama sat in a Chicago Church for 20 years and listened to a preacher spew hatred for America and preach black liberation theology, and when Obama chose friends and acquaintances such as revolutionary radicals Bill Ayers and Bernadine Dohrn, and when he received endorsements from people such as Louis Farrakhan, Muamar Qadaffi and Hugo Chavez, nobody seemed to care.

When he surrounded himself in the White House with advisors who were pro-gun control, pro-abortion, pro-homosexual marriage and wanting to curtail freedom of speech to silence the opposition, people said it didn't matter.

And even when he took over insurance companies, car manufacturing companies, and banks, somehow it was no big deal.

And somehow, we are now a Communist nation.

Our biggest enemy is not China, Russia, Iran or any other foreign nation. Our biggest enemy is a contingent of politicians in Washington, D.C. bent on "change."

We are witnessing the utter Communization of America. Nikita Sergeyevich Khrushchev warned in 1960, "We will bury you," and Obama is doing it within the two generations that the commies said it would take—and without firing a shot.

The danger to America is not Barack Obama but a citizenry capable of entrusting a man such as this with the presidency. It will be far easier to limit and undo the follies of an Obama presidency than to restore the necessary common sense and good judgment to a depraved electorate willing to have such a man for their president. The problem is much

THE BIRTH CERTIFICATE CONTROVERSY

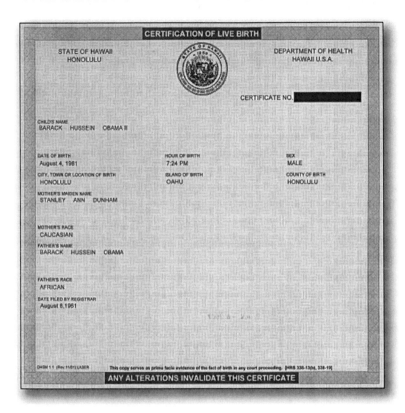

Above is Barack Obama's "Certification of Live Birth" from Hawaii. It is not a birth certificate, *per se*, but a modern computer-generated form on modern stock. While it may be believable that he does not possess his real birth certificate, it is hard to swallow that not one hospital in the Honolulu area (in which city Obama claims he was born) has any record of his mother, Stanley Ann Dunham, giving birth in its facility. Another peculiar anomaly is that the father's race is listed as "African" instead of "Negro," as one would expect having inspected other birth certificates from the era. At the same time, witnesses claim a very pregnant Dunham was seen in Kenya, a nation that proudly proclaims Obama as a native son.

deeper and far more serious than a Barry Soetoro, who is a mere symptom of what ails America. Blaming the prince of the dunces should not blind anyone to the vast confederacy of dunces that made him their prince. The republic can survive even a Barack Obama, who is a far greater danger to it than a mere fool, but it is less likely to survive an ongoing multitude of fools such as those who made him their president.

Everything he ever told us was a lie.

ENDNOTES:

1 Charles Tisdale, the late editor and publisher of Mississippi's only black-owned newspaper, used to delight in exchanging stories with me at breakfast in Jackson once a week or more for nearly a decade. Once, when I had driven him to Oxford for a speech at the university, he introduced me to the Ole Miss journalism class as his "token honkie," and nobody laughed as loudly as I. He used to tell about standing with a group of Negro reporters in front of the Tallahatchie County Courthouse during the 1955 trial of the killers of Emmitt Till, when the sheriff came ambling up the walk and greeted them with, "G'mornin', nigras." Those reporters from the *Chicago Tribune, New York Times* and *Washington Post* were appalled, but Charles, having been raised in Athens, Alabama during the "Stepin' Fetchit" days of the Depression, took no umbrage. He knew that they simply had been addressed with the Southern slang that inferred no disparagement. Unlike the others, he also knew that a common greeting at that time in the South from a black to a white stranger was often, "Mawnin', white folks."

2 On the afternoon of January 21, 2009, Obama's first day in office, Chief Justice John Roberts spent two private hours in the Oval Office with the new "president," but their discussions remained secret. By this time the Supreme Court had already resisted many lawsuits regarding the issue and has since ignored many more. Was some kind of treasonous agreement between the two most powerful men in the executive branch and judicial branch, protecting Obama's unlawful election, reached this day?

3 During the Clinton era, these were known as "Arkancides," and the suspected number went into three figures.

*"The trouble with socialism
is that you eventually run out
of other people's money."*

—PRIME MINISTER MARGARET THATCHER

THE MOON LANDING:

THE BIGGEST MEDIA HOAX IN U.S. HISTORY

Fifteen years ago Pat Shannan told William Bicket in *I Rode with Tupper* (page 89) that he didn't know if we (man) had been to the Moon or not, because he had no real evidence that we had *not*; but Bicket then posed the question to his readers, "How do you know that we *have*?" Indeed, with such rampant lies by government officials in so many different venues, endorsed and perpetuated by a cooperative news media, it is difficult for Americans to detect myth from truth.

Here we are confronted with probably the most controversial chapter in this whole book—more so even than the upcoming chapter about the 9-11 fraud on America, which no one in the U.S. *wants* to believe, even though, at last count, 84% didn't buy the ridiculous "official" story anyway. The reason that this one so much more grates on the credulity of the able-thinking American is that the idea has hardly ever been challenged. After all, everyone in my generation *watched* the @#%$ thing on TV! But while only 16 percent of Americans still believe the official explanation of the multiple 9-11 atrocities, and that number is shrinking, almost two-thirds of the world public never believed the way-out "Fantasyworld" production by the team of NASA/Nixon/Armstrong/et al. from the first hour. For the record, I was not one of the skeptics at the time and wouldn't be for 20 years.

(While most *Americans* still believe the official story of Armstrong walking on the Moon, hardly more than 33% of the rest of the world accepts it as fact to this day. Many other nations' citizens chuckle under their breath at our naiveté. Maybe what follows will help some of the deluded [by propaganda] Americans agree or at least think it further through. Meanwhile, we know we are strolling on the fringes and risking "insanity by association" to be even covering this topic.

However, the facts now require it. Today these facts showing that the event never took place far outweigh those that have been sold to the world public as proof that the U.S. astronauts performed a successful Moon landing with Apollo 11. In fact, there is no proof whatsoever that Armstrong, Aldrin and Collins got any farther than a few hundred miles into space following the successful launch in July of 1969, but there is much proof that they did no more than orbit the Earth from a couple of hundred miles for a few days while the world watched the fantasy unfold. And the truth appears to be that they've been lying to us all along.

"Evil men and imposters will proceed from bad to worse, deceiving and being deceived." See 2nd Thessalonians 2:11.

"Cosmic Conspiracies" is a website out of England that has been challenging the Apollo missions for years, and it receives several letters from Apollo believers on an almost daily basis saying they are completely wrong in their scoffing. In retort, they point out that the distance that man allegedly had to travel to get to the Moon was the equivalent of 30 Earth diameters. Now compare that with the greatest distance that man has traveled since then (in the shuttle), which is 400 miles. That is the equivalent of just 1/2 an inch from the Earth compared to the distance allegedly traveled to the Moon.

Chief NASA wing-ding of the era Werner Von Braun said in his book *Conquest to the Moon* (published in 1953) that it would be impossible to send anyone to the Moon because of the sheer size of craft needed to do the trip. In fact, taking Von Braun's calculations into consideration, a spaceship that needed to travel that distance would have had to be 266 times bigger than the Saturn 5.

Also consider the recent announcement from NASA that it would take scientists 15 years from now to design and build a craft to go back to the Moon. Why, when we have supposedly been there six times already?

J.F. Kennedy announced in 1962 that man would travel to the Moon by the end of the decade. This was with little knowledge of the unknown mysteries of space. Just seven years later man allegedly did just that. But more than 40 years later in a world that is vastly technologically superior to the

1960s, why would it take over twice as long to do the same thing today? This article about "missing" Moon videotapes makes one wonder. . . .

MISSING VIDEOTAPES MAY HAVE BEEN FOUND
June 30, 2009, Fox News
www.foxnews.com/story/0,2933,529476,00.html

Just in time for the 40th anniversary of the first Moon landing, NASA may have found the long-lost original Apollo 11 videotapes. Back on July 20, 1969, the raw video feed from the Moon was beamed to the Parkes Observatory radio telescope in southeastern Australia, and then compressed and sent to Mission Control in Houston. Because of technical issues, NASA's images couldn't be fed directly to the TV networks. Instead, the grayish, blotchy images Americans saw on their TV sets were the result of a regular TV camera pointed at the huge wall monitor in Houston—a copy of a copy, in effect. Those images survive, and anyone can see them on YouTube. But the original, sharp, black-and-white tapes that were recorded at Parkes vanished. NASA had thought they'd been shipped to the Goddard Space Flight Center in Greenbelt, Md. But a search there a couple of years ago turned up nothing. Around the same time, though, a cache of tapes containing data from Moon-surface experiments from the entire Apollo program was discovered in a university basement in Perth, Western Australia, on the other side of the country from Parkes. According to the Sunday Express, NASA has combed through those tapes and found the original Apollo 11 video footage. "We're talking about the same tapes," an unnamed NASA spokesman told the newspaper, though he added that "at this point, I'm not prepared to discuss what has or has not been found."

Isn't it amazing that NASA could lose these invaluable tapes? There are many strange questions surrounding these issues, and the surfacing of these tapes just in time for the 40th anniversary is just one more to strain our credulity. Other attempts at perpetuating the lie were carried out at the same time, such as Buzz Aldrin's folly of rapping on record.

On the night of July 20, 1969, I sat in front of my TV just as mesmerized as everyone else, marveling at this scientific conquest, and because I trusted as fact everything that the news media reported at that time, not only did I have no reason to doubt what (I thought) I had just seen but scoffed at the few fools around me the next few years who did doubt it.

After all, President Nixon had talked to the astronauts from the Oval Office on live television. Nobody realized that we didn't even have the technology at that time to conduct such interviews from city to city or nation to nation on Earth, let alone into outer space.

As philosopher Dresden James said, "A truth's initial commotion is directly proportional to how deeply the lie was believed. It wasn't the world being round that agitated people, but the fact that the world wasn't flat. When a well-packaged web of lies has been sold gradually to the masses over generations, the truth will seem utterly preposterous and its speaker a raving lunatic."

Two full decades after Apollo 11, then in the early days of pursuing a career of investigative journalism, I began to read many things outside the scope that never reached the daily newsstands. One of these pieces was a short booklet by a former NASA engineer named Bill Kaysing, called *We Never Went to the Moon*. It was mostly filled with circumstantial evidence that could be taken either way as well as engineering data considerably over my head, but it did contain a few penetrating facts and questions that at least made one think. It wasn't a lot of irrefutable evidence, but it was enough to get my attention.

I began to realize that Neil Armstrong's walk on the Moon had to have been the biggest thing in modern history to happen since Jesus walked on the water, yet Armstrong would go for years without a public appearance. *"How come this man is such a recluse?"* I wondered. *"Maybe Kaysing's stuff has some merit."* I still had a lot to learn, but my investigative juices were flowing, and I realized that we Americans didn't know a blasted thing about Armstrong and Aldrin's alleged Moon walk except what the government had reported through its controlled media, and I had long since had my fill of "official" reports.

Charles Lindbergh's feat was "elementary Mickey Mouse" compared to this, yet he was a national hero for the rest of his life, everywhere he went—from 1927 to his death in 1974, Charles Lindbergh was revered as a *bona fide* hero. And yet now Neil Armstrong is (supposedly) a multiplied-by-many-times hero who was far more than the first to cross the ocean in a solo flight. Armstrong *walked on the Moon* for goodness sakes! Are you listening? Can anyone think of a greater feat since Jesus walked on the water?

This is an absolutely magnified and multiplied real-life Christopher Columbus, Capt. Cook or Thomas Jefferson or George Washington walking around in our midst. Why isn't he speaking on the college circuit, and why is he not even accessible? Not only is he seldom seen and photographed anywhere, he makes no public appearances whatsoever. This is the man who was just as obscure as Lindbergh had been one week and had jumped to the forefront of history the next. I certainly would delight in sitting with him and picking his brain. What a GIANT of history! Or was he? Is he really for real? After two decades, I didn't think so. I had begun to suspect that he is ashamed of his fraud, and as a fair-minded investigator, I began to listen to others who had more facts and a far better scientific background than I.

I wanted to be sure, and I must admit that I still am not able to make a statement of fact, but I am willing to go out on a limb. (After all, what power of fact and weight would a declaration from this non-scientist carry anyway?) While there is almost no evidence that the 1969 Moon Mission (and others that allegedly followed) ever actually took place, other than news reports which have no basis in fact and quote only the government deceivers, there is much evidence—enough to convince a jury of reasonable doubt, in my opinion—that not only did the event *not* happen as reported, but that it was impossible to have happened—violating many laws of physics—and was probably engineered by a team of high-level experts that not only fooled the world public but most or all of the engineers at the NASA bases of Houston and Cape Kennedy as well.

(One of the favorite defenses of the conspiracy scoffers is, "You just can't get that many people to keep a secret for this long"—and that is true. However, if the ground crew and technicians at Houston were fooled, too, then we can understand their lifelong pride of having been associated with such an historic event. It now appears that this was the case—that they were only victims of the deception and fraud and never even suspected it. Those that were aware were either bought off or rubbed out.)

The accessories *before* and especially *after the fact* were the news media. The hoax could not have been pulled off without this cooperation.

The most outspoken and renowned of the scoffing group are Bill Kaysing of course, because he was first, Ralph René of New Jersey, Jim Collier and the Johnny-come-lately Bart Sibrel, who, through the benefit

In mid-July of 2009, the British press reported that spaceman Buzz Aldrin had teamed up with a rap star to record a song marking the 40th anniversary of his Apollo 11 Moon landing. The single with Snoop Dogg—*Rocket Experience*—was dreamt up by Aldrin, 79, to boost waning interest in the U.S. space program.

of the combined research of the others before him, has now produced the most convincing work of all. If you check out these four with an Internet search, you will find at least three interesting points to ponder about the disparagement of each that is found; (1) the juvenile attacks on each researcher are based upon the character and questionable education and intelligence of the individuals, with no logical argumentation to the factual claims of each; (2) usually there are no signatures or identification of the ones supplying the disparaging critique; and (3) instinctively, you will begin to wonder about the aforementioned control of the alleged "free press."

(This is in the style of the Anti-Defamation League, whose personnel constantly feed the media by defaming any person or group that in any way challenges with facts the ADL's false claims. Rather than debate sensibly with logic and facts, the ADL chooses to disparage its opponents with ungrounded and unrelated defamation that never meets the subject at hand. My friend and colleague in deception exposure, talk show host Dave von Kleist, refers to the ADL as the "Anti-Defecation League" because they are "so full of it." My personal message, after a half century of witnessing these lies and those of Morris Dees and the so-called Southern Poverty Law group and others similar is: when you stop telling lies about me and my colleagues, then we'll stop telling the truth about you.)

When a man can think of no other way but imprisonment to rid himself of a verbal opponent, it is because he has no arguments. When a man is reduced to making up stupid lies, it is because the truth is against him. —Phillipe Henriot

The first discrepancy to be cited by the "authentic" scoffers—those who did the in-depth research and study of the pictures, lighting, previous history, and capabilities of NASA at the time—was the multiple shadows from the pictures on the Moon. With the Sun as the only source of light on the Moon, the researchers logically claim that there can be but one shadow at only one angle. Most of the still photos taken by the astronauts of each other show various shadow angles suggesting more than one source of light.

The second early discrepancy was not so obvious to us uneducated laymen, but for the scientists around the world it was just as easy to spot as the multiple shadows. The consistency of the lunar surface—that gray powder—as shown on the film to the world public is not what the surface really looks like, according to the experts.

The surface of the Moon is not this smooth, flat, dry, powdery, dusty surface that we saw but rather a black, rough, jagged lava base, say the scientists such as the one who follows here.

CORNELL PROFESSOR JAMES MCCANNEY

"Whom do you know that has any first-hand knowledge that we ever went to the Moon?" asks Jim McCanney, who says that after a quarter-century of looking he hasn't found any but has sat with many scientific experts who know that we didn't go, that such a feat was impossible.

Indeed, the testimony of almost all of us old enough to remember is only, "I know they went there because I saw it on TV!"

So who is Jim McCanney, and what does he know? He was a college student at the time of the Apollo program and because of his study and research was one who happened to know just a little bit more about the situation than most of Americans and one who a few years later was to become very suspicious of the whole sham.

In the 1980s and into the '90s, archeologist and astronomer McCanney worked with some of the top Russian scientists, who just laughed at him when the subject arose, saying, "Your people never went to the Moon."

These Russian scientists were well versed and experienced on the 1950s discovery of the Van Allen Belts by an Iowa university professor and knew that no man could get through that thick belt of radioactivity and emerge alive. (A spaceship with the required 12-inch-thick lead shield completely encapsulating the outside skin would be far too heavy to be even lifted off the launch pad.) Russia was miles ahead of us in space research, and they knew better than to try to break through this deadly belt. This is why they sent up monkeys instead of humans in their early experiments. (More details on Dr. James Van Allen's discovery to follow.)

Russia, McCanney learned from the scientists, had a far more advanced space program than the U.S. could even claim, even with its constant disingenuous habit of deception. Russia tried to send men to the Moon long before we did and had launched over 1,600 small spacecraft into space from 1962 to 1976—sometimes sending up two and three craft a day with four to six people going at a time. During this time they never went to the Moon, of course, with their massive program that was so much bigger than ours, but at no time was anything ever reported in the Western press about this tremendous space program going on in Russia.

"When we thought it was so great that the U.S. was launching a couple of times a year," says McCanney, "Russia had the Kosmo series shuttle. That shuttle alone had over 1,200 flights during those years. I then realized that the American press had not been honest with us."

Many other problems began to surface, he found, once he embarked upon his own investigation.

He reports that only a week before the scheduled Apollo 11 launch (the one that allegedly landed on the Moon with Armstrong et al.) they still couldn't get the lunar lander to work. There was an accident where it flipped upside down and crashed during a test flight.

"Then we learned that the landing vehicle itself was not stable and could not land on the Moon," he said, the aforementioned rough surface being another problem. "That's when I realized that there was something seriously wrong here. And that's when I learned also of a lot of other deception that was happening within NASA, and I started seeing first hand, for instance, how data would come in from a space probe and be totally changed around and then presented to the public. What they were doing was trying to promote their own pet theories. The scientists were very arrogant, and it was the beginning of a lie that has perpetuated throughout the United States.

"Then at the end of the Voyager program was when they started animating test results. It turned out that it was easier for them to hire Disney animators and present results. So NASA learned that they didn't have to do anything and still would get that 15 to 20 billion dollars a year, and that's where this lie is leading. NASA realized that it does not have to show much to the public to get that money, and much of it today designated for the space program is actually going into people's pockets."

McCanney points out that the Apollo 13 "mishap" was a hoax, too. An entertaining rendition can be found in the Ron Howard movie production by the same title, *Apollo 13*, with Tom Hanks playing the lead role of astronaut Jim Lovell.

It really is an entertaining movie, watched again by this author only a few nights before writing these words, in order to obtain research information. But McCanney says that this was another staged incident (why not, after the first one worked so well?) designed to make the public (whose interest had been waning since the alleged Moon walk that so few believed) pay more attention to the space program.

Another thing that defies the laws of physics is the severe temperature change from the dark side of the Moon to the sunlit side. These temperatures vary in a 14.8-day period from more than 200 degrees below zero F to well over 200 above zero F.

Not only can this present a tremendous problem to any human not wearing enough protection against the extremes, but Bart Sibrel, who was supplied with most of his early research by Ralph René, claims that the 12-volt batteries, the same used to power an ordinary golf cart, could not function for the many hours that they appeared to be used.

Anyone who has gone 18 holes with a battery-powered golf cart would agree. And another important detail: the batteries of 1969 had not nearly the power and longevity of those now 40 years more modern.

Bart Sibrel, producer of the best-selling video of all on the subject, *A Funny Thing Happened on the Way to the Moon*, has been screaming for more than a decade that the Apollo Moon landings are science fiction.

In addition to the scores of non-qualified but logically thinking laymen who agree, there are many highly educated engineers and scientists who are willing to refute as "impossible" the wild and erratic claims made by NASA surrounding the whole five-year span of Moon hoaxes.

The space shuttle, Sibrel points out, has killed 14 people so far, with the mere attempt to attain an orbit about 250 miles above the Earth.

How is it then, that nearly half a century ago, with less computing power in the entire rocket than in a present-day $20 Wal-Mart watch, NASA claims to have gone 100,000% farther, six different times between 1969 and 1972, landing on another celestial body and then returning, without ever killing anyone?

How could they have powered air conditioning in 224-degree heat for three days with only batteries?

Why is the "second round" of "returning" to the Moon estimated to be no earlier than half a century after the first? (Few people remember that in 1927 the second trans-Atlantic flight took place only weeks after Lindbergh's, and there were several more before the decade was out. There were also many who went before him, and he may not have even been the first to do it solo, but such it is with recorded "history.")

"If the Moon landings were, as we now believe, a government deception," says Sibrel, "then George Orwell's comment, 'whoever controls the past controls the future' is a scary wake up call to insist that our government reform to the truthfulness of our founding father 'who could not tell a lie.' Otherwise, the powers that be will continue their addiction to deception, and we all will be worse off for it."

Ralph René (1933-2008), from whom Sibrel learned the early information that provoked his own temperament and spawned his initial inquiry, has had much influence on the more publicized researchers that have followed.

René showed the folly of the double shadows in the pictures of "Man on the Moon" from the 1969 shots.

Kaysing brought the initial questions to the public in 1985. Jim Lovell called him a "wacko" but nearly stuck his head in the noose by doing so, because Kaysing sued him for defamation of character, thereby setting the stage for getting an astronaut on the witness stand under oath.

Certainly, some high-ranking strings had to be pulled behind the scenes to get this stopped, and soon a federal judge dismissed Kaysing's suit without comment.

Kaysing found out quickly that he was battling a lot more than just a single defendant that defamed him.

The dismissal of his federal lawsuit against astronaut Lovell made the alleged cover-up seem to be not only real and constant but universal and omnipotent.

Kaysing had sued for defamation of character because Lovell had publicly proclaimed him to be nuts. And a liar. So how does this get dismissed just because the defendant is a former astronaut, or is there is something deeper to conceal?

Of course, most of this so far is still speculation, so let's get into some more definite facts.

THE EARTH'S MOON

"The Earth may have only one Moon, but it's a big one! The Earth's moon is the fifth largest in the whole Solar System. But it is still much smaller than the Earth, so objects weigh less on the Moon than they do here. That's why the astronauts could enjoy bouncing around on the lunar surface."

Oh, yeah?

The above deceptive claim is made at one of the "search" hits we made on the subject. The contrasting problem with this is the claim in the last sentence and the fact that the astronauts *did not* "bounce around on the lunar surface," as shown by the film evidence.

In all the videos and still-shots published of the astronauts singing & dancing, running & jumping, and just generally frolicking for fun on the Moon's surface, none shows anyone jumping higher than a foot in the air, about the height that would be expected on Earth with a 60-pound pack on one's back.

However, with the Moon's gravity pull being but one-sixth of that of the Earth (something we learned in elementary school), the weightless-

Even though NASA says there was a bar holding the flag stiff, Moon-landing skeptics ask: "Why is the flag billowing when there is neither wind nor atmosphere?" The flag is clearly rippling for some reason. Inset top right, the distinct footprint left by Armstrong should have been more like the indentation you leave in dry sand at the beach.

ness on the Moon means that the astronaut's ordinary and effortless hops and skips we see on film from the Moon's surface should have bounded him to five or six feet in air—a real "giant leap for mankind—displaying kangaroo leaps that would have been humanly impossible on Earth! They did not because they could not. They were not on the Moon.

We can think of nothing that would have been more convincing of man's presence on the Moon than to have seen these kangaroo leaps. Then the only claim the scoffers could have possibly had of this feat would have been that "the pictures were faked"; and that the feat was not really performed on the Moon but only appeared so with trick photography. It would have been an argument much easier for NASA to defend than the ones we are left with.

We must remember, too, that we never saw any faces behind those face shields of the spacesuits. Could this and the other alleged "Moon" pix have been filmed say in Area 51 of Nevada? Did the spacesuits in the film contain three other people not even known to Armstrong, Aldrin and Collins?

But because the extraordinary leaps never took place, it certainly appears as convincing evidence, instead, that the official photos were, indeed, faked; but not with the results that the fakers had intended.

Actually, as anyone who looks meticulously at the stills and video film of the 1969 Moon walk and others you may have seen, there is no convincing evidence that there is a real presence on the Moon of humans from Earth. Yet there is very convincing evidence—beyond a reasonable doubt—that the pictures were taken somewhere on planet Earth.

The photo on the facing page is another object of scorn. It is purported to be that of Armstrong's first "small step for man . . ." etc. However, because there is no atmosphere on the Moon, there also is no moisture, which would seem to render such a footprint in the dust impossible.

A decade after Professor McCanney's revelations and Kaysing's book, Ralph René of New Jersey, a brilliant physicist who would later be berated by critics not for his factual data but because of his lack of formal education, wrote a book called *NASA Mooned America*, a masterpiece that later inspired videographer Bart Sibrel to produce his documentary. René took a copy to investigative journalist Jim Collier in New York, and Collier became fascinated with it.

Jim Collier and his brother Ken had just completed and published a 20-year work exposing the computer vote fraud in America—*VoteScam*—and Jim was sufficiently ignited to do his own video documentary on the subject. He called it *Was It Only a Paper Moon?*

Collier began his own investigation and proved a couple of other things that had only been speculative doubt to René. After visiting NASA in Houston and the Air & Space Museum in D.C. with a videographer at his side, Jim showed how the seating section of the Lunar Module, popularized at the time as the "LEM"—the small craft that took them the short jaunt from the spacecraft to the Moon's surface—allegedly—was just about the size of two phone booths, allowing a "phone booth" apiece for each of the two astronauts aboard.

However, the video pictures also make it obvious that an astronaut wearing his inflated space suit, with his oxygen tank and other equipment in the backpack strapped on behind him, simply could not have first fit into the seat provided nor been able to emerge from the contraption because *the exit door actually opened to the inside.*

The LEM never flew on Earth. The one time Armstrong tried it, he had to bail out prior to its crashing. When Collier visited the developers of the LEM, Grumman Aircraft, he was told that all the paperwork had been destroyed.

Collier exclaimed, "A $30 billion project and the most historic venture in the history of mankind, and they destroyed the paperwork?"

Then he speculates as to *why* NASA would be foolish enough to allow anyone to use this craft that had never flown on Earth in another "test" flight on the Moon. "And why would their wives have even allowed this insanity without protest?"

Moreover, the famous "Moon buggies," the lunar roving vehicles (LRVs), that the astronauts cruised around in and allegedly left up there on the Moon's surface, were actually *too large* to have fit into the LEM and could not have been hauled by it.

Having studied the pictures supposedly snapped on the Moon surface, Jim Collier observed that the multiple shadows of varying length and from more than one light source, the phony Moon rocks, the distinct footprints where there is no moisture, and the impossibility of the LEM and LRV, all show that the performance never really happened as reported and was instead a grand production in a desert studio, most likely the government protected site of Area 51 in the Nevada desert.

I still had found no evidence whatsoever that any human had ever reached the Moon, but there seemed to be plenty that *no one* ever had. Here's more:

THE VAN ALLEN BELTS

While we don't claim to possess a scholastic background qualifying us as capable of making any scientific points of our own regarding this situation, we do know how to read. A mere listener in the audience can see that the most glaring scientific obstacle standing in the way of the veracity of the official story are the Van Allen belts. In 1958, James Van Allen, professor at the University of Iowa, discovered a belt of radiation surrounding the Earth.

On January 31, 1958 a Jupiter C rocket was launched and carried the *Explorer 1* satellite, and as soon as it reached altitudes of several hundred miles, the Geiger counter began to register the frantic clicking of thousands of particles passing through the satellite every minute. Professor Van Allen remarked in surprise "Space is radioactive!" Additional satellites such as *Explorer 3* and *Explorer 4* confirmed this discovery. The *Pioneer 1* and *Pioneer 3* space probes were launched late in 1958 and carried radiation detectors with them on their unsuccessful trips to the Moon, but the data showed just how the Van Allen belts were shaped in space. It was soon thereafter that Van Allen began to issue his warnings to the newly born NASA that anybody traveling in a spacecraft for an extended time through this belt of radiation would have to wear some kind of yet-to-be-determined protection. The spacecraft would have needed lead shielding several inches or even a few feet thick.

From James Van Allen's own words in his autobiographical sketch we learn: "Following the Soviets' successful flights of the first Earth satellite *Sputnik I* and then *Sputnik II*, the Army's rocket vehicle Jupiter C was adopted as a U.S. alternative to the planned but faltering Vanguard vehicle for placing an early U.S. payload into Earth orbit. By virtue of preparedness and good fortune, the Iowa cosmic-ray instrument was selected as the principal element of the payload of the first flight of a four-stage Jupiter C, launched on 31 January 1958 (1 February GMT).

"Both the vehicle and our instrument worked. The data from the single Geiger-Mueller tube on *Explorer 1* (as the payload was called) yielded the discovery of the radiation belt of the Earth—a huge region of space populated by energetic charged particles (principally electrons and protons), trapped within the external geomagnetic field. The attempted launch of *Explorer II* was a vehicular failure, but the launch of *Explorer 3* on 26 March 1958, with an augmented version of the Iowa instrument, was successful. The *Explorer 3* data provided massive confirmation of our earlier discovery and clarified many features of the earlier body of data.

"Soon thereafter we were invited to provide radiation-detecting instruments for two satellites for the observation of the effects of several nuclear bombs to be detonated after delivery to high altitudes by rockets. On a time scale of less than three months Carl McIlwain, George Ludwig and I designed and built the radiation packages for these satellites—using much smaller and more discriminating detectors, chosen for the first time with knowledge of the existence of the natural radiation belts and the enormous intensity of charged particles therein.

"*Explorer* 4 was launched successfully on 26 July 1958. Our apparatus operated as planned and provided the principal body of observations of the artificial radiation belts that were produced by the three high altitude nuclear bursts—called Argus II and III. The back-up launch of our apparatus on *Explorer* 5 was a vehicular failure. *Analysis of our* Explorer *4 data on the natural radiation belt as well as on the artificial radiation belts from the Argus bursts propelled the entire subject to a new level of understanding and broad scientific interest.*" (emphasis added)

RALPH RENÉ

The first Soviet confirmation of the existence of natural radiation belts came from *Sputnik 3*, launched in May 1958.

"Late in 1958, the Iowa group supplied radiation detectors on two missions, *Pioneer 1* and *Pioneer 3*, which were intended to impact the Moon. The lunar objective was not achieved but our data established the large scale structure and radial dimensions of the region containing geomagnetically trapped radiation. Another lunar flight, *Pioneer 4* (also unsuccessful in reaching the Moon), of our apparatus in early 1959 provided a valuable body of confirmatory data."

Van Allen's early research, more than a decade before Apollo 11 blasted off, showed among other things: the radiation belts are of importance primarily because of the *harmful effects* of high-energy particle radiation for man and electronics:

• It degrades satellite components, particularly semiconductor and optical devices;
  • It induces background noise in detectors;
  • It induces errors in digital circuits;
  • It induces electrostatic charge-up in insulators;
  • It is also a threat to the astronauts.

This is the synthesized result of lengthy scientific research by University of Iowa Professor James Van Allen: However, upon seeing a controversial television presentation a few years ago questioning the validity of the 1969 Moon shot, Van Allen (1914-2006) referred to *no less than his own work* as "nonsense":

> The recent Fox TV show, which I saw, is an ingenious and entertaining assemblage of nonsense. The claim that radiation exposure during the Apollo missions would have been fatal to the astronauts is only one example of such nonsense.

Why would Van Allen do this?

I have a problem with his later, degrading opinion of himself because it is so typical of what goes on in this Orwellian era in which we live. With the ability to create money out of thin air, governments have an enormous behind-the-scenes power. Cognizant of the death threats and other CIA power moves that followed the Kennedy assassination, the OKC investigation, TWA Flight 800, Waco, Ruby Ridge and the inside job of 9-11, to name but a few, I find it to be no stretch of the imagination to see that "they" got to Dr. Van Allen in recent years when their hoax was in jeopardy. We will also see in subsequent chapters how easily assassins can be purchased to take care of the uncooperative players on the opposite side of the fence. Knowing what we know, and what we see above as Van Allen's lifelong claim to fame being scattered to the winds, we can easily suspect that he got a visit from the guys in the dark glasses and tan trench coats telling him how they knew what time his grandchildren got off the school bus and how easily they could be abducted and "disappeared" forever.

These remarks were made by Neil Armstrong at the White House on Wednesday, July 20, 1994 during a ceremony commemorating the Apollo 11 mission: "Today we have with us a group of students, among America's best. To you we say we have only completed a beginning. We leave you much that is undone. There are great ideas undiscovered, breakthroughs available to those who can remove one of the truth's protective layers. There are places to go beyond belief. . . ."

And just what is this protective layer of truth he would like to see removed by the next generation? We can imagine only one, and it is being presented right here. The poor guy is wrung out with despair and, guilt-ridden, would like to rectify the deceiving position in which he was placed and cleanse his soul before he dies. At his worst, he is trying to open some doors here of "I tried to tell you." At best, he could come forward before he dies with an affidavit of truth.

We the People would appreciate the latter. If he does not, he will remain on the same level of Revisionist history of government tools as Lee & Harvey Oswald, (coming up), James Earl Ray, Sirhan Sirhan, Arthur Bremer, John Hinckley and Tim McVeigh et al. Neil Armstrong, Edwin "Buzz" Aldrin, Michael Collins and all those who followed were similar patsies in a different venue, sucked into a scheme without consent from which they could not escape. How wonderful it would be for us here, as well as his eternity, if just one would muster the courage to tell the world the truth. At their ages today, none has very long to repent.

It was not the first time that Armstrong threw in a subtle hint that all may not be exactly as it seems. In previous press conferences shortly following the alleged walk on the Moon, Armstrong not only inadvertently contradicted one of the others, as all three were very vague in their answers to the press, but issued other subtle hints that could be taken in a whole different vein. In general, Neil Armstrong appears to be an emotionally tortured man who hates himself for the lie that he has lived the last half of his life. But if he is under a death threat, as many suspect today should he come forward himself, perhaps he just might delight and revel in the prospect that someone after him might expose the fraud of which he never wished to be a part.

That would not be enough. He must put in an affidavit now, and if he does not have the courage to fight (how much longer does this wimpy pacifist expect to live?) now, then at least leave it in a *published* document to be read to the world at his wake.

During the few occasions that Neil Armstrong does appear publicly, he seems to be very uncomfortable. Is he under a threat of death should he expose the truth? We believe that he and the others have been under exactly such a threat since being fished out of the ocean in 1969 and probably even before they ever committed to the fraud and stepped into the phony Moon rocket that launched them into the stratosphere but not to the Moon.

Moonfaker Neil Armstrong said he "never even *dreamed* of going to the Moon."

MOONFAKER NEIL ARMSTRONG (born 1930)

"Astronot" Neil Armstrong—allegedly the first man on the Moon—was totally opposite to Werner von Braun in personality. Neil kept a very, very low profile and that probably saved his life. Here is a quote from an authorized biography of Neil Armstrong:

NEIL ARMSTRONG

"When Neil started as a professor at the University of Cincinnati in 1970, news executives from the area's radio, TV, and print media were summoned to a downtown restaurant to hear an ultimatum: They were not to request interviews with the space hero who would be living in their midst, because none would be granted; they were to totally ignore his presence and not consider it legitimate news.

Amazingly, the group agreed—with one exception. Lawrence H. Rogers, then head of Taft Broadcasting Corporation, owners of a chain of television and radio stations in the region, howled in protest. "The reason they gave was that Neil had no secretary and would be overwhelmed with requests. I raised my hand and said, 'That's the most preposterous thing I have ever heard.' I told them Armstrong was the most famous explorer since Christopher Columbus; it would have been criminal journalistically to not write about him and praise what he had accomplished." (Wagener, *One Giant Leap*, pp. 298-99)

After the ploy to fake the Moon shot and to just let the guys orbit the Earth for a few days before being dramatically dropped into the ocean, the three began to behave fatuously, obviously resenting the roles into which they had been thrust and frustrated that they could do nothing about it.

When he was first handed the slip of paper on which his famous script for the ages was written—*"One small step for a man; one giant leap for mankind!"*—astronaut Neil Armstrong scoffed, *"Who wrote that crap?"* As the astronauts walked to the launch pad that morning, he was heard on his helmet radio facetiously requesting a window seat, asking the location of the duty free shop, what was the in-flight movie and what were they serving for dinner.

All of this shocking evidence is very difficult for any American, inoculated by government educational deceivers for 12 years or more (especially while carrying what is likely to be a case of "Red, White & Blue Fever"), to grasp as fact; even when it is so blatantly presented here.

But somewhere between "here and there," Americans and the deceived world lost their investigative way—mostly through the combined efforts of a disingenuous news media, both electronic and print.

The official government reports of the era said that Oswald killed Kennedy, all by himself as a "lone nut"; James Earl Ray killed Martin Luther King, Jr. and was stupid enough to dump the self-incriminating evidence on the street as a "lone nut assassin"; Arthur Bremer wounded Alabama Governor George Wallace four times (early reports first said "five") and three others at least once each with a Smith & Wesson, Model 36, five-shot revolver (for you neophytes on weaponry, that's a gun that holds and fires a maximum of five rounds). And Americans bought it. We were being filled with propagandizing lies.

Then we have the assassination attempt on President Ronald Reagan that pointed to another inside job a decade later. We'll have more about that shortly, but let us get back to the subject at hand. The point is that whenever government gets away with another lie, it will eventually have the people believing the completely illogical if not the impossible.

And another quote from Moonstruck Neil Armstrong:

"As for walking on the Moon, sometimes I wonder if that really happened. I can honestly say—and it's a great surprise to me—that I have never had a dream about being on the Moon. It's a great disappointment to me." (Wagener, *One Giant Leap*, p. 303)

Confronted on camera unexpectedly by Bart Sibrel, who had a microphone in one hand and a Bible in the other, Armstrong was totally speechless for several seconds before finally refusing to swear that he had been to the Moon. Sibrel offered him $5,000 (or to the charity of his choice) if Armstrong would simply place his hand on the Bible and swear before God that he had actually performed the famous feat. Instead, Armstrong ran like a rabbit. (Actually, after a few minutes of reflection, we found this escape to be far more admirable than lying under oath before God.)

Without evidence in hand, let us tell you what likely transpired: Armstrong, Aldrin and Collins were told early in 1969 that they would be the first astronauts to go to the Moon. They were led to believe it, told their wives so, and even NASA authorities believed that if everything went right and as planned, the three, indeed, would be the chosen ones.

The problem for the rest of the year, however, was that nothing *did* go according to plan, and by July, the NASA brass realized that they were going to have to revert to "Plan B" and activate the deception that had not only already been approved by the White House advisors and President Nixon but had been actually conceived by those high-ranking officials.

ENTER 2001 SPACE ODYSSEY PRODUCER

At the time of the Moon shots, the Cold War was at its height and a major coup such as landing a man on the Moon would have tremendous value, so this became a war of images.

Gen. Alexander Haig first came up with the plan to fake the actual Moon landing in a Hollywood movie set, and Donald Rumsfeld brought it to Nixon. He agreed, and they went into rapid production, using Walt Disney's studios in part. Stanley Kubrick was the man to pull it all together. Ralph René, Bill Kaysing, Jim McCanney, Jim Collier and, most recently, Bart Sibrel would pull it all apart a generation later.

STANLEY KUBRICK

Stanley Kubrick had just produced his sci-fi mega-hit movie in 1968, and he owed NASA a favor for having borrowed their super special camera for some of his difficult movie shots the year before. Pressured by the top officials in the U.S. government, including Richard Nixon, to repay the favor, Kubrick reluctantly agreed to help America score mega-points in the propaganda war.

After Kubrick died in 1999, his widow decided to come forward with the truth, knowing that her husband had hated for the rest of this life the role he was coerced into playing in order to falsify history. She came forward with the truth in a documentary suppressed by the Western MSM but found later on the Internet from British releases.

In this mystifying (why would they say this now?) conglomeration of interviews in a documentary including those of Mrs. Kubrick, Henry Kissinger, Don Rumsfeld, some military generals and a host of others, the whole scheming scenario is laid out. We even watch President Richard Nixon rehearsing a speech he would have to make if the men did land on the Moon and failed to return.

There are interviews with: Christiane Kubrick, Godfrey Hoffman—CIA, Fahrouk Elbaz—NASA, David Scott—Apollo 15 astronaut, Jack Torrence, Buzz Aldrin—astronaut, Lois Aldrin—wife, Eve Kendall—Nixon's secretary, David Bowman—NASA Houston, Richard Helms—CIA, Gen. Vernon Walters—CIA, Dimitri Muffley—CIA/KGB, Ambrose Chapel—CIA; and the most revealing information comes from interviews with: Donald Rumsfeld, Gen. Alexander Haig, Henry Kissinger and Lawrence Eagleburger.

Many of the production crew that worked on the production met with strange—and sudden—deaths, including Gen. Vernon Walters.

The rest became illegitimate history and a chapter in the lives of the three "astronots" that would haunt them for the rest of their lives, and not one can relish the facing of it to this day. A visit from the boys in the dark glasses and beige trench coats, with a few words of instruction and threat, was all it took.

Today, we have to wonder, *"Okay, those guys are all 75 or 80 or so now. Why won't one of them come forward with the truth at the last days of their lives?*

The answer to that is here, too, if you can read the white part of this page.

Astro-not #2, Buzz Aldrin, was tormented from the beginning. In the 1970s, according to family members, Aldrin became a pathetic, gutter-vomiting alcoholic. They were proud of him a decade later, though, when he claimed to have sworn off the booze and become a Christian. It was after another full decade of the cleaner living that Sibrel confronted him in a Los Angeles hotel lobby.

Upon being asked by Sibrel to place his hand on the Bible and swear to God that he had walked on the Moon in 1969, Aldrin lacked the restraint shown by Armstrong. Instead, this "born-again Christian" swung a roundhouse right and nailed the interviewer square in the left cheek. Hardly the reaction expected from an honest man, let alone a peace-loving "Christian."

Meanwhile, Michael Collins remains silent, too. He was later confronted by Sibrel and his cameraman and asked the same question. "Will you swear on a Bible that you went to the Moon in 1969?" Collins also refused, taking similar umbrage and threatening violence before storming away.

But the faked pictures (proven by the multiple shadows), lack of atmosphere and temperature extreme on the Moon, and dubious abilities of the "LEM" all aside, there is now a new source of evidence that is irrefutable and proves how NASA shot itself in the foot with its overzealous attempt to legitimize the lie. It is all the proof laymen such as you and I should need.

We speak here of the evidence found by Jack White, who is most renowned for his forensic photographic research from the Dealey Plaza assassination site in Dallas. However, it does not take an expert of any caliber to understand, along with all the other things they claimed to have done up there, that the astronauts would not have been capable of taking a picture almost every 50 seconds. That's right. In a total occupation time on the Moon with all the alleged visits—from NASA's official records—of 4,834 minutes (80.6 hours), the astronauts brought back 5,771 pictures.

Mr. White goes into much more detail in his report showing everything that the astronauts claimed they did while on each mission, rendering the taking of a picture every 50 seconds absolutely impossible.

So we now have to believe without reservation that a few people in very high places and only a few more at NASA pulled off this hoax and that even the ground crew at Houston was fooled. And anyone who looks at the evidence without prejudice can come up with no other conclusion. Evidence of this is expressed by the many testimonials from men and women who looked at Bart Sibrel's DVD *A Funny Thing Happened on the Way to the Moon* in recent years:

"NASA has admitted in 2002 that it cannot adequately protect the astronauts working in the International Space Station from radiation, yet it was able to do so with our lunar adventurers in flimsy Apollo modules back in 1969? Ridiculous. I absolutely enjoyed your documentary, and Buzz Aldrin simply punched you because he had no other recourse: you uncovered the truth." —Michael (IN)

* * *

"I just saw the presentation of your documentary in one of my writing classes where we were discussing the difference between opinion and belief. In my entire educational experience I have never seen a more convincing piece of evidence, which disregards the American pride of being the first to land on the Moon. And I agree that many of our beliefs are false as we need a scientific approach to prove them. The world ought to know the truth!" —Angad (CA) "I was watching Jay Leno last night, and what did I see? You getting decked by Buzz Aldrin for apparently asking him to tell the truth. That seals it for me. There is no way we landed on the Moon." —Eric (NH)

* * *

"I don't believe we ever went. Some think Apollo 11 was the only fake one, but I think they all were. The thing that sells yours is the filming of Earth from the capsule, the reflection in the window. If this is really authentic (and I believe it is) then what else can they say? Also, when you watch Armstrong's reaction to Collins at the interview following that segment, you can see he is stressed and ashamed, and Aldrin is in a perpetual haze. Collins, what a liar, and Armstrong...the guy almost broke his neck when you turned to look at Collins, he obviously wanted to say 'SHUT UP, MAN!' Am I the only one seeing this? Thanks for the great DVD! I purchased your video some time ago and have shown it to quite a few family and friends—the majority of whom now believe that man never landed on the Moon. . . . Here in Ireland, we have had numerous tribunals into political sleaze and corruption, and it seems to me that the truth about this should come out. —Matthew (Ireland)

* * *

"I've been telling people since 1986 that there is no possible way that they could have gone to the Moon. Your research will prove my years of talking to really be the truth. I have the tape and I am not shocked, but relieved that the truth is no longer covered. —Corey (MO)

* * *

"Excellent film. I found it extremely timely. I teach a course in Canada called 'history's mysteries'. Used this film along with NASA's great achievements in American space exploration as points of discussion. My students loved it." —EV

* * *

"I have never used an educational tool with the sheer impact of your documentary…. After watching it in class last Monday, my students looked like stunned fish. First they were speechless, then they couldn't stop talking. I am using your film in my college classroom to teach students basic principles of proof, refutation, and examining the foundations of their own beliefs. Frankly, I have never had such an effective teaching tool for thawing intellectual inertia among students." —Doug (CA)

* * *

"[E]xcellent video. As a professional photographer, I see that the evidence is clear that the photographs have numerous technical errors. I am convinced these photos are staged as anyone with minimal experience in photography will quickly see. The footage of them staging this fake event actually coming from NASA leaves no question the Moon landing was a fraud. Another unsolved mystery solved." —J.D. (IL)

* * *

"Excellent documentary. Stunning. Even my grandparents were speechless. The video of the crew faking the shot out of the window sealed the coffin shut as far as our opinions are concerned. Neil Armstrong and the rest of the crew are nothing but liars and tricksters, and that's how history WILL end up remembering them. This evidence is far too damaging to go unnoticed." —Rich (CA)

* * *

"After seeing this movie, I totally questioned the government's involvement in many other cases, like the existence of aliens and other so-called hoaxes. This documentary was excellent and I think everyone should know about how dirty our government is to the people. . . ." —However, in *A Funny Thing Happened on the Way to the Moon* it appears to me that the only agenda the director has is a desire for truth and exposing government lies. Job well done! I look forward to seeing more of Sibrel's work." —Pastor Rick Strawcutter (Mich.)

* * *

"I find it questionable whether there is really any need for a documentary proving that NASA never sent men to the Moon. Even if they had managed to reach the Moon alive, it would have been an engineering miracle for them to have succeeded in leaving the Moon's surface and returning to Earth. Actually, to say it was an engineering 'miracle' is being too generous. It was an engineering impossibility, and it simply did not happen." —LEJ Brouwer

* * *

"If you want facts, you've gotten them here," says Bart Sibrel at his website. The U.S. has never accomplished a Moon landing, but it did prove how strong American propaganda is."

APOLLO 13 DID IT AGAIN

Jim McCanney tells us that even the Apollo 13 alleged accident in April of 1970 was a fundraising hoax, later made famous with the movie in recent years starring Forrest Gump (ooops, I'm sorry, I mean Tom Hanks) in the leading role of Chief Astro-not Jim Lovell.

McCanney says that the mission was another hoax staged from the beginning to re-ignite interest in the waning space program, and from my perspective at the time, I now think he is right. The world public—especially the American taxpayers—needed a little drama.

I lived in Biloxi, Mississippi in 1970 and remember having a "ho-hum" attitude about the third mission myself and really paid little attention to it until the "explosion" on board rocked the headlines of TV and newspapers. It was particularly focused in the gulf coast media because Biloxi was the hometown of astronaut Fred Haise, Lovell's right-hand man.

Knowing what I know now, I recently pulled out my copy of the Ron Howard production by the same name of *Apollo 13* and watched the details a little more intently than when it had first hit the big screen a decade or so ago. The scenario was actually more outlandish than that of Apollo 11 and Neil Armstrong et al. the previous year.

The public bought it and hailed it as a great story, but the experts saw it as but one more propaganda hoax to stimulate interest and continue the huge payments to the near-nonexistent NASA space program. Howard made millions, and the public remained hoodwinked.

Everything they ever told us about it was a lie, and if you are still supposing that those hoaxsters should have little to fear in these advanced years of life on this Earth and you are wondering why none will come forward now with the truth, let me remind you that these men now have several grandchildren whom they love dearly. Nothing would frighten them more today than the thought that one would be kidnapped and sent into child slavery in a foreign nation. And you can bet that these three "astro-nots" still receive periodic, anonymous reminders of this in the mail or by telephone.

(If I had more space I would tell you a little more about Mrs. Alexander Stephens in Memphis, Tennessee, who, without a trial or even an official record of her arrest, disappeared into an insane asylum for 10 years in 1968 for failing to succumb to intimidation and for refusing to lie in favor of another government deception.)

But what about the American people from my generation? Those who watched the 1969 fantasy with child-like gullibility? What is it that petrifies these people into total mental gridlock? What makes them scream in defense of NASA? At first I was befuddled and reflected a why-are-you-angry-with-me stare back at them.

With nothing resolved, some even stalk away as if I had cursed their dead parents. Others become very indignant because they worked in the space program or had relatives that worked in the space program and say something like, "My brother would never have lied about this."

[My unspoken response is: "Of course he wouldn't, but what if he never had any reason to know about the deception or to doubt it? If that were the case, wouldn't he be living in pride of his contribution to this "accomplishment" for the rest of his life?"]

Yet with $30 billion having been already spent (say that times about 16 to compute the silver dollars of the '60s against the fiat Fed note "dollars" of today to get aligned with an accurate measurement of comparison), one can see, from the perpetrators' perspective, why a sham had to be performed. Not only did it allow the money flow to continue from Congress to the space program but it justified the additional tax dollars being sucked up from the trough. After all, the great United States of America had just won the space race with the Soviet Union, had sent a man to the Moon, and brought him home safely—just as the martyred president had promised to do in 1961. How much prouder could Americans possibly be of the three astronauts, even if they had somehow disappeared behind locked doors for the next many decades?

And conversely, how much hokier could any hare-brained scheme have sounded on the surface, when first presented to Nixon and the others? Yet it worked, proving once again that the naïve American people will believe just about any lies their government wants to present—particularly if it is through the TV voice of Walter Cronkite or his current equivalent colleague of today. Nixon always loved the limelight and even managed to get into the act with a split-screen telephone conversation with the "astro-nots" on worldwide television. I believe it was the first time the world ever saw that electronic technology displayed. I was so impressed that I snapped a 35mm picture of the TV screen at the so-called historic moment, and it is still in my photograph album at home today.

But (30 and 40 years later) the unmanageable anger tantrums from others who had previously professed to be my friends happened so often that I then began to prepare for this kind of response each time. It's more than a knee-jerk, hands-covering-of-the-ears refusal to admit being fooled. It is their subconscious realization that an organized conspiracy had occurred from the inside, and to acknowledge it would mean that the great red, white & blue was tarnished and rusting. Much as when they were shown a video of JFK being shot from the front after being told for years that it was one man from the rear, news people still continue to parrot the government lie to this day—that of one "lone nut" gunman.

And certainly, when Neil Armstrong passes on, this book will not affect the media reports within his obituary that "he was the first man to walk on the Moon," closely followed by his alleged first words about "small steps and giant leaps."

The public must not be allowed to know the disdain and contempt with which Armstrong had actually treated this folly and how well deserved that contempt was.

Nope. Just as with all the other lies, this Revisionist history is already written.

Armstrong was the first man to set foot on the Moon. Buzz Aldrin was the second. That's the official story, and they're sticking with it.

Concluding his two-hour video documentary, Jim Collier (now deceased) deduces, "In the final analysis, it appears to me that the major media and the scientific community at the time of the Apollo flights abrogated their duty to ask critical questions.

"I suspect that the politically charged atmosphere of those times, that is to beat Russia to the Moon by the end of the 60s, caused NASA problems. It is probable that NASA had not solved those technical problems by the end of 1969, but they couldn't admit it or their funding would be cut. All those billions would dry up.

"In the end," he asks, "did they have to fake it?"

STILL NOT CONVINCED?

Check out this from a British website—posted by a longtime truth seeker

29 THINGS THAT NEED TO BE ANSWERED:

1) There should have been a substantial crater blasted out under the LM's 10,000 pound thrust rocket. [Some] would have you believe that the engines had only the power to blow the dust from underneath the LM as it landed. If this is true, how did Armstrong create that famous boot print if all the dust had been blown away?

2) Footprints are the result of weight displacing air or moisture from between particles of dirt, dust or sand. The astronauts left distinct footprints all over the place.

3) The *Apollo 11* TV pictures were lousy, yet the broadcast quality magically became fine on the five subsequent missions.

4) Why, in most Apollo photos, is there a clear line of definition between the rough foreground and the smooth background?

5) Why did so many NASA moonscape photos have non-parallel shadows? Skeptics will tell you because there are two sources of light on the Moon—the Sun and the Earth. That might be the case, but the shadows would still fall in the same direction, not two or three different angles and Earthshine would have no effect during the bright lunar day (the time at which the Apollos were on the Moon).

6) Why did one of the stage prop rocks have a capital "C" on it and a "C" on the ground in front of it?

7) In Ron Howard's 1995 science fiction movie, *Apollo 13*, the astronauts lose electrical power and begin worrying about freezing to death. In reality, of course, the relentless bombardment of the Sun's

rays would rapidly have overheated the vehicle to lethal temperatures with no atmosphere into which to dump the heat build-up.

8) Who would dare risk using the LM on the Moon when a simulated Moon landing was never tested?

9) Instead of being able to jump at least 10 feet high in "one-sixth" gravity, the highest jump was about 19 inches.

10) Even though slow-motion photography was able to give a fairly convincing appearance of very low gravity, it could not disguise the fact that the astronauts traveled no further between steps than they would have on Earth.

11) If the rover buggy had actually been moving in one-sixth gravity, then it would have required a 20-foot width in order not to have flipped over on nearly every turn. The Rover had the same width as ordinary small cars.

12) An astrophysicist who has worked for NASA writes that it takes two meters of shielding to protect against medium solar flares and that heavy ones give out tens of thousands of rems in a few hours. Russian scientists calculated in 1959 that astronauts needed a shield of four feet of lead to protect them on the Moon's surface. Why didn't the astronauts on *Apollo 14 and 16* die after exposure to this immense amount of radiation? And why is NASA, if they have sent 12 men already, only now starting a project to test the lunar radiation levels and what their effects would be on the human body?

13) The fabric space suits had a crotch-to-shoulder zipper. There should have been fast leakage of air since even a tack hole deflates a tire in short order.

14) The astronauts in these "pressurized" suits were easily able to bend their fingers, wrists, elbows and knees at 5.2 psi and yet a boxer's 4 psi speed bag is virtually unbendable. The guys would have looked like balloon men if the suits had actually been pressurized.

15) How did the astronauts leave the lem? In the documentary *Paper Moon* The host measures a replica of the lem at the Space Center in Houston. What he finds is that the "official" measurements released by NASA are bogus and that the astronauts could not have got out of the lem.

16) The water-sourced air conditioner backpacks should have produced frequent explosive vapor discharges. They never did.

17) During the *Apollo 14* flag setup ceremony, the flag would not stop fluttering.

18) With more than a two-second signal transmission round trip,

how did a camera pan upward to track the departure of the *Apollo 16* lem? Gus Grissom, only minutes before he was burned to death in the *Apollo 1* tragedy, said, *"Hey, you guys in the control center, get with it. You expect me to go to the Moon, and you can't even maintain telephonic communications over three miles."* This statement says a lot about what Grissom thought about NASA's progress in the great space race. Previously, Grissom had not only disparaged the program publicly but further displayed his contempt by hanging a lemon on the dashboard of his spacecraft.

19) Why did NASA's administrator resign just months before the first Apollo mission?

20) NASA launched the TETR-A satellite just months before the first lunar mission. The proclaimed purpose was to simulate transmissions coming from the Moon so that the Houston ground crews (all those employees sitting behind computer screens at Mission Control) could "rehearse" the first Moon landing. In other words, though NASA claimed that the satellite crashed shortly before the first lunar mission (a misinformation lie), its real purpose was to relay voice, fuel consumption, altitude and telemetry data as if the transmissions were coming from an Apollo spacecraft as it neared the Moon. Very few NASA employees knew the truth because they believed that the computer and television data they were receiving was the genuine article. Merely a hundred or so knew what was really going on; not tens of thousands as it might first appear.

21) In 1998, the space shuttle flew to one of its highest altitudes ever, 350 miles, which was hundreds of miles below the beginning of the Van Allen radiation belts. Inside of their shielding, superior to that which the Apollo astronauts possessed, the shuttle astronauts reported being able to "see" the radiation with their eyes closed penetrating their shielding as well as the retinas of their closed eyes. For a dental X-ray on Earth which lasts 1/100th of a second we wear a ¼-inch lead vest. Imagine what it would be like to endure several hours of radiation that you can see with your eyes closed from hundreds of miles away with 1/8 of an inch of aluminum shielding!

22) The *Apollo 1* fire of January 27, 1967, killed what would have been the first crew to walk on the Moon (had they gone) just days after the commander, Gus Grissom, held an unapproved press conference complaining that they were at least 10 years, not two, from reaching the Moon. The dead man's own son, who is a seasoned pilot himself, has in his possession forensic evidence personally retrieved from the

charred spacecraft (that the government has tried to destroy on two or more occasions). Gus Grissom was obviously trying to make a big statement as he placed that lemon in the window of the *Apollo 1* spacecraft as it sat ready for launch!

23) CNN issued the following report: "The radiation belts surrounding Earth may be more dangerous for astronauts than previously believed (like when they supposedly went through them 40 years ago to reach the Moon.) The phenomenon known as the 'Van Allen belts' can spawn (newly discovered) 'killer electrons' that can dramatically affect the astronauts' health."

24) In 1969 computer chips had not been invented. The maximum computer memory was 256k, and this was housed in a large air-conditioned building. In 2002, a top-of-the-range computer required at least 64 Mb of memory to run a simulated Moon landing, and that does not include the memory required to take off again once landed. The alleged "computer" on board Apollo 11 had 32k of memory. That's the equivalent of a simple calculator.

25) If debris from the Apollo missions was left on the Moon, then it would be visible today through a powerful telescope; however no such debris can be seen. The Clementine probe that recently mapped the Moon's surface failed to show any Apollo artifacts left by Man during the missions. Where did the Moon Buggy and base of the LM go?

26) In the year 2005, NASA still did not have the technology to land any man or woman on the Moon and return them safely to Earth.

27) Film evidence has recently been uncovered of a mis-labeled, unedited, behind-the-scenes video film, showing the crew of Apollo 11 staging part of their photography. The film evidence is shown in the video *A Funny Thing Happened on the Way to the Moon!* The film was mistakenly mailed to Bart Sibrel when he had issued a Freedom Of Information Act request to NASA.

28) If this was one of history's greatest accomplishments, why did the blueprints and plans for the lunar module and moon buggy get destroyed?

29) Why did NASA need to airbrush out anomalies from lunar footage if there is nothing to hide?

Nope, it's time to face it, RWB American devotee. Of all the evidence we could dig up (and so much was buried, literally), *all* of it indicates that no spaceship, Russian or American, ever traveled farther than 300 miles from the Earth's surface; and *none of it* shows any proof whatsoever that there actually was any human strolling on the Moon, ever.

It is fair to say to your neighbor now that everything they ever told us about the Apollo Moon missions was a lie. Or, if you want to be a little more direct and blunt, quote the researcher Ralph René, who did more in-depth research on the case than anyone. René concluded, "The bastards hoodwinked us."

RONALD REAGAN
'THE REST OF HIM'

During Ronald Reagan's campaign and popularity during the rest of his life, he was remembered whimsically by columnists and authors for a few movie characters he played and lines he spoke on screen. One of these utterances was from his character that had lost his legs in an explosion, and upon waking up in the hospital bed and lifting the sheet, said, "Where's the rest of me?" The line later inspired a 1970 book title. Here is some of the rest of Reagan that the MSM shielded from the public during the 1980 campaign and later. It now appears likely that this was done in order to position George Bush, who (like Lyndon Johnson riding the political back of JFK) could never have gotten near White House residence without Reagan's charisma to pave the way. It is still amusing to hear bridge club and barbershop conversation lamenting the passing of the Reagan years and his great "conservatism." No lie was ever better sold to Americans than this one.

One of the slickest public relations transitions in the 20th century was the selling of the liberal socialist Ronald Reagan (a professional actor who later performed magnificently for the world's stage) to the American people as the savior of the republic and the wonderful "conservative" reformer that he never was. In actuality, Ronald Reagan was the biggest fraud to occupy the White House since Abraham Lincoln, and not only do most Americans not know it yet but still speak of him in reverence. (After all, much as with Obama right now, what was there not to like about this man's public persona?) His quotes, most of which were plagiarized from others over the years, such as Will Rogers[1], are now going down in history as Reagan's great insight. It was all just one more lie.

Reagan was a fraud far before his appearance on the national scene. First he had to fox the California voters. On October 22, 1964, after it was obvious that the Republican Party, under the control of Nelson Rockefeller, had scuttled Barry Goldwater's chances of defeating Lyndon Johnson for the presidency, Ronald Reagan felt it safe going on TV and presenting his "Rendezvous with Destiny" speech that launched him into destiny. This enthralled the conservatives, some of whom decided to support and finance him for the governor of California race coming up in 1966. But just who was this man?

Until the recent fraudulent occupation by Barack Hussein Obama, never had a man occupied the White House that Americans knew so little about. However, a look at the background of Ronald Reagan's earlier life, his philosophical background and political activities seems to shed some much needed light on why there is a paucity of information on him and why the value of his public relations staff was determined more on what they concealed than on what they revealed. Just about everything they ever told us was a lie, and when it came to true conservatism, Reagan was a bigger fraud than little Georgie Bush 43 (but probably not his deceptive daddy, Bush 41).

Politics is a vocation that comes equipped with a license to lie, and in this game of make-believe an actor is constantly pretending to be something or someone he is not. He is already trained for the political arena, and the combination can be lethal.

By 1947, after a decade in Hollywood, Ronald Reagan had become president of the left-wing Screen Actors Guild. During his tenure he was called to testify before the House Un-American Activities Committee in connection with the Communist writers and actors within the union. According to Lou Cannon's book *Reagan*, he insisted the Communists formed a political party and he would be hesitant to see any political party outlawed on the basis of its political ideology. In taking this position, Reagan was parroting the typical party line of that time. During this time, he was collaborating with James Roosevelt and Dore Schary, president of the Anti-Defamation League.

Surprise! Ronald Reagan became a charter member of the Fabian So-cialist-controlled Americans for Democratic Action in 1950. The same year he campaigned for and raised money for one of the era's most no-torious left wingers, Helen Gahagan Douglas. He had traveled the country in 1948 publicly campaigning for Harry Truman and castigating Repub-licans for causing inflation.

The California Senate Committee on Un-American Activities had identified the National Advisory Committee of the American Veterans as a Communist front organization in 1952, but Reagan saw no reason not to become a member in 1958 and did so.

During this earlier period of his life, Reagan had played an up-front role in an organization called the "California League for a Democratic Far East-ern Policy." This gang was closely linked to and followed the lead of the Communist-dominated "Institute of Pacific Relations" (IPR) in its drive to bring the Communist butcher, Mao Tse-tung, into control in China.

The Senate Committee chaired by Sen. Pat McCarron investigated the IPR and reported, "The IPR is an instrument of Communist policy, prop-aganda and military intelligence." When the FBI later raided the offices of IPR's *Amerasia* magazine, the agents found 1,800 stolen and very sensitive government documents.

These Communists, working with George Marshall, Joseph Stillwell and President Truman, were instrumental in bringing the murderous Mao Tse-tung to power in China by conspiring against America's anti-Communist friend and ally Chiang Kai-shek. Without a Communist China and the Red butcher Mao to run it, there would have been no Korean or Vietnam wars, which did not benefit anyone except the Communists and the international banksters. Ronald Reagan was a willing and active cheerleader.

In 1954, Reagan was hired by General Electric Corporation as a TV spokesman and all-around PR man. The man who hired him was GE's longtime president Gerard Swope, the author of FDR's National Recovery Administration plan, which became the blueprint for corporate socialism in America.[2] This was the beginning of Reagan's transition from liberal to conservative, at least in the public's eye, and he found his "hat-switch" from cowboy to bankster's Homburg to be quite lucrative, as well. His *as-sumed* new political and economic stance was the only one the American public would ever hear about for the rest of his life.

Upon being elected California's governor in 1966, after campaigning on the basis of a promise to "squeeze, cut and trim" the size of state government, he immediately dumped the conservatives who had ensured his new position and brought in Nelson Rockefeller's California staff of radicals to run his administration in Sacramento. Many of the same crowd followed him to the Oval Office in 1981.

Most Americans have been the victims of the propaganda taught in the humanistic government school system and have difficulty figuring out why a socialist would become a capitalist. The untaught fact is that socialism is the mongoloid child of capitalism. Capitalists realized long ago that socialism is the road to wealth, as long as they control it. This explains why the Wall Street and the international banksters financed the Russian Revolution and takeover by the Communists. It explains why the CFR and Trilateralists[3] are still supporting and financing Communism's spread to finally attain their objective of a one world socialist government where their appointed emperor and his mattoids can own everything and control the mass of serfs.

It doesn't take one as politically cynical as I to conclude early that if you want to identify a politician's real character, you quit listening to his rhetoric (except to compare it to the lie he tells later) and examine what he actually did. As much as his staff managed to conceal it at the time, Reagan's "spend and tax" record as governor of California was available for anyone (not mesmerized by his star status) to look at before voting. Of course, the Hobson's choice was the Republican socialist who denied it versus the Democratic socialist who embraced it.

Reagan was a spendthrift—a "tax and spend" Keynesian with no regard for the constitutionally protected rights or economic needs of the electorate. He increased the state budget from $4.6 billion in 1967 to $10.3 billion in 1974. He increased the sales tax 248%, the personal income tax 404%, the corporation tax 160% and gasoline taxes 40%, while property taxes doubled. During the Reagan tenure, welfare was up 43%. So much for "cut, trim and squeeze."

When Ronnie ran for president in 1980, he campaigned vigorously on two main platforms: reversing the legalized government-funded abortion ("Thirteen million babies have been aborted since the 1973 legalization by the Supreme Court," he screamed throughout the Bible Belt) and balancing the budget. Nothing could warm the ears of Christian, conservative America more than that. The problem was that after eight years the Reagan administration had surpassed the "spending" of all 39 of his predecessors totaled. That's right! The 39 administrations from Washington through Carter could not equal the total of what the 40th president "spent" in two terms. And when he left office in January of 1989, the daily rate of legal abortions had reached 4,400 nationally and totaled nearly 40 million since 1973, but it was the "conservative" rhetoric that was important at the time.

While campaigning for governor in 1966, Reagan promised to resist any effort that would take from the American citizen his right to own and carry firearms. However, in 1968, then Governor Reagan signed into California law the Mulford Act which was the most sweeping and repressive gun control legislation passed in the United States to that date. This law nullified any citizen's right to defend himself and banned loaded guns from any public street or highway in California unless the owner could prove *he was in imminent danger of attack.* (Who can possibly know of an impending attack before it happens? Hmmm. Well, maybe one who is running from the cops.)

Not yet satisfied, Governor Reagan enthusiastically stifled the Second Amendment rights of Californians further by embracing the plan proposed by the federal Law Enforcement Assistance Administration (LEAA) that would eventually provide for the confiscation of guns. Gov. Reagan agreed with the LEAA to make California a model or pilot state for the entire country.

Under the guise of "reform for criminal justice improvement," Reagan appointed and arranged for financing the State Office of Criminal Justice Planning. With a large office staff they were to be the task force to carry out the LEAA program of *prohibiting the private possession of handguns* by January 1, 1983. He appointed the executive director and staff, who were responsible only to the governor. The Council on Criminal Justice and 17 subcommittees were also appointed to study this and report directly to the governor. Reagan was scheduled by these task forces to put the LEAA controls into effect by executive proclamation on December 31, 1974, at a time when most Californians would be more interested in New Year's celebrations than in watching the machinations of their state government.

WHO SAYS YOU CAN'T BEAT CITY HALL?

However, a committee of California patriots had been following every move of the Reagan gang the whole time, and they knew several weeks in advance of the planned proclamation exactly what was coming down. This committee, with Bernadine Smith[4] at the helm, arranged a meeting with Gov. Reagan in his Sacramento office on December 3, 1974.

Mrs. Smith, the committee's spokeswoman, said later that when Reagan was confronted with the committee's knowledge of the proclamation, he feigned astonishment, bewilderment and innocence. In other words, in the mode of a typical politician, he lied.

She said to the governor, "It is inconceivable that the LEAA and your own Office of Criminal Justice would have scheduled you to make such an important gubernatorial proclamation without first consulting you and obtaining your permission."

Faced with irrefutable facts that seven months previously he had approved the plan and appointed a large task force to carry it out, and it was his own committee that had arranged for him to make the proclamation that would outlaw handguns, Reagan still insisted he did not know about the existence of plans for the proclamation. A professional actor with 50 years of training and experience, he wiggled out of the situation but was not convincing. Everyone there knew that he was lying. However, because of the confrontation, the proclamation was not signed and the action was stopped, at least temporarily.

Reagan and the international banksters headed by the Rockefellers, who backed him and gave him his marching orders the whole time he was posing as a great "conservative savior" of the country, much earlier had realized that there was no better position from which to advance their own fortunes and liberal, subversive ideas than through a self-avowed political "conservative." The amusing part amongst the sad facts is that almost *all* of the simple dolts in TV-land not only bought it but still to this day refuse to face the facts. (Reagan was not the great conservative hero of the 20th century that we are supposed to believe he was. It is the offspring of this deluded group that today still believes that the Bush family is (1) Christian, (2) conservative and (3) for the advancement of American ideals. None of that is true, either.)

What we have brought to the surface here is only a small part of the liberal record of Reagan but should be far more than enough to bring any thinking American to the conclusion that Ronald Reagan was never a political conservative and that America and its conservative Republican voters were duped by the powers that be and the news media.

As usual, everything they ever told us about the "conservatism" of Ronald Reagan and George H.W. Bush[5] was a lie.

ENDNOTES:

1 "It isn't what we don't know that gives us trouble. It's what we know that ain't so." Reagan got great mileage out of this without giving credit. Maybe, because Rogers wrote it more than fifty years earlier, Reagan figured the statute of limitations had run.

2 From *Wall Street and FDR* by Anthony Sutton, 1975. According to Sutton, GE was but one of the many multi-national corporations actively involved in expanding the military/industrial complex in foreign countries through the massive transfers of U.S. technology, as the foundation for world government was being laid.

3 The Council on Foreign Relations and Trilateral Commission are longtime globalist organizations created and controlled by the nation's elite and dedicated to the destruction of the United States and the construction of a world government through the United Nations.

4 This hard-nosed octogenarian is still at it, writes to me often and is my heroine of the 2nd Amendment movement. If there is a living activist more committed to the Colonist's slogan, "Don't Tread on Me," I would like to know who it is.

5 In any honest police investigation, G.H.W. Bush would have been the No. 1 suspect in the attempted murder of Reagan on 3-30-81, as the facts will show in a later chapter.

A SECOND LOOK AT 'HONEST' ABE

The previous mention of the historical distortion of Abe Lincoln takes us to a second opinion. Nothing could be truer to this book's title than the following information, most of which was supplied by two of the most prolific truth-tellers alive today—Lew Rockwell and Thomas DiLorenzo—and posted on the Internet for the benefit of truth-seekers on the anniversary of Lincoln's 200th birthday —February 12, 2009.

I don't know what they teach in U.S. history classes today. But back in the middle of the last century, when I was in elementary school, there was absolutely no question about how we were to regard Abraham Lincoln. We were taught to feel a reverence bordering on awe for "Honest Abe," the "Great Emancipator," the eloquent martyr who saved the republic.

We were required to memorize the *Gettysburg Address*. And if we were lucky enough to join a field trip to our nation's capital, one of the most significant events was our visit to the Lincoln Memorial. (A few of us rapscallions spoiled the solemnity of the moment by sliding down the sides of the monument.)

That was what we were taught in the elementary schools in the heart of the former Confederacy—the same fabrication and exaggerations that the young and fertile minds swallowed in Cedar Rapids, Sikeston, Chillicothe and Pawtucket. The winners get to write the history.

It wasn't until I became an adult and started reading history on my own that I began to doubt the version of events I was taught nearly six decades ago. For example, how many Americans know that Lincoln suspended civil liberties in the North, including the writ of habeas corpus?

That he filled the jails with more than 13,000 political prisoners, all incarcerated without due process? And when the Maryland Legislature was about to vote to become state No. 12 in the Confederacy, Lincoln sent his troops to the home of each legislator during the night and arrested and jailed them one by one. Then 100 or so state lawmakers spent the duration of the war behind bars. How come that's not in the history books?

The Supreme Court protested Lincoln's disregard for our Constitutional protections, but the president replied he had a war to fight. Since he commanded the Army, Lincoln won that argument.

And speaking of the war, guess who uttered these words:

"Any people anywhere, being inclined and having the power, have the right to rise up and shake off the existing government and form a new one that suits them better. This is a most valuable—a most sacred right—a right which, we hope and believe, is to liberate the world. Nor is this right confined to cases in which the whole people of an existing government may choose to exercise it. Any portion of such people that can, may revolutionize, and make their own, of so much of their territory as they inhabit."

Okay, I'll admit this is a trick question. The speaker was Abraham Lincoln. But he was not talking about the Southern states that tried to secede from the union. No, these remarks were made in 1847, when Lincoln was defending the right of Texans to demand their independence from Mexico. A dozen years later, when 11 Southern states tried to declare their independence, Lincoln's response was to wage war on them.

As a child, I never questioned the assertion that the South was wrong to secede. And that Lincoln was right to use as much force as necessary to preserve the Union. Later, as I grew to understand the strength and uniqueness of our constitutional republic, I began to question both assumptions.

The U.S. Constitution, I came to believe, was a contract—a contract between the various states and the federal government they created. Note that the Constitution had to be approved by the states, not a majority of the citizens. There was no "majority rule" here, no popular vote taken.

But this raises the question, if it was necessary for the states to adopt the Constitution, why wouldn't it be legal for some of those states to rescind that vote, especially if they felt the contract had been broken? More and more, I found myself thinking that the South was legally and morally right in declaring its independence. And the North, by invading those states and waging war on them, was wrong.

And what a terrible war it was. By the time it was over, nearly 625,000 Americans were dead—more American servicemen than were killed in World War I, World War II, the Korean War and the Vietnam War *combined*. Fully one-fourth of the draft-age white male population of the South was dead.

The devastation in the former states of the Confederacy is hard to imagine. Sherman's march from Atlanta to Savannah is notorious for its savagery. But he was far from the only Northern officer who ordered his troops to lay waste to Southern farms, fields and plantations. Union troops routinely destroyed crops, sacked homes and even stabled their horses in Southern churches.

As H.W. Crocker III puts it in *The Politically Incorrect Guide to the Civil War* (Regnery Publishing, 2008), "If abiding by the law of a free republic and fighting a defensive war solely against armed combatants be flaws, the South had them and the North did not. Lincoln ignored the law, the Constitution and the Supreme Court when it suited him. His armies waged war on the farms, livelihoods and people of the South, not just against their armies."

Of all the big lies about the "War of Federal Aggression," the biggest of all may be that it was necessary, to end slavery. The truth is that many illustrious Southerners, including Jefferson Davis and Robert E. Lee, recognized that slavery had to come to an end. But it should not come by force of arms, they felt; not at the point of a gun, but rather through the free consent of the owners, with the proper preparation of the slaves. To get them ready for their own freedom, for example, Lee's wife insisted the family's slaves be taught to read and write, and the women how to sew.

Seek out the famous quotes of Frederick Douglas, certainly the most astute black man of the era. You will be surprised to learn that he was the creator of the myth (and not until 1863) that the war was fought over slavery.

FRANKLIN ROOSEVELT
AND THE SOCIAL SECURITY PONZI SCHEME

Very few Americans remember anymore the facts about Franklin Roosevelt's introduction of the Social Security (Federal Insurance Contributions Act, i.e., FICA) Program. Almost everything he ever proposed about it was a lie. He promised:

1) That participation in the program would be completely voluntary [actually it still is, but few know it];

2) That the participants would only have to pay 1% of the first $1,400 of their annual incomes into the program; [whatta' joke today!];

3) That the money the participants elected to put into the program would be deductible from their income for tax purposes each year [Not for long!];

4) That the money the participants put into the independent "trust fund" rather than into the general operating fund, and therefore, would only be used to fund the Social Security retirement program, and no other government program; and

5) That the annuity payments to the retirees would never be taxed as income.

Since many of us have paid into FICA for years, if not many decades, and are now receiving a Social Security check every month—and then finding that we are getting taxed on 85% of the money we paid to the Federal government to "put away"—the reader may be interested in knowing that there is no trust fund managing the retirement funds anymore. Lyndon Johnson and his Democratic-controlled Congress did away with that and moved the Social Security monies into the General

Fund in order to provide more for the weasels to spend.

Understand that LBJ's theft happened in preparation of the "Redeem your Fed Notes Here" window to be slammed shut at all the banks on June 24, 1968, rendering every Fed note of any denomination to be 100% inflationary. There was no longer any "taxpayer's money" in existence; it was all government money that could now be created at will for whatever was deemed necessary.

Here's what a 1936 government pamphlet on Social Security said: "After the first three years—that is to say, beginning in 1940—you will pay, and your employer will pay, 1.5 cents for each dollar you earn, up to $3,000 a year .... beginning in 1943, you will pay two cents, and so will your employer, for every dollar you earn for the next three years. .... And finally, beginning in 1949, twelve years from now, you and your employer will each pay three cents on each dollar you earn, up to $3,000 a year." Here's Congress's lying promise: "That is the most you will ever pay." Let's repeat that last sentence: "That is the most you will ever pay." Compare that to today's reality, including Medicare, which is 7.65 cents on each dollar that you earn up to nearly $107,000, which comes to $8,185.[1]

The Social Security pamphlet closes with another lie: "Beginning November 24, 1936, the United States government will set up a Social Security account for you. . . . The checks will come to you as a right." First, there's no Social Security account containing your money, but more importantly, the U.S. Supreme Court has ruled on two occasions that Americans have no legal right to Social Security payments.

We can thank public education for American gullibility.

All this is why the fear-mongering scheme by one party against the other that "Social Security is going broke etc" is a joke. How can the Social Security system go broke when it is funded by the push of a computer button? It cannot go bust until the whole financial structure disintegrates—an inevitable crash has been accelerated today by the trillion-dollar infusions of Obama's alleged "bailout."

Meanwhile, everything they ever tell us about the Social Security system will be at best a temporary truth that will soon evolve into a lie. And, by the way, it was Jimmy Carter in the 1970s who authorized the Social Security payments at age 65 to illegal immigrants that had moved into this country, even though they never paid a dime into it. The point here is for you not to blame the Bushes, Clintons or Obamas for this planned failure of America. What you are witnessing is the coming-to-fruition of the Luciferian world government plan that has been going on since before you were born. You will soon have the choice of either bowing down to it or rebelling against it in the name of Jesus Christ.

No other wars exist. All the others labeled as wars are but mere minor battles in the bigger war between good and evil, more definitively as Christ vs. Satan. Need we remind you that Satan is the author of lies? And everything they ever told us was a lie. Are we starting to see who "they" really are?

ENDNOTES:

1 It is important to remember the lawful money lesson here. With silver at $21 an oz., it takes 16 of today's counterfeit dollars to equal one lawful dollar in 1964 (when the surreptitious switch to counterfeit took place).

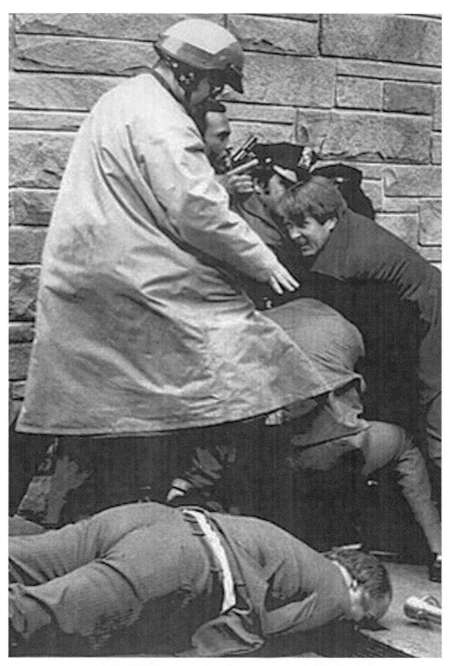

There is no doubt that Hinckley shot Jim Brady and probably (most of) the others, but the news video reveals that someone else was firing as well. NBC newswoman Nancy Dickerson initially reported another shooter but quickly fell silent about it.

ASSASSINATIONS

AND THE NEWS MEDIA COVER-UP

JOHN HINCKLEY AND GEORGE H.W. BUSH

W ere you aware that George Bush the First, as in Ronald Reagan's vice president, was friends with John Hinckley, Sr. in 1981 and had performed various oil deals with him? (You probably were not.) In fact, their sons were friends, too. Scott Hinckley was scheduled to have dinner with Neil Bush on the night on March 30, 1981. Now think of this! The brother of one principal and son of another were close friends. Do you remember the significance of that date? It was the day that John Hinckley, Jr. allegedly shot President Ronald Reagan following a luncheon at the Washington Hilton. And do you remember who had most to gain from the president's demise? Well, let's have a look-see.

From his own records, John Hinckley, Sr., the owner of Vanderbilt Oil, had made the maximum donations allowable by law to the various political campaigns of George Bush, the owner of Zapata Oil as well as his Houston neighbor, since the latter first ran for Congress. These stories first hit in the *Houston Post* and were later carried nationally via Associated Press.

The other aspect of the case that should have merited more careful scrutiny was the relationship of John W. Hinckley Sr., the gunman's father, to the U.S. intelligence community. The line in the press right after the assassination attempt was that "the father of John Hinckley is a devout Christian who did work in Africa." Some papers also included the fact that John W. Hinckley Sr. had worked with World Vision, beginning in 1976 (the year that Bush was appointed CIA director). World Vision describes itself as the largest "international Christian relief and development agency" active in the Third World. It is officially a joint activity of the Episcopal and Presbyterian churches.

"Jack" Hinckley, as the gunman's father was frequently called, during the 1970s became a close associate of Robert Ainsworth, the director of U.S. Ministries for World Vision, Inc. Jack Hinckley's profile was that of a born-again Christian. Jack Hinckley and Ainsworth traveled together to the Sahel region of Africa, Zimbabwe and South Africa. Even before joining World Vision, Jack Hinckley had carried on "relief work" in Guatemala. "Jack and I became very close," Ainsworth said. "Jack was a successful businessman. On occasion he would ask us to pray for his son. It's not that Jack felt that John would do something bad, just that John had no direction. John had not found himself."

As Caspar Weinberger recounts the moments following Vice President Bush's return from Houston that evening: "[Attorney General Bill French] Smith then reported that all FBI reports concurred with the information I had received; that the shooting was a completely isolated incident and that the assassin, John Hinckley, with a previous record in Nashville, seemed to be a 'Bremer' type, a reference to the attempted assassin of George Wallace."

But, as usual, the official story is full of a lot more holes than just those from bullets.

Those who were not paying close attention at the time may have missed the fact that just a few minutes after George Bush had returned to Washington and walked into the room, he had presided over the sweeping under the rug of the decisive question regarding Hinckley and his actions: was Hinckley a part of a conspiracy, domestic or international? Not more than five hours after the attempt to kill Reagan, on the basis of the most fragmentary early reports, before Hinckley had been properly questioned and before a full investigation had been carried out, a group of Cabinet officers *chaired by George Bush* had ruled out any conspiracy. The scene was reminiscent of Lyndon Johnson's infamous call to Dr. Crenshaw at Parkland Hospital, as the doctors were struggling to save the life of Lee Harvey Oswald in 1963. Johnson wanted a "deathbed" confession and even had an armed agent already in the operating room ready to take down the words.

Alexander Haig, whose later memoirs discussed the great possibility of a conspiracy, does not seem to have objected to this incredible decision at the time.

From that moment on, "no conspiracy" became the official doctrine of the U.S. regime, for the moment a Bush regime and the most massive efforts were undertaken to stifle any suggestion to the contrary.

This assassination attempt was only nine weeks after Reagan was inaugurated. *NBC New's* John Chancellor reported the Bush/Hinckley connection on its nightly TV report, but it was first noted by the *Houston* Post and then carried nationally by Associated Press. Then, the *Washington Post* passed it off in the next day's edition that this was an "interesting coincidence." Indeed it was. We must suppose that if Robert Oswald, Lee's brother, had been dating one of Lyndon Johnson's daughters in 1963, this would have been *an interesting coincidence*, too. And *weird, too.*

From *Dutch*, a Reagan biography by Edmund Morris, on the subject: "Most chilling of all was the phenomenon of the *random accuracy* of John Hinckley's bullets. Four men mown down in less than two seconds by a person *impossible to see* either before or after the chattering explosions; rain; ricochets; a mad scrimmage; yet within the chaos, an *accidental geometry* so precise as to bring Reagan to the edge of death." (2nd author's emp.)

Yes, indeed. One need only view the newsreel tapes from the Washington Hilton that day to see the discrepancies and the likelihood of another shooter. The *History Channel* televises this documentary a couple of times a year. On the far right we can see what is purported to be John Hinckley, Jr., unrecognizable at the bottom on the "scrimmage" and beneath a half dozen government agents and others. Then the camera moves left and we see President Reagan frozen in fear as he realizes what is happening. Swinging into action, Secret Service Agent Jerry Parr grabs "Rawhide"[1] and pulls/pushes him into the back seat of the Cadillac limousine.

During this melee, another agent (of maybe 200 lbs. and six feet in stature), Tim McCarthy, steps between the president and the "danger zone," as he is trained to do. However, he is not facing the pile of humanity on his left (our right) but to the left screen area of the camera, far away (maybe a 35 or 45 degree angle) from John Hinckley and the pile of humanity.

Gunfire is still being heard and suddenly McCarthy takes one "in the gut" that literally lifts him off his feet, as we see his heels rise before his toes leave the ground by an inch or so.

That Hinckley could have been responsible for this, even if he had been kneeling and firing from a prone position and head-on, would have been very doubtful, considering he was firing a mere .22 caliber pistol. But when this impossible angle was "officially" explained away by claiming that a ricochet bullet off of the limo had hit the agent, it became even more incredible. A ricocheting .22 bullet, while it could still be deadly if it hit a vital organ, would be so weakened in velocity that it would be far less likely to have enough impact to even budge a 200 lb. man. So, yes, let's call it "accidental geometry."

The ricocheting theory as the manner in which Reagan was wounded is just as questionable. Let's examine the president's own testimony:

"I was almost to the car when I heard what sounded like two or three firecrackers over to my left—just a small fluttering sound, *pop, pop, pop*. I turned and said, "What the hell's that?" Just then, Jerry Parr, the head of our Secret Service unit, grabbed me by the waist and literally hurled me into the back of the limousine. I landed on my face atop the armrest across the back seat and Jerry jumped on top of me. When he landed, I felt a pain in my upper back that was unbelievable. It was the most excruciating pain I had ever felt. "Jerry," I said, "get off, I think you've broken one of my ribs.

"John Hinckley, Jr.'s bullet probably caught me in midair at the same moment I was being thrown into the back of the car by Jerry Parr. After they took it out of me, I saw the bullet. It looked like a nickel that was black on one side; it had been flattened into a small disk and darkened by the paint on the limousine. First the bullet had struck the limousine, then it had ricocheted through the small gap between the body of the car and the door hinges. It hit me under my left arm, where it made a small slit like a knife wound. I'd always been told that no pain is as excruciating as a broken bone; that's why I thought Jerry had broken my rib when he landed so hard on me. But it wasn't Jerry's weight I felt; according to the doctors, the flattened bullet had hit my rib edgewise, then turned over like a coin, tumbling down through my lung and stopping less than an inch from my heart. As I said, someone was looking out for me that day."

Once again, one must view the newsreel video report to see that such a theory is next to impossible. Reagan's wound was in his left side, under the heart, but it was his *right* side that was vulnerable to any ricocheting missile bouncing off the vehicle. By the time he was in a position for his left side to have been facing the "small gap between the body of the car and the door hinges," the shooting had ceased. This is not how the president was wounded and nearly killed.

The iron curtain came down on the truth about Hinckley. There doesn't seem to be any reason to suspect that Reagan is not telling the truth or at least what he *believes* to be true, but one's knowledge is only as good as his information. Almost everything about his story—after being thrown into the car—is what he has been told by others. Whatever flattened bullet he was shown did not necessarily have to have been removed from him.

When the president was shot, as we see from the newsreels, he was pushed into the car by his Secret Service guard. Jerry Parr fell on top of him and later the *Reader's Digest* had Jerry Parr telling his "valiant story."

Then the limousine tore off, presumably heading for safety. It was then some five minutes later that the ambulances arrived for the other wounded personnel. They put the Secret Service agent McCarthy, the Washington D.C. policeman and the most seriously wounded Jim Brady in the ambulances and they roared off. Using normal time/rate/distance, who should have arrived at George Washington University Hospital first? You know the answer, but it didn't happen.

The ambulances actually arrived some 15 minutes before the president. When asked, "What happened?" the Secret Service driver simply responded, "We got lost."

Yeah, right. (Glance at this book's cover to review the title once more, please.)

The Secret Service does not get lost in Washington, D.C. They don't get lost in Beijing or Moscow or any other place in the world. They have detailed and solid plans of escape routes and nearest hospitals already laid out in the case of any emergency wherever they might be with the president. But we are to believe that they got lost in their own hometown?

And so, now the investigation starts to get a little interesting. When they take President Reagan in, they see that he is convulsing and there's blood on his lips. They know he's hurt, seriously. But they can find no wounds. They X-ray him three times and can find nothing.

Finally, a nurse notices a tiny entrance wound right at the seventh rib, underneath the armpit. And a doctor takes a probe and very carefully, because they couldn't see it on X-ray, the doctor is able to extract what he said was a planchet, thinner than a dime, that was one-quarter inch from Ronald Reagan's aorta.

Then Ronald Reagan said (this came right out of *The Washington Post*): "I knew I had been hurt, but I thought that I'd been hurt by the Secret Service man landing on me in the car. As it was, I must say it was the most paralyzing pain. I've described it as if someone hit you with a hammer. But the sensation, it seemed to me, came after I was in the car and so I thought that maybe his gun or something had broken a rib. I sat up on the seat and the pain wouldn't go away—and suddenly, I found I was coughing up blood."

Was there really a bullet in there or was Reagan "spiked" with another weapon inside the limo during the missing 15 minutes? To consider what follows in the next paragraph's revelation is to then further wonder if even President Reagan may have been just parroting stories fed to him while really knowing better but valuing his life more than the truth at this point.

Retired Army colonel, author, operative in Bush's CIA and former Populist Presidential candidate James "Bo" Gritz reported from a deeper perspective:

"In Mesa, I met with Cleon Skousen and I said, 'Why in the world did Ronald Reagan sell us down the tube by taking George Bush as his running mate?' And I really didn't know that Cleon knew Ronald Reagan rather well. But he told me: He said, 'Bo, George Bush was Ronald Reagan's greatest opponent,' (if you'll remember, back in the 1980 elections), 'and Ronald Reagan said he would never have him. Then Reagan was invited to New York to go see David Rockefeller. When he saw Rockefeller, he was told, 'If you do not take my head of the Trilateral Commission, George Bush, as your running mate, the only way you'll see the inside of the White House is as a tourist.'"

What was the truth of the matter? The Roman common sense of Lucius Annaeus Seneca (who had seen so many of Nero's intrigues and who would eventually fall victim to one of them) would have dictated that the person who would have profited most from Reagan's death be scrutinized as the prime suspect. That was obviously Bush, since Bush would have assumed the presidency if Reagan had succumbed to his wounds. The same idea was summed up by an eighth grade student at the Alice Deal Junior High School in Washington D.C. who told teachers on March 31: "It is a plot by Vice President Bush to get into power. If Bush becomes president, the CIA would be in charge of the country." The pupils at this school had been asked for their views of the Hinckley assassination attempt of the previous day.[2]

But how did Bush get on the ticket as the 1980 V.P. candidate in the first place? He had been one of the front-running presidential candidates until Reagan came along. So during the Republican convention but after Reagan was nominated, David Rockefeller flies Reagan to New York and instructs him to appoint Bush as his running mate under threat of losing the election or maybe his life if he does not. If this is true, then in March of the following year, the reason for the forced appointment became obvious in that Reagan was there only to get Bush elected. After that he was dispensable.

Neither Lyndon Johnson nor George Bush stood a chance of being elected by the American people in 1960 and 1980. Kennedy and Reagan were their tickets to the eventual occupancy of the White House and it might be said that former head of the CIA George Herbert Walker Bush finally did become the official president, but it was nearly eight years after he meant to.

The first thing any modern detective is trained to do in a murder case (or as in this case, attempted murder) is to ascertain exactly who has the most to gain from the crime. Were agents of that great investigative agency known worldwide as the FBI so dense that they did not know to pursue this lead? Of course not. They were pulled off. Just as in Dallas in 1963, when the world was told that they had their man and no other investigation was necessary. And just as the fighter jets were turned around on September 11, 2001, as we shall learn. Much goes on behind the curtain.

IS TIM MCVEIGH IN HELL OR ON PARADISE ISLAND?

The following is from Pat Shannan's "Musings" column published in Media Bypass magazine in 2001.

Recently, Stan Solomon had me on his Indianapolis talk show along with Clay Douglas. Clay is our friendly competitor and stays on top of the current issues as well as anyone. We seldom disagree on anything, but during the dual interview on *The Solomon Show*, the day after Tim McVeigh's alleged execution, Clay made the remark that "Tim is now probably down in Argentina drinking rum and enjoying the beach, with plastic surgery and a new ID."

I countered with something about that I had seen all that conspiracy paranoia on the Internet and did not believe it. After all, Tim was far better off to "them" dead than alive. Dead men tell no tales. Besides, Tim McVeigh's face may be more recognizable these days than Tiger Woods', and it would take a modern-day Chester Gould (remember him?)[3] wigged-out on LSD to distort Tim's mug enough to not be recognizable in public.

However, on an airplane the next day, I did a little thinking, and a few days later a little research and found enough to at least make me wonder: is Tim McVeigh really dead?

I obtained a copy of Tim McVeigh's death certificate, upon which it says under Item 11, Decedent's Usual Occupation: "Soldier," and under Item 12, Kind of Business: "U. S. Army." This is dated June 11, 2001, some nine years after Tim reportedly separated from military service. Was this his current occupation in 2001? (If not, how simple would it have been to pencil in: "Unemployed"?) It brings all sorts of speculation to the surface, and, if really a fact, answers a whole Ryder truck full of questions.

Let us explore a new scenario; not that of Tim being an unwitting participant and only on the fringes, as we have always acknowledged; but that of a willing participant, a government agent, from day one, which might even precede the Waco incident and even account for his presence there. And this would not only explain his foolhardy sprint up I-35 at 85 mph in his old Mercury with no license plates, immediately following the blast(s), but his failure to shoot Trooper Charlie Hangar to avoid being arrested. After all, sooner or later, it would have to have been Tim's job to get arrested.

No, it doesn't change any facts. The building was blown from the inside, and no one can ever refute that certainty with any honest evidence or explanation. Since Gen. Ben Partin came on the scene in May of '95, no one has even tried to do so with any vigor.

And it would immediately explain the government's cover-up of everything: Cary Gagan's torpedoed multi-attempts to expose the "Middle East connection" and the investigative reporting of the same by KFOR-TV's Jayna Davis; Tim's ability to travel the country with no visible means of support; the clamming up of Gov. Frank Keating, after he announced to the world his knowledge of the "unexploded bombs found at the scene"; the FBI's refusal to acknowledge the existence of any perpetrators who did not fit the description of McVeigh and Nichols; "defense" attorney Stephen Jones's duplicity with prosecutors in allowing the expedited demolition of the Murrah Building shell only 34 days after the incident, without detailed examination; the dismal defense performance at trial by Jones and the continual suppression of evidence by Judge Matsch; and the failure of the FBI to ever produce the surveillance tapes commandeered from across the street, from cameras focused on the front of the Murrah Building.

Yes, Tim as a hired gun would make the whole !@#$% cover-up more understandable.

Most of all, it would explain Tim's alleged confession of taking the rap and being solely responsible; "the sole architect" of the bombing, the facts of which we know to be impossible, considering the evidence.

After a week of pondering, it was not so absurd anymore. As stated here before, no one loves a good conspiracy more than I, but the bit about faking Tim's death and sending him away with a new ID was more than even I could swallow—at first.

But then there was the on going, seemingly never-ending snow job by the media. Everywhere we looked—TV, newspapers, magazines—were the Buffalo newsmen touting their new fairytale about McVeigh's alleged confession. They claimed to have talked with the death-row inmate for 75 hours via telephone but said they could not produce the tapes because they "had promised not to." Dubious evidence, indeed. (Bravo Sierra, more likely.)

Nancy Grace of Court TV said on the day of the "execution" that a decoy hearse was used and "It's a good thing because those militia kooks might want to steal the body!" How ridiculous can one get? As hard as they tried, the liberal media were never able to connect McVeigh to any militia movement, but the spin was in. The ever-sensational Geraldo, at every opportunity with an interview with anybody on the subject, delighted in saying time and again that McVeigh was a "monster" and a "scumbag." Overkill.

Speaking of the "wacky conspiracy theorists," Frank Keating said in an interview with Court TV's Catherine Crier, "We can never prove them right and have a system of law that survives." Hmmm. Ponder that statement for a moment. Who was it who said that if you tell a lie big enough, anybody will believe it?

Okay, if it is a lie and Tim's execution was a fake, then how did they do it? Craig Roberts is an investigative reporter and a former cop with all sorts of sordid experience in his background, including that of being a sniper in Vietnam. He is not buying the government story, either. He offers cogent food for thought on how the sham could have been pulled off.

A few days before the proposed execution date Roberts said, "What I tell people when they ask about McVeigh confessing [that he was the lone bomber] is that the media hacks don't understand that McVeigh is playing the good soldier. He thinks he is expected to take the blame by himself and cover for his cohorts since he is totally compromised. It is exactly the same as if he was on a patrol behind enemy lines and got captured. He would tell his captors that he was alone, lost and no one else was out there so his buddies could get away. That's what is happening here. McVeigh is still trying to be the "good soldier" hero to his mates. He can only hope that they can do something to interfere with the execution or to engineer something to reduce his sentence (such as this timely release of FBI documents after a change in administration).

"Few people who have never been in the military would understand the above. Most who have been in the military, especially combat veterans, would know exactly what is going on here."

A few days after the supposed execution, Roberts was our radio guest on *Pat Shannan's Investigative Reports* and gave us more benefit of his military experience.

Okay, let's just imagine for a moment that the "fix" was in.

1. McVeigh, being part of some covert action team of soldiers or mercenaries (the Mission Impossible scenario types), has a guarantee that if he is caught, they will not help him until he goes through the judicial system and is out of the spotlight. They will place a large amount of money in an offshore account under a bogus name (whatever name Tim is about to assume).

2. Time passes, and McVeigh is no longer on the front page. He is instructed to take all the blame, leaving "others unknown" out of it. He does this by feeding information to two gullible reporters who write a book full of errors that basically puts the issue to rest in the minds of the general population of ostriches. (This is the common MO. The fairytale by Lou Michel and Dan Herbeck, whose title we refuse to publicize, was likely ordered and delineated by the CIA. From the same venue a few years ago came *Case Closed* by Gerald Posner, which whitewashed the Warren Commission's deception and named "Oswald" as the lone culprit.[4] While ignoring all the evidence to the contrary, he and it attempted to give credence to the Warren Commission's indictment of "Lee Oswald". It was another diversion straight out of the CIA cookbook. Whether delusional or by design, the efforts of all these authors are way out in left field.)

3. McVeigh then demands his execution date be set—since he knows he isn't going to be executed, it will actually be his release date, assuming he is not double-crossed.

4. The stage is set for a show. Witnesses will have to be convinced that he is dead. This is easy to accomplish if the actors are convincing in their roles in the death chamber.

5. Special chemicals are mixed "in some other city" (perhaps Langley, Va.?). These are capable of feigning death by slowing the heartbeat and respiration to the point that observers think Tim is dead—especially when "someone" announces it from inside the room, and then they cover him with a sheet or close the curtains. Such chemicals exist. Curare is one that can be used if mixed with other chemicals. Others can be obtained from the Caribbean from voodoo priests who use the ground leaves of certain plants to create "zombies." Zombies are only drugged people who appear to die to the observers, then come back from the dead later. They have a paleness to their skin and glazed eyes appearing like spooks, which is a

continuing drugged state. The priests keep them drugged when they feed them and use them to show power—and as slave workers. (A program on this subject was done on one of the major satellite network educational channels recently.)

6. The executioner is brought in from somewhere else, and is anonymous, "for his own protection."

(Terre Haute is supposed to have a "state of the art" execution chamber. Why do they need to bring in the chemicals from elsewhere?)

7. The chemicals are injected and McVeigh goes into a deep sleep, his heart rate and breathing decelerate to what appears to be a halt. He is pronounced dead by someone in on the plan, and the visual play ends. The curtains close, and his "body" is wheeled out to a waiting hearse.

8. He is driven to a funeral home, where he is allegedly cremated, as a judge has already ordered "no autopsy." Therefore no autopsy photos or report will ever surface. This also ensures that there is no body to exhume later to make sure Tim is really dead, should questions arise.

9. An urn of ashes and a death certificate are produced, and the story ends here.

Or does it? The key players, "in the know" and paid off handsomely,[5] would have to be the executioner, whoever pronounced him dead and someone at the funeral home who does the "cremation." (This has more than one precedent—the Lincoln/Booth case, for instance.)

Also, since there were two hearses, or more, it might be possible to time this execution with a body similar to McVeigh's which is delivered to the funeral home. If still sealed in a box or cardboard coffin, surrounded by "federal agents," even the funeral home personnel would be convinced and not need to become part of the act (thereby eliminating one or more from "need to know" status). Neither would the county coroner who signed the death certificate as they would have a real corpse to burn, leaving no dental ID or fingerprints to check later. Also the coroner doesn't check dental records or fingerprints of a corpse that is already identified in the normal course of duties. The ashes are to be scattered "in a secret place."

McVeigh, transported away in one of the ambulances driven by one of the operators wakes up later in a safe house. He is transported at night, by air, to South America or the Orient, where he undergoes facial surgery and gets a new ID. His money is waiting, and he's retired or saved for future missions.

And, finally, there is the one remaining scenario: Tim did all of the above, came to his agreement with his controllers to take the rap in exchange for a bundle of money and a new life; but true to form, the deceiving dogs shoot him with the real juice and kill him anyway. (We are sure you thought of that!) However, Mr. Roberts counters with more persuasive input.

I asked Roberts: "Why don't they just get rid of him? After all, he's a live witness to the ID of others involved and can tell what really happened in OKC at any time."

Roberts responded, "It's simple. The rest of the team has the same guarantee as McVeigh, and they will be watching to see if he is taken care of as promised. Their loyalty is now assured for future operations. Of course, there is nothing to stop the upper echelon from getting rid of the whole team as they are actually expendable, unless they are too valuable due to time spent recruiting and training them. McVeigh would serve as an example that their Manchurian Candidate system works, and the other operators are not a threat to the conspirators."

So it is not so "way out" as it may appear on the surface. The government has pulled it off before. It has long been speculated that John Wilkes Booth did not die in that burning barn in 1865.

Now we can prove it. In our research in recent years, we came across a gem—a book written by Booth's granddaughter in 1937, who as a young child was kept in the dark by her mother and most family members about Booth's escape. But the older she got, the more she became so intrigued that she pursued the case during her whole adult life and sorted out the facts. In her twilight years, she produced the irrefutable evidence that Booth survived at least to middle age. If one wants to read the whole story, one need only go to the articles published in two editions of THE BARNES REVIEW magazine. These article were contained in the May/June 2008 and the November/December 2008 issues. Additionally, a small booklet has been published about the escape with additional material not published in TBR due to space constraints.[6]

No, we are not 100% convinced that Tim is still alive, but we also have no way of knowing that he is really dead. And you don't either.

THE VINCE FOSTER MURDER

Investigative Reporter Hugh Sprunt of Dallas, Texas did as much or more than anyone in exposing the government cover-up of the Vince Foster murder in Washington in 1993. Most of the facts and information following here were learned from him and attorney John Clarke more than a decade ago. The following is a list of 64 anomalies regarding the Vince Foster "suicide" that needs to be answered:

64 SUSPICIOUS EVENTS AND CIRCUMSTANCES

Vincent Foster was a lifelong friend of Bill Clinton, having spent their childhood together in Hope, Arkansas. As Clinton's political star rose in Arkansas from a young (30) attorney general to the governorship, Foster rode along with him.

When Clinton attained the presidency in 1993, Foster packed up and went to the White House as chief counsel. On the way and during his six months there, he had picked up a lot of baggage—more than he needed to carry, apparently.

On the warm summer afternoon of July 20, 1993, Vince was found shot to death on a grassy slope in Fort Marcy Park, across the Potomac River from Washington, D.C. and only a stone's throw from the Central Intelligence Agency Headquarters in Langley, Virginia. It was obvious that his body had been placed there, but the official cause of death was "suicide." The popular slang term of the day regarding the subject was "Arkancided," because of the large number of strange deaths coming out of the state during Bill Clinton's Arkansas governorship and later U.S. presidency.

Foster was the highest-ranking White House official to be killed since John F. Kennedy in 1963. The official report was but another dose of Bravo Sierra.

Here follows a list of suspicious events, observations and circumstances, taken from the 2,726 pages of the 1994 Senate Hearings and Report Volumes that cover the death of Vince Foster.

1. No fingerprints on the gun.
2. No proof that it was his gun.

3. Suspicious people seen in and around victim's car just before the body was found.

4. Eyewitnesses saw the victim's briefcase in his car, yet the briefcase later vanished. So did the files index in his office.

5. All 35mm film of crime scene was either "overexposed" or it vanished.

6. Most of the Polaroid photos of the crime scene vanished.

7. "Independent" investigator Robert Fiske was forced to concede that the victim's head had been moved—after death had taken place and before his body was photographed.

8. Car keys were not found with victim at crime scene, nor were they to be found in his car, yet the conclusion immediately arrived at . . . was suicide! (Does this make any sense whatsoever?)

9. The first non-official to see the body said there was no gun in sight; so did the first official to see the body.

10. No blood splatter found. (High-velocity .38 bullets through the mouth and head leave "blowback" and splatter!)

11. No bone fragments were found at the scene, yet part of the victim's skull was missing, according to the Fiske report.

12. X-rays vanished with no explanation. (Was it to conceal the fact that Foster had other head injuries besides that of a single bullet?)

13. Dr. James Beyer, the examining physician, has a history of mistaking homicide for suicide. In some instances he stated X-rays had been taken; in other instances he stated they had not. Why the inconsistency?

14. According to some reports, Foster's head wound not consistent with a high velocity .38 caliber bullet. Dr. Donald Haut's statement to the FBI was that the exit hole was very small. In contradiction, the Fiske report says Dr. Haut's observation was that the exit-hole was very large.

15. No fingerprints were found on the torn-up "suicide" note, but a palm print was. How can you tear up a piece of paper without leaving any fingerprints on it, when the paper is "receptive" enough to take a very clear palm print?! (No determination was made that it was Foster's palm print.)

16. A wound was seen on Foster's neck by paramedics. One described it as a bullet hole.

17. Dr. Haut and paramedics said they viewed the body in a location

that is 200 feet from the site officially described.

18. The cannon near where some witnesses say the body was found has been removed from the park.

19. In his report, one paramedic listed the death as a homicide.

20. Numerous hairs and carpet fibers covered Foster's clothing. But his car was never checked to see if any of the same fibers could be found on the driver's seat, as surely there would have been found, had he actually driven himself to Fort Marcy Park.

21. Whereabouts of victim in hours before death remains a mystery.

22. The list of items in his "suicide note" could simply have been some reflection of his plans to resign his White House position, which his wife said he was seriously thinking of doing.

23. Only two bullets in the gun. No matching bullets were to be found in his home or car.

24. The victim had planned to give his visiting sister a tour of the White House the next day.

25. The victim's friend and attorney, Jim Lyons, was coming from Colorado to meet with him the next day.

26. Foster had a full lunch before leaving the White House to (supposedly) kill himself. He was jovial, and told his staff he would be back later in the day.

27. In spite of an exhaustive search, no bullet was ever found that matched the cartridge in the revolver reportedly found at the scene.

28. The attitude of the body was not consistent with suicide. It was laid out straight, with arms neatly at his sides.

29. No one is known to have heard the shot. Few people in the surrounding area were even asked. The closest house, which was under construction at the time, was only 400 ft. away.

30. The FBI was kept out of the initial investigation. (This was certainly because the clumsy bungling needed to be blamed on the inexperienced Park Police.)

31. The lead investigator assigned to go to the body site was thereby performing his first homicide investigation.

32. Victim's appointment book was never found.

33. Victim had been making *overnight* trips to Switzerland (go one day, come back the next) which his wife didn't know about. Indications are

that he had a Swiss bank account which had been mysteriously emptied of $2.7 million a week before he died. His last planned trip to Switzerland, for reasons unknown, had been canceled.

34. Foster had, until coming to Washington, been employed as a $300,000 a year lawyer. His house in Washington was not especially impressive. Yet in the last weeks before his death he had a chronically overdrawn checking account.

35. Police were prevented from searching the victim's home and office.

36. Victim's widow was not interviewed for 10 days after the death. Apparently she was shown a stainless steel or nickel revolver which was identified as the weapon used. She said it looked like the "silver-colored revolver" she had previously seen at home. The ABC photo very clearly shows a black gun in Foster's hand.

37. No proof that the gun found with the victim actually fired the fatal shot.

38. Photos and reports in the possession of the Park Police and FBI are being kept from public view. (Just like the Zapruder film in 1963 and OKC surveillance of 1995.)

39. The Fiske Report contains numerous factual errors regarding time and geography at crime scene. It reports a large pool of blood under Foster's head, even though no one who was at the site made any such report. In fact some of those who viewed the body, including Dr. Haut and Corey Ashford, specifically stated to the FBI that there was no blood on the ground. (Ashford is one of the medical technicians who helped pick Foster's body up, to remove it from the scene.)

40. One vehicle seen at park by police and rescue eyewitnesses is ignored in the official record of the case.

41. Park Police concluded their investigation before they sent the gun for testing to see if it could fire.

42. Death was ruled a suicide before the investigators viewed the body.

43. The crime scene was never totally secured. (There are access roads near the body site, in the opposite direction from the parking lot where Foster's car was found. Access to the body, from these roads, was never blocked off in any way.)

44. No damage whatsoever to victim's teeth from the recoil of a .38, allegedly placed in his mouth. This pistol has a rather substantial steel

aiming device mounted at the top of the end of the 4-inch barrel.

45. Wildly conflicting testimony about the time at which the victim was identified.

46. There is no evidence to support the Fiske report that the victim had lost weight. The only evidence is that he had *gained* weight.

47. Conflicting testimony as to when the White House was told of the death—from as early as 6 p.m., according to the initial report from Chelsea's nanny, to the official time of 8:30 p.m.

48. The phone number of a Secret Service officer was found in the notebook of Park Police investigator Rolla. Immediately following this entry was the address and phone number of Vince Foster. When asked about this during his deposition, the record shows that Rolla got nervous and flustered.

49. Eyewitness testimony is in disagreement as to whether victim's car was initially found locked. Some say it was locked. But the car keys were "found" much later, at the morgue, in a front pocket that had already been searched at the scene. How then was Foster's car opened up?

50. Because of interference with prosecutor Rodriguez's inquiry into this case, he resigned in protest.

51. Marsha Scott met with Foster, her friend of 20 years, in an unusual one- to two-hour closed-door meeting the day before he died. After Foster died, the *only* thing Ms. Scott said she could remember discussing, from her long meeting, was that Foster had a good weekend.

52. The ABC News photo published showing Foster's hand with the gun is not consistent with eyewitness accounts of the scene.

53. The victim's office, a secondary crime scene, was immediately cleansed of evidence and documents by Clinton administration officials.

54. The victim's personal effects including his pager were returned to the White House within 24 hours—before they could be analyzed by the police.

55. Certain White House personnel, whose names are (for reasons unknown) not in the official record, were prepared to break into Park Police Officer Rolla's desk drawer to obtain a key to the evidence locker where Foster's possessions were being kept. (From p. 91 of Hugh Sprunt's report.)

56. The neighborhood around the crime scene at Fort. Marcy Park was

not canvassed by police, to see if anyone had heard a shot, until *two years* after the shooting took place.

57. Several police officers in Arkansas, two of them on duty at the governor's mansion, have given sworn depositions that they were told of Foster's death, by phone, at 6 p.m. EST. But this would be *before* police and rescue workers arrived at Fort Marcy Park! One of these officers immediately informed the governor's wife—more than an hour before White House personnel say they found out about Foster's death.

58. It is unclear when and where the victim's car keys were actually found. One rescue worker says they were found on the way to the morgue. Another says they were found at the morgue.

59. Police and rescue workers have been forbidden to discuss the case.

60. No mention has ever been made as to whether there were powder burns inside of Foster's mouth and whether they were consistent with the bullet and spent shell found in the gun at the scene.

61. Shortly before his death, Foster asked his executive assistant to put two, inch-thick ring binders, from the National Security Agency, into Bernie Nussbaum's safe. However, Foster did not have the security clearance necessary for possession of such binders. When Foster's assistant revealed, under oath, in an interview by Senate Banking Committee investigators, that she had placed these binders in the safe after Foster gave them to her with this request, no follow-up questions were asked, and no mention was made of any of this in the public hearings what followed. Why not?

62. The gun allegedly found at Fort Marcy Park was composed of parts from *two different guns*, and the serial numbers had been ground off both parts.

63. Lisa Foster was given more than $250,000 just prior to her husband's death. It was channeled to her via Vince Foster's sister who works at the Department of Justice. Why was Lisa given this money? Was it hush money?

64. Web Hubbell, in his testimony to the recent Whitewater hearings, when describing his actions *following* notification of Foster's death is reported to have said, "We searched for Vince Foster's gun in his house." Could Web Hubbell have taken the silver-colored gun from Foster's house, so that the FBI could later show Lisa Foster the "suicide weapon"?

THE $64,000 QUESTION:

How could the first independent prosecutor, Robert Fiske, have possibly missed *all* of the preceding 64 points? How could a truly independent and objective investigator honestly and totally miss all this?! And if he missed it on purpose, what was he trying to hide, why was he hiding it, and for whom was he hiding it?

And the answer is,[7] everything they ever intend to tell us will always be a manufactured lie, geared to the protection of the establishment, unless the truth somehow enhances the position of the controlling faction, which seldom happens.

The foregoing list of suspicious events, observations, questions and circumstances was taken, almost entirely, from the 2,726 pages of the 1994 Senate Hearings and Report Volumes (three of them) that cover the death of Vince Foster. A 165-page synopsis of this material was put together by fellow investigative reporter Hugh Sprunt. Sprunt has an MBA and JD from Stanford, as well as a BS (it's those BS degrees that have always worried me, *just kidding, Hugh*) and an MS from MIT. He is the lead author of a two-volume, 750-page tax reference work. His words have been published in *The New York Times, The Washington Times, The Wall Street Journal* and *Forbes* magazine. He also happens to have been the person to find his grandfather, minutes after the elderly gentleman had blown his brains out with a .38 revolver (the barrel of which had been placed in the mouth). So he knows, personally and vividly, what such a scene looks like and also knows that from all descriptions of the Foster body site, no high velocity .38 caliber bullet through the mouth and head could have possibly taken place at this location.

All but two or three of the items on the list can be found both in Sprunt's booklet as well as in the Senate Hearings Report just mentioned. The two or three others can be found in Jim Norman's *"Fostergate"* article, which was carefully checked by the staff at *Media Bypass* and the staff at the *Jerusalem Post*, where the article was finally published.

Everything they ever told us about the Foster "suicide" was a lie. Vince Foster was murdered—probably in the White House. There were phone calls to indicate this.

Additional circumstantial evidence, too vague to present in court, but

The long-circulating rumor that Vince and Hillary carried on an affair while they worked together in Little Rock's Rose Law Firm was confirmed to this author by a retired Arkansas State Police trooper who was often used as Gov. Bill Clinton's chauffeur.

nevertheless enlightening, came to me from a longtime, trusted friend who is a retired Delta Airlines pilot. He spoke to me in 1996 or so about a co-pilot with whom he had flown, who told him that his brother had been a Secret Service agent in the White House in 1993. His brother had told him this story. Take it for whatever it is worth.

The Delta captain told me that his co-pilot had said that when his brother had gone to work at the White House the next morning (Wednesday, July 21st), the entire carpet had been removed from Vince Foster's office and replaced with new carpeting, and that the carpet-laying crew, who had obviously been there since the wee hours of the morn, were just leaving when he arrived for work at seven.

Hearsay? Indeed. But ahhh, what juicy seeds for a novel, and sooooo Clintonesque.

ENDNOTES:

1 Reagan's Secret Service code name.

2 Out of the mouths of babes!

3 I soon found out that nobody did remember him, and it was one more reflection of my using stuff too old for my audience. Chester Gould, for the information of all the young readers, was the artist and creator of the "Dick Tracy" comic strip character and series (that I always read first on Sunday mornings), and he also was a wizard at creating all kinds of evil characters with distorted faces. All this led to the Warren Beatty cinema creation that you probably did see a few years ago.

4 A decade later, Vincent Bugliosi, who once held some stature as an author in the true crime venue of writers and was even admired by this author, fell from grace when he wrote and published a 1,600+ page epic of a multiplied Posner-type deception that ignored truths and made him a laughing stock of the private investigative world. Most of us agreed that Bugliosi was far too smart to have arrived at these conclusions on his own and must have been paid handsomely to be the new distorter of the JFK case in this decade. Another will come along, around 2020.

5 This is another benefit of legal tender and the ability to create "money" out of thin air. Prior to the creation of the FED, the states had to fund federal projects through "apportionment." In the old days the states would not have bothered with even the doctor and the needle and would not have funded much more than the cost of a rope and scaffold.

6 The 90-page book—*The Great Escape of John Wilkes Booth*—can be ordered from LIFE & LIBERTY PUBLISHING, P.O. Box 2770, Stafford, VA 22555 for $15.

7 During the presidential Impeachment (so called) hearings in 1998, Bill Clinton's infamous response to a question at one point was his ridiculous "that depends on what the definition of 'is' is." However, just as with his four-hour deception in front of the special prosecutor and TV cameras (but also somehow avoiding submitting to grand jury questioning), where he lied under oath throughout most of his testimony by saying, "I don't remember that," with Orwellian predictability, the rascal got away with all of it.

"Lying is deadly and highly contagious. The man who receives his information from a liar will spew out lies when he passes the information on. When you have liars trained in the demonic arts controlling the highest seats of governmental authority, you will have liars controlling the information channels. When their lies fill the printed pages, loud speakers, and TV screens, you will have liars administering the workplaces, marketplaces, schools, churches and homes. Without realizing it, your nation becomes possessed by demons. Your nation practices the politics of witchcraft."

—From "The Politics of Witchcraft," the epilogue to *Tennessee Waltz* by F. Tupper Saussy—a book Saussy wrote with James Earl Ray that told Ray's story of being "framed" for the murder of Martin Luther King.

THE MULTI-FACETED
JFK MYSTERIES AND OTHERS

C heck out this quote by Johann Wolfgang von Goethe (1828): "The truth must be repeated again and again because error is constantly being preached around us, and not only by isolated individuals but by the majority! In the newspapers and encyclopedias, in the schools and universities, everywhere error is dominant, securely and comfortably ensconced in public opinion, which is on its side."

Well, 1828, huh? So what else is new?

After reading *Who Killed Kennedy* by Thomas Buchanan in 1964, I became passionately interested in the government's dubious story of the public execution of President Kennedy. There were lots of questions but few answers. Soon thereafter the Warren Commission released its gigantic fraud, and private investigators countered with a flurry of books challenging this fiction with logic, laws of physics and previously unpublished and/or ignored facts. I was quickly hooked and, over the 45 + subsequent years, my thirst for more and more led me to the accumulation of what now must be one of the largest private collections in the world—research reports from the experts on the subject in the form of books, magazines, and both audio and video tapes. One large (7'x 5') bookcase is jam-packed full of nothing else but this Kennedy memorabilia. I am what they call a "JFK buff," and it wasn't long before I would become an "assassination buff," and yes, even a "conspiracy factist" who will forever poke fun at the "coincidence theorists."

When New Orleans District Attorney Jim Garrison uncovered his case against Clay Shaw—weak as it finally appeared—he was met with a vicious attack by the press and solid roadblocks by the federal judiciary. U.S. attorneys, as well as the attorney general himself—all of whom should have been on Garrison's side—refused to honor his subpoenas for witnesses or cooperate with his investigation in any way. Even Texas Governor John Connally, who had sustained multiple wounds himself, disallowed the extradition papers of two key witnesses.

And a million of us wondered *why would this be?* Gov. Connally was a shooting victim who was nearly killed along with President Kennedy that fateful day. Wouldn't he be the first to want the truth to come out? But Jim Garrison had not yet begun to realize who the real enemy was and what high-powered pressure could be applied from the inside.

The following year, 1968, Martin Luther King and Sen. Robert Kennedy were murdered only two months apart—April 4th and June 4th. The railroading of James Earl Ray in the first case became so obvious a blind man could see it,[1] and further investigation showed that somebody in addition to Sirhan Sirhan had been firing a weapon at the New York senator who was about to get the Democratic nomination for president. Either someone else was shooting or Sirhan performed the magical feat of firing his eight-shot revolver at least 11 times without reloading.

The later evidence showed that even such a ridiculous scenario as that would not fly because the autopsy showed that *Sen. Robert Kennedy had three wounds fired from a different weapon from behind,* two of which were fired, beyond doubt, from only 1 to 3 inches away—proven by the powder burns present, and the fact that Sirhan was never anywhere near that close to the senator.

JAMES EARL RAY & MARTIN LUTHER KING

When M.L. King was murdered in Memphis on April 4, 1968, the same pattern of honest news reporting followed by FBI "correction" (that was evident in Dallas in 1963 and later in OKC in 1995) came to be obvious in Memphis and once again witnesses had to be intimidated in order for their testimony to change. For instance, the witnesses inside Canipe Amusement Shop said they saw two men jump into a white Mustang and speed away from the scene after dropping the bag of evidence in their doorway. This eyewitness report would coincide with Jim Green's story that follows, which tells us exactly who these two men were. However, the FBI soon changed its reports to read that only one man (Ray, of course) was rushing from the scene.

In only five minutes, the police conveniently found a .30-06 hunting rifle wrapped in a bundle at Canipe's front door, a shop next to the rooming house. Along with the rifle was found a pair of binoculars, two unopened beer cans with Ray's fingerprints, a tack hammer and pliers, a shaving kit, a hair brush, a pair of men's shorts and undershirt, the April 4th issue of the Memphis *Commercial Appeal* and a radio with the number 00416 (Ray's inmate number at the Missouri State Penitentiary) etched on it. The dumbest cop on the planet could see it was planted evidence.

Two weeks later the fingerprints on the rifle were identified as belonging to James Earl Ray. The largest FBI manhunt began and on June 8, 1968, James Earl Ray was apprehended at the Heathrow Airport, London as he prepared to go to Brussels.

In this case, Ray, an escaped convict from the Missouri State Penitentiary, was the chosen patsy. Ray was a petty thief who had never committed a violent crime in his life and had no history of any racial hatred. Ray, it was learned much later from his brother, John, was "allowed" to escape in the back of a bread truck. Upon reaching a main road and out of sight of anyone, Ray jumped out, and John, following closely in his car, picked up his brother and took him to his home in East St. Louis, Illinois "for about 30 days." This was in late April of 1967, some 50 weeks before the King murder the following April.

In June, Ray made his way to Chicago,[2] where he bought an old Chrysler for $100, cash presumably supplied by his brother, but before two weeks had passed, the Chrysler fizzled out, he sold it for $40 and bought a 1962 Plymouth for $200. From there he went to Detroit, crossed the border into Canada and spent a night in Toronto, where he somehow sought out pieces of phony ID of four men who looked somewhat like him, such as "John Willard," who would later check into the flophouse at 422 South Main in Memphis. (James claimed that he chose these at random from a Toronto telephone book, but the astronomical odds against such a thing made his claim preposterous.) It was "Harvey Lowmeyer" who would purchase the 30.06 rifle later in Birmingham, even though Ray was spending most of his days under another name from the Canadian list, "Eric Starvo Galt." After the murder, "Ramon George Sneyd" acquired the passport and traveled to Europe where he was captured two months later.

From Toronto, Ray made his way to Montreal, a place where he had spent some time committing petty crimes in 1959. There in only two days he managed to meet and befriend the elusive "Raoul," who told James he could use him in a smuggling operation. It was the initial contact of a frame up that would last for nine months until the following April 4th.

"Raoul" had cash, and James needed that. "Raoul" bought him a white Mustang, took him to New Orleans, sent him to Acapulco, and paid for some plastic surgery in Los Angeles to round out some of his pointy features in order that he look more like the ID pictures of Galt, Willard et al. James stayed in touch through a "504" area code in New Orleans.

The following March, "Raoul" had Ray drive the Mustang back across country from Los Angeles to New Orleans. From there the two rode together to Birmingham, Alabama to purchase a rifle.

Another incident illuminating the obvious set-up of Ray took place at the Aeromarine Sports Supply Shop in Birmingham. "Raoul" stayed in the motel and told Ray to go buy a "good deer rifle," handing him several hundred dollars. When he arrived at the sports supply shop, Ray told the salesman that he wanted to buy a gift for his brother-in-law and purchased a Winchester .270 and returned to the motel. "Raoul" immediately began to complain that this was inadequate and a weapon with "a larger bore" was required. Ray flung him a catalog and told him to pick one out because he didn't know anything about firearms.

The next day James returned to Aeromarine Supply and asked to exchange the new rifle for one of a larger caliber. The salesman remembered telling him, "You tell your brother-in-law that this gun will bring down any deer in Alabama."

He did, however, agree to take it back and sell James a Remington semi-automatic 30.06.

The obvious real purpose of this exercise was not to exchange a perfectly good "murder weapon" for another but to make certain that the Aeromarine salesman would not forget James Earl Ray. We are talking about an eventual shot in Memphis that would take place from only 210 feet away. A K-mart .22 rifle could have performed successfully.

The trap was set, and as the world now knows, James Earl Ray fell right into it. In November of 2000, I was in Dallas for a JFK Researchers Conference and recognized Jerry Ray, James Earl's brother, from his pictures. He was sitting at a table in the Adolphus Hotel bar with a man he introduced me to as Jim Green. Jim's story so fascinated me that I later visited him at his home in Hudson, Florida, took pictures of the real weapon that killed Martin Luther King, and later featured him on the cover of *Media Bypass* (May, 2001) holding the gun and with a long feature story inside.

Green's story can hardly be told in a nutshell, but we shall try here with a "Readers Digest condensed version" of the more detailed report as seen in my *Media Bypass* magazine article a decade ago.

May 2001 issue of *Media Bypass* magazine featuring Jim Green, who said he was part of the MLK assassination.

James Cooper Green was born in 1947 and became a car thief for the St. Louis mob before he reached the age of majority. In 1968, he had known "Raoul" for a couple of years, but he knew him as an FBI agent and only as "Paul." Earlier in the game, Paul had shown Jim his FBI credentials briefly and too quickly for him to see and remember the last name.[3] In any case, Paul/Raoul was calling all the shots (pun intended) for months prior to the King murder. He had been leading the patsy, James Earl Ray, around on a money leash since July of the previous year, when they "accidentally" met in a Montreal bar.

With an FBI agent in charge of the set-up, a local police detective placed in position to murder the patsy, and mob thugs used as the trigger men on the targets, this whole scenario typifies an "inside job." J. Edgar Hoover and the FBI always utilized outside help for their dirty work. In case any were ever caught red-handed, the agency would not be implicated. (Hoover took gifts from Mafia dons for decades while publicly denying even the existence of such "families.")

On the day of the murder, Green and a confederate named Butch Collier—a Caruthersville, Missouri policeman and former bad boy with Green in his youth—had collected $5,000 (with five more to come following completion of the operation) to handle the assassination of King. Collier, stationed in the brush down the hill from the backside of the flophouse, would be the shooter (and Jim Green said that indeed he was), and Green was to be the "protector." He was stationed on a rooftop two blocks south of the flophouse hotel where Raoul and James Earl Ray were checked in. His assignment was to shoot and kill James Earl Ray in the event that Memphis police detective John Talley failed to do so. Green was armed with a .357 rifle to match the slugs in the .357 magnum pistol carried by Talley, who was stationed at the corner west of the fire station, awaiting and prepared to shoot and kill Ray.

Here was the ploy: Raoul had instructed James Earl Ray, because they "would need some travel money," to go downstairs and stick up Jim's Grill to obtain some cash. Then Ray was to walk (run!) south on Main Street for three blocks to the Arcade Restaurant, where he and Raoul could meet up.

It was a set-up within a set-up, and Ray either recognized it or just was not up to the task; but in either case, he did not participate. He left the flophouse at 5:50 p.m., but instead of pulling the armed robbery, as instructed, he got into the Mustang and calmly drove away—not with a hurried exit with screeching tires, as described by the news media and falsified FBI 302 reports, but without incident. Jim Green said that he witnessed this from his rooftop perch two blocks away, while John Talley waited on the street corner below him. Because Ray went the other way, neither Green nor Talley would fire a shot.

A few minutes later, after Collier had delivered the fatal bullet to King and Raoul had posed as the bathroom shooter, the second Mustang indeed did leave the area at a high rate of speed, but not with only one person inside, as so deftly twisted by the FBI reports (after multiple witnesses said there were two in the "white Mustang") but with Raoul and Butch Collier, as witnessed by Jim Green from the rooftop.

Jim Green spent the last half of his life as a schoolteacher, coach and raising a family. A smoker who wouldn't quit, even after he got sick, he died in May of 2003. He had told me that Butch Collier had died about 10 years earlier of cancer. He never learned what had happened to Raoul/Paul but was certain that he was an FBI agent and that he was the one in the bathroom[4] of the flophouse who had run down the hall after the shooting, had been seen by Grace Stephens, had stuffed the duffle bag with Ray's possessions and dumped it on the street a minute later.

"I saw him do it," Jim said, speaking of the dumping of evidence and his grandstand seat on the rooftop only a block away.

A few minutes later, Butch Collier picked Jim up at the vacant building and drove the two of them back to Caruthersville, Missouri. Jim kept the murder weapon at a friend's house for 29 years before retrieving it and allowing me to photograph it for his story.

What is related above is the condensed version of a 5,000 word article we published in the May 2001 issue of *Media Bypass* magazine with a picture of Jim Green holding the rifle on the cover (see page 155).

Ray told the sequel to this in his book *Tennessee Waltz*, published by Tupper Saussy in 1987, just before Saussy was forced to go underground for more than 10 years out of fear for his own life.[5]

Ray said he heard the news on the car radio and beat a path to Atlanta and caught a bus to Toronto. However, the New Orleans district attorney, during his post-JFK assassination probe, managed to get a video interview with a CIA operative named Jules Ricco Kimball from federal prison (where he is serving two life sentences for murder), wherein Kimball said that he was the pilot who flew Ray to Canada out of Charley Brown Airport on Atlanta's west side. Garrison later said that everything Kimball ever told him proved to be true.

Throughout Ray's autobiographical testimony, it seemed as though he almost always told the truth but never quite all of it. Up until his death in prison of liver cancer in 1998 he always maintained his innocence and that he was framed; and the facts of the case supported this. However, he also seemed to always want to be protecting somebody. It is an unwritten code, and whether he was protecting someone out of simply being honorable or out of fear for his life (after all, he was an easy target in prison) it will never be known. What is certain is that James Earl Ray did not murder Martin Luther King, Jr., and even King's children know that today. Everything the FBI ever told us about it was a lie.

As mentioned, Jim Green's revelation fit too many pieces (confirmed with the FBI's own documents) to have been contrived from his imagination. He had told it to one official long before James Earl Ray told his story in *Tennessee Waltz*, which Green did not read until 1998, after he had begun his own book. Jim Green had attempted to "clear his soul" as far back as 1973, when he told journalist Kay Black of the *Memphis Press-Scimitar* the same story printed here with only slightly fewer details. It was never published but frightened Ms. Black enough for her to report it to law enforcement authorities. This led to Green's appearance in front of the House Select Committee on Assassinations (HSCA) in 1976. There his testimony was obliterated from the record and never made public. So much for government inquiries.

One of James Earl Ray's brothers has now come forward with information corroborating the FBI's cooperation in James' escape as well as the Chicago mob's participation in the assassination, under the direction of Sam Giancano. John Ray admits that it was he who picked up his brother after his 1967 "escape" in the bread truck and drove him to a safe house in East St. Louis.

Lyndon Barston's detailed research shows powerful evidence implicating the FBI in a CIA plot.

1] In late 1964, the FBI had tried to get King to commit suicide prior to his departing to Europe to claim his Nobel Peace Prize. This was accomplished by sending an alleged surveillance tape of King in an extramarital sexual relation to the SCLC with a letter warning that all would become public if King didn't kill himself prior to his collecting his Nobel Prize.

2] Lab work relating to the murder of King at FBI Headquarters was dreadfully inadequate. The Remington 30.06 rifle purchased by Ray in Birmingham and deposited at the scene of the crime was not even swabbed to see if it had been fired! Today it still remains as the "official" murder weapon of the MURKIN case. Yet, for some reason, this test was run on even the rifle James Earl Ray had returned to Aeromarine Supply in Birmingham in exchange for the Remington prior to the murder!

3] Atlanta FBI informant, J.C. Hardin, is documented in the MURKIN file as contacting James Earl Ray in Los Angeles just prior to Ray's packing up and heading east to Atlanta and Memphis.

4] On the 29th of March, the FBI, through its "friendly" press contacts, placed King in the open and insecure Lorraine Motel by criticizing him in the press for patronizing "white owned hotels."

5] Journalist Louis Lomax, who later died in a mysterious car crash, was investigating Dr. King's death when visited by two FBI men who instructed him to abruptly end the series of fruitful articles he was producing for the N.A.N.A. Louis Lomax, described as being "no good" in an FBI memo (HQ 44-38861-3196); was a highly respected journalist. It was Lomax who uncovered the deception of the false fingerprints sent out by Jeff City for escaped prisoner James Earl Ray. This strongly suggests the duplicity of both state and federal agencies in the ploy.

The intelligence community's relationship with the mob and union racketeers, as described by Jim Green, is highly documented in the post-World War II era. Chicago mob boss Sam Giancana often described the CIA and his organization as "two sides of the same coin."

The King assassination was every bit as much an "Inside Job" as those of both Kennedys and several more to come in the future.

The purpose of this resurrection of these old cases is not to attempt to solve them here (this has already been done to a conclusive point many, many times in previous publications) but to point out that the real culprits could not get away with these crimes without a culpable and cooperative news media assisting in the deception.

SIMILARITIES TO BREMER & WALLACE

At a 1972 campaign rally in Maryland, Arthur Bremer offered to shake hands with presidential candidate George Wallace, but shot him four times instead. He also fired three more times and wounded three more people with his five-shot .38 revolver, according to the official story. An amazing feat that can only be believed by those with Red, White & Blue Fever.

Check the microfiche at your local library for the 5/16/72 issue of the *NY Times* to see all these facts. Are we to believe that no newsman of the era was smart enough to count to seven? Or is it more likely that any mention of this was cut by his editor before it saw the light of day? Everything they ever told us was a lie.

It didn't take a seasoned investigator to spot the obvious discrepancies in the attempt on the life of this presidential candidate. Anyone could spot this discrepancy by simply reading the next day's newspaper, but not one peep was ever seen or heard on the national news. If any reporter ever did question this, it apparently was nipped in the bud by his editors, and nothing more was ever seen in print.

How illuminating it was to learn from a 1978 *Playboy* interview that Sara Jane Moore, who took a shot a President Gerald Ford in 1975 and was serving a life sentence for the dastardly deed at the time of the interview, had been a paid FBI informant! Why could the establishment press not discover this? Or had they? Yes, it was true. Ms. Moore even named her FBI control officer in San Francisco, Bert Worthington. The FBI, true to form, refused to comment, because everything they ever told us was a lie. The problem was, almost always, that not even their dumbed-down street agents had a clue. Theirs was/is the most galloping case of RWB fever[6] in the country. They are worse than the military dolts who think they joined up to defend freedom.

This pattern of FBI intimidation of witnesses in high profile cases, double-talk, and general cover-up of federal crimes becomes obvious when one does the historic research. It all came home to me when I studied the systematic hunting down and murder by federal agents of Gordon Kahl in Arkansas on June 3, 1983. It was the first case I investigated on my own, and later I wrote about it in *I Rode with Tupper*. My involvement had finally moved from passive to active. I had no choice. It was either begin writing and speaking about these lies and cover-ups publicly or swell up, explode and burst into flames; a personally provoked suicide by the withholding of too much explosive information.

Study of the JFK murder, with the benefit of hindsight and facts of other political assassinations both before and since, reflects an interesting pattern. We find this pattern to be either a cleverly designed arrangement—prior to the fact—by those in charge or, in every single case, a mutual thread of stupidity shared by each "lone nut" assassin, which was so incompatible with their otherwise (alleged) shrewd and clever planning. It takes no more than elementary logic—and certainly far less than that of a seasoned investigator—to understand the truth of the situations.

Let us examine just the surface of a few of the "official" stories:

Five and a half months prior to the Kennedy murder in 1963, on the night of June 11, 1963, we are led to believe that Byron De La Beckwith lurked in the woods for several hours before blasting, with his own 30.06 deer rifle, Mississippi NAACP leader Medgar Evers with a single shot through the back. Then, before jumping in his car to beat a hasty retreat for his home 90 miles north, De La Beckwith stashed the gun under some brush just a few feet away. (*Nobody will ever find it there.*) Ten days later, Beckwith was arrested and charged with the murder, after his thumb print was conveniently found on the telescopic sight.

On November 22nd that year—the spinmeisters tell us—Lee Harvey Oswald, a 24-year-old Marxist, fired three shots from a sixth-floor warehouse window from a cheap Italian rifle, which he then stashed behind some boxes (*no one will ever find it there!*) before rushing out of the building toward his escape. But 40 minutes later he killed a cop and got caught. Even though the paraffin test, administered by the Dallas police that afternoon, showed that Oswald had not fired a weapon, the FBI never sought anyone else and quickly charged Oswald with the murder of the policeman and the presidential assassination.[7] Independent investigators from outside of police and government ranks produced so much contradicting evidence over the ensuing years that we now know far beyond any reasonable doubt that Oswald was a patsy set up to take the fall by his employer, the U. S. Government. One need only read the later segment on "Lee and Harvey" to understand how this was done.

Five years later, escaped convict James Earl Ray, who was never known to have committed a violent crime or even to have fired a rifle in his life, is said to have killed Martin Luther King with a single shot from the rear, second-floor bathroom window of a cheap hotel in Memphis, Tennessee. Then Ray, who must have been the stupidest of all (if we are to believe the FBI), ran down the hall to his room, stuffed the rifle back into its box, and crammed the container into a duffel bag already stuffed with James Earl Ray's clothes, a beer can with his fingerprints thereon, and a prison radio from the Missouri State Penitentiary. This radio just happened to have Ray's prison I.D. number *engraved* into the back of it. How convenient! He then dropped it in the doorway of a business entrance next to the hotel where he had been staying. (*"No one will ever find it there!"*)

Sirhan Sirhan, who killed Robert F. Kennedy according to the official story, supposedly wrote a few hundred times in his notes, "RFK must die!" However, handwriting experts later determined that the handwriting was forged and not that of Sirhan. Officially speaking, he fired his eight-shot pistol eleven times.

In September of 1975, President Gerald Ford had a bad month in California. On the 5th, Lynette "Squeaky" Fromme, of Charles Manson "family" notoriety, clicked a .45 automatic at him in Sacramento at point blank range. However, the 100-pound airhead and would-be-assassin didn't know—even though the magazine was full—that a cartridge must be chambered before a semi-automatic pistol can fire. She had never fired such a weapon before and probably would not have been strong enough to pull back the mechanism on the hefty .45 anyway. Who put this moron up to this maniacal act? She was finally paroled from her life sentence in 2009 but is not commenting on the subject.

On the 22nd, as President Ford emerged from his limo to enter his San Francisco hotel in a large crowd, Sara Jane Moore fired a single round from a .38 revolver from *across the street*. Fat chance of scoring that one. Could both of these airheads really have been this stupid, or were they under some kind of mind control? The CIA's MK-Ultra[8] experiments were in full force by then.

If the attacks on Ford are considered to be serious ones, then the reader must remember who the waiting-in-the-wings vice president was at the time. Even Moore herself said from behind the prison walls, ". . . It would have elevated Nelson Rockefeller to the presidency, and then people would see who the actual leaders of the country are."

While the attempts on Ford seem to have involved some type of mind control and/or manipulation of the would-be assassins, the cases of Wallace, King and the two Kennedys are textbook CIA, and always with the designated patsy being but a fringe player at best. These suckers learn their real stage parts too late and are defined to the public as the latest "lone nut." The fringe player is led around by his handler, usually on a money leash, until such time as he/she can be cleverly placed in the incriminating position of no return. (We believe we can safely add Tim McVeigh of Oklahoma City notoriety to this list.) With the passing of time, the lie becomes historical "fact," and we have the perfect crime.

There are many ongoing perfect crimes such as with the daily operations inside the conglomerate of Federal Reserve Banks, the Internal Revenue Service, the huge medical establishment and other powerful corporations. Usually the perfect crime is so big that nobody questions its legitimacy.

The Federal Reserve Bank creates credit from thin air and foists on the people counterfeit currency and slug coins with no intrinsic value. Its crime is protected by a regulatory agency called the IRS, which also continually operates outside of its written statutes.

The recipe for the perfect crime may be laced with a variety of spices as long as it includes four prime ingredients:

The perfect crime is justified by government legislation.

The force of law and police power of the state protect the perfect crime.

The people are inundated with continual propaganda by the controlled media and public education systems, which "justify" the perfect crime(s).

Politicians, bureaucrats, and newsmen—honest at heart and patriotic in their speech—are corrupted with financial reward and promotion for protecting the system.

The facts of the old and well known murder cases that follow were never accurately reported to the American people. Here on these pages we want to concentrate on the many obscured facts in evidence vs. the contrived and distorted "official" versions as seen in the mainstream media and school books. Today, people might refer to my writings as "Revisionist" history, but I disagree, because that term should apply to the corrupted versions and those who revised the truth in the first place, rather than those of us who have always attempted to report the honest and factual history. Our mission is to report the facts as they actually happened, and theirs is always to twist the truth into their agenda-driven, politically useful propaganda mold and codify it forever in the government-sanctioned publications.

We will begin with a party held at the home of the wealthy oil baron and longtime Lyndon Johnson financier, Clint Murchison, on the night before the John Kennedy assassination. In attendance for an hour-long parlay in a smoke-filled room—in addition to Johnson and at least two of his future appointees to the Warren Commission—were Richard Nixon, J. Edgar Hoover, George Bush, Henry Kissinger, H.L. Hunt, George Brown and R.L. Thornton, among many others unaligned with the Kennedy administration. Our information was derived from personal interviews with two sources, unknown to each other, who were guests at the party. The report will include the most damning evidence of all—from his own mouth—that Lyndon Johnson had foreknowledge of the next day's rubout.

The FBI, whose watchwords have long been "Fidelity, Bravery, Integrity," destroyed, altered and withheld evidence from the Warren Commission; carried on a vicious vendetta against Martin Luther King; and illegally conducted its own counterintelligence program ("Cointelpro") which included break-ins and domestic spying. Another federal agency, the CIA, we would learn, worked hand-in-glove with the Mafia in trying to kill Fidel Castro; planned and carried out assassination plots against other foreign leaders; experimented with drugs and behavior control, using unwitting human guinea pigs; and conducted its own massive and illegal domestic spy programs. These shocking and disgusting revelations match perfectly with ingredient No. 2 from the recipe above.

Deborah Davis wrote that Katherine Graham, the *Washington Post* publisher and subject of *Katherine the Great*, is said to have stated in a 1988 speech given at CIA headquarters: "We live in a dirty and dangerous world. There are some things the general public does not need to know and shouldn't. I believe democracy flourishes when the government can take legitimate steps to keep its secrets, and when the press can decide whether to print what it knows."

Indeed, the democracy does flourish, while the republic disintegrates.

ENDNOTES:

1 When Mrs. Grace Stephens said that it definitely was *not* accused King assassin James Earl Ray that she saw running down the hallway in the cheap hotel where she lived, authorities swept her up the next day and hauled her away to the insane asylum, unbeknownst to her family. She did not surface for 10 years. This helped prevent anyone else coming forward to dispute the official story.

2 Three decades later, indefatigable researcher Lyndon Barston of Minneapolis unearthed an FBI "302" form (via Freedom of Information Act) written by an agent stalking Ray and pinpointing his presence in Chicago. The significance of this is that here was documentation that the FBI had the whereabouts of a known fugitive but failed to contact Missouri authorities. Ray's fingerprint card was found altered with bogus prints in order that he not be arrested should be detained at a traffic stop. Both of these facts indicate that not only was Ray being set up as the chosen "patsy," but that the FBI was playing the lead role. It also led many to believe later, even Ray himself, that his "escape" was actually allowed by the authorities.

3 James Earl Ray had speculated in *Tennessee Waltz* that Raoul "might have been" the lead marching tramp seen being arrested in the famous news pictures from the streets of Dallas taken less than an hour after the JFK assassination. However, when we showed it to Green, he said that it was not Paul (Raoul).

4 The evidence shows that it was "Raoul" in the bathroom. He was there but never fired a shot. The ploy was only to further that deception of Ray being the killer.

5 See *I Rode with Tupper*, the story of my 25-year association with this remarkable man, including being his trusted friend and confidante during the decade he was on the lam. It is available from First Amendment Books at AFP.

6 That's "Red, White & Blue Fever." It is usually isolated within the ranks of military personnel and Reagan/Bush-loving, Judeo-Christian conservatives. The fever prevents otherwise intelligent Americans from seeing the truth going on all around them and causes them to behave, vote (especially while on a jury) and speak very stupidly.

7 Col. Fletcher Prouty, critic of the Warren Report and official JFK-Assassination baloney from day one, was a high-ranking military and CIA muckety-muck and had been on a trip to the South Pole the week of the assassination. He always believed that he was intentionally sent there to keep him "out of the loop" because his superiors knew that he would not go along with this "palace coup." He was returning to the U. S. and stopped at Auckland, New Zealand when he got the news (Saturday morning in N.Z., some 17 hours ahead of Dallas time where it was still Friday afternoon) of the murder. Quickly buying a newspaper, Prouty was amazed to see not only the world-wide news of the implication of Oswald but the immense compilation of information about him ranging from his "communist affiliations" in New Orleans and Dallas to his actual "denunciation of the United States and defection to the USSR." Prouty didn't know who had done the dirty deed, but from his experience in "black ops," he already knew it wasn't anybody named "Oswald."

8 MK-Ultra was/is a CIA mind-control program in experimentation since the late 1940s.

Lyndon Baines Johnson was certainly no choir boy.

LYNDON & MADELEINE

Larger factions than anyone could imagine at the time carried out the murder and cover-up of the murder of President John F. Kennedy. It was the "crime of the century," and they got away with it. The orders came from the very top of the "shadow government."

Lee Harvey Oswald was possibly the most maligned man of the 20th century. Unlike John Wilkes Booth of assassination notoriety a century earlier, he was not the main player in the nefarious plot to murder the president. Confused and reluctant to speak in the early hours after his arrest—not knowing exactly what he should say—Oswald came to the realization of the enormity of what had just been dropped on his back, demanded legal counsel and announced to the news cameras one of the few truths reported about the case for years to come: "I am a patsy."

Indeed, he was (or they were). But what the world never knew was that there were at least two Oswalds masquerading in various CIA roles for not only months but for *years* prior to November 22, 1963. They were such natural lookalikes that, even though unrelated, they could have passed as twins. We shall explore the astounding and illuminating evidence of this fact later in this book.

There were many potential motives and suspects explored and projected over the subsequent years—once the Warren Commission Report was released and immediately debunked—with maybe a half dozen being worthy of consideration:

  • The motive of Southern extremists angry over the shoving of
school integration down their throats faster than they (already upset

with JFK's liberal policies), wanted to swallow it.

• Left-wing Cubans, under the direction of Castro, in retaliation for the several attempts on Fidel's life by the American CIA. This was Bobby Kennedy's initial reaction. He was cognizant of the "contract" out on Castro and had approved of the plan. Barely an hour after the murder he told a CIA contact, "One of your guys did it," believing the shooter(s) to be (a) double agent(s).

• The mob, under the direction of three main players—Carlos Marcello, Santos Trafficante and Sam Giancana—who were disturbed by the intervention of Attorney General Bobby Kennedy's Justice Department into their affairs. Marcello had been illegally kidnapped and deported, Trafficante had served time in prison, and Giancana had been "snubbed" by the administration after using his influence to swing the key city of Chicago to JFK in 1960's election.

• Lyndon Johnson and the Texas oil cartel.

• The military/industrial complex. JFK had ordered 1,000 "advisors" home from Vietnam by Christmas and the balance was to be removed by 1965. This was removing the potential for billions to be earned by the warmongering complex.

• The (almost) never-mentioned Israeli connection. JFK was doing everything he could to prevent Israel from obtaining nuclear weapons and gaining world power. Israel's first prime minister, David Ben-Gurion, hated him for it. See *Final Judgment* by Michael Collins Piper.

While appearing to be reasonable motives on the surface, especially during the immediate aftermath, numbers 1 and 2 simply do not stand up to in-depth scrutiny. The high-tech precision of the hit, the lack of a related suspect and the foolhardy assumption that this would have changed any governmental policy, all eliminate motive No. 1. LBJ had scarcely settled into office before civil rights packages were coming out of Congress like candy bars from a vending machine. And while Fidel Castro may have had an ego as big as a cathedral, he is not stupid. If such a plot could have been tied to a foreign enemy, it would have meant a full-scale war by the next morning. In Cuba's case, this would have meant total annihilation in a matter of hours. Cuba would have been blown off the map.

Lee Oswald had been affiliated with Cuban right-wing gunrunner David Ferrie, a defrocked, sodomite Eastern Airline pilot, since 1955, while still in the Civil Air Patrol and before joining the Marines the next year at age 17. But he was a current member of the *anti*-Castro group in New Orleans. His distribution of "Fair Play for Cuba" leaflets on the streets of New Orleans and his embrace of Marxism on a local radio interview were a Machiavellian ruse—designed to portray him as the opposite of what he was and to further cement one or both of the theories that "Castro Did It" and with the help of a "lone nut." This also became the foundation for the news media to forever portray Oswald as a left-wing extremist, but it simply wasn't true. As illustrated by the pre-planned set-up, Motive No. 2 was more likely an arranged subterfuge designed to sway the spotlight away from the real culprits. Both of these motives are also eliminated as potential theories by the same factor that sets aside the next one, only more so.

The mob played an active part and was a tool of the assassination plotters. But then so were the hierarchy of the Dallas police and the county sheriff's department. (Just how much more brazen can conspirators be than to stage the crime of the century in full view of Sheriff Bill Decker outside his office window?) The underworld used Jack Ruby to both help set up Oswald and then eliminate him in the Dallas Police Station. But these "tools" simply did not have the ability and wherewithal to 1) forcibly steal the body at gunpoint from the rightful Texas jurisdiction, 2) sabotage Washington-area telephone communication for an hour, 3) falsify the D.C. autopsy results on the spot, 4) remove all evidence from custody of the Dallas Police and Sheriff's Department and deliver it to the FBI; 5) manufacture false evidence, deliver it to the Warren Commission and leak it to the press on the same day and 6) create lifetime liars out of the highest elected and appointed officials in the land, as well as news commentators. However, this is not to suggest that the mobsters were blameless.

The overall operation required the cooperation of the palace guard (with which "they" can utilize any and everyone) and the details of the plot point straight to the elite princes in the ivory tower. It involved numbers 3, 4 and 5. This murder was a palace coup far more intricate but just as blatant as the one 2,007 years earlier when the senators personally rammed the knives into the helpless body of Julius Caesar. In our era's assassination, the victim never had a chance to utter a sound, but before sundown millions would be issuing the query for him: "Et tu, Lyndon?

Another of these anti-Castro mercenaries and former CIA operative was Gerry Hemming. According to the 1981 publication *The Fish is Red*, Hemming confided to authors Warren Hinckle and William Turner that he had grown weary of the revolution in 1960 and left Cuba. He formed an instruction corps called Interpen in order to train others in revolutionary combat. His quest to raise funds for the operation took him to Texas where he received donations from no less than Clint Murchison and Nelson Bunker Hunt.[1] Once, in 1962, when the subject of assassination came up at the Texas Club in Dallas, where Hemming was lecturing, one of the oil men piped up that Castro was not the one who should be killed but his boss, Jack Kennedy. Hemming complained that he had little success in collecting any substantial donations from the other wealthy oil men on his list. "They wanted nothing less than a Normandy Invasion for their money," he said.

But this may have been where and when the seeds were planted for the crop that was to be harvested at Dealey Plaza on November 22, 1963. It was Nelson Bunker Hunt who had co-sponsored the black-bordered "Welcome Mr. Kennedy" screed, which was published in Section One of the *Dallas Morning News* that day. Hundreds of "Kennedy—Wanted for Treason" posters were handed out on the street during the parade.

In 1994, I began a series of interviews with a former CIA pilot which lasted more than two years. Col. Russell Bowen had fallen from grace a decade earlier after he began to blow the whistle on the agency's part in the American drug activity. He had been confined for more than six years in the Springfield, Missouri federal "hospital" and force-fed mood and mind altering drugs. George H.W. Bush wanted him killed there and except for the intervention by Bowen's longtime friend (and Bush's right-hand man in the CIA) Ted Shackley, his life would not have been spared. Bowen was quietly pardoned by President Bill Clinton in 1996, which freed him to travel. Shortly thereafter, he moved to Peru and has not been heard from again. If still alive, he would have reached his 86th birthday on August 12, 2010.

The colonel, himself, is a book walking around waiting to be published, but it probably never will be. He was an OSS pilot in WWII and moved over to the CIA in the year of its birth, 1947. He admitted committing some despicable acts "in the name of democracy" (such as piloting the murderous crew into Iran in 1953 in order to install the "U.S.-approved" shah—a mission headed up by Norman Schwartzkopf, Sr., father of the celebrated Army General) but finally put his foot down in 1983, when it came to drugging American kids.

"I was flying my second load of cocaine into the United States from Colombia when it hit me," Bowen told me, as we sat poolside behind his Winter Haven, Florida home. "This is no good. Now I am drugging my own kids," he had realized.

Previously, he had told me that when they (the CIA) went into foreign countries, "We were kingmakers. We could topple the local and national governments with drugs, all in the name of so-called democracy."

But when he flew his first load into America he felt guilty. And by the time he was halfway across the Gulf of Mexico on another assigned delivery, his conscious and second thoughts drove him, as soon as he could get a land line in Texas, to call the sheriff in Sylvania, Georgia to say that he was bringing in a load of cocaine from Colombia and was ready to name names, all the way to George H.W. Bush.

It was not the prudent thing to say or do and it was remarkably naïve for a man of Bowen's position and experience; and when he landed his twin Cessna at the Sylvania airport a few hours later, he saw that his plan had backfired. Right there on the strip was the DEA jet, whose designation numbers he recognized from Homestead AFB, already waiting for him. The sheriff had made a call and Bowen's plans of exposure were quickly shot down.

He was arrested and the local papers heralded the story of the biggest drug bust in county history. The sheriff was the hero and Bowen was the goat. And that's how it works in the real world. He spent six and a half years in Springfield, Missouri's federal hospital/prison being shot daily with drugs to keep him stupid. Only Ted Shackley, his longtime friend in the agency, prevailed over George H.W. Bush, who wanted to kill him, to spare his life.

The colonel would always wince when reminded of the tap dance of "the only two adults in America" who couldn't remember where they were the day Kennedy was shot—George H.W. Bush and Richard Nixon.

"I knew where both the lying bastards were," he said to me with a beaming grin. "They were right there in Dallas with me. We were at Clint Murchison's house at a party the night before the assassination." The colonel said that it was he who had flown the "triangular assassination team" into Dallas, but he was reluctant to discuss any further details either then or in our several subsequent interviews, finally becoming visibly angered at my repeated inquiries.[2]

Private investigation had already turned up the Murchison party that took place on Thursday night, November 21st, but the reports were all third party hearsay with no participants or eyewitnesses willing to talk. A book or two had mentioned it in passing, but there was nothing solid until now. Suddenly the unasked question became *Did The Colonel read this somewhere, or had he really been there?* He recited a whole laundry list of Washington high-falootin' muckety-mucks that I was fairly confident had never been published before. In addition to Nixon and Bush and including Henry Kissinger, the list included J. Edgar Hoover, H.L. Hunt and Lyndon Johnson. I wanted to believe, but it was out of the mouth of only one source, so the interview was tucked into a file drawer for future reference. I needed some confirmation and that would be four more years in coming.

At the Dallas Preparedness Expo in 1998, I stopped by the book booth being attended by Madeleine Duncan Brown, the 73-year-young author of *Texas in the Morning,* the story of her 21-year intermittent love affair with senator, vice president and president Lyndon Baines Johnson. We traded books and I learned a little more than the newspapers had told me about their affair. In 1950, she had given birth to Lyndon's out-of-wedlock son and began to receive a cash delivery of $500 a week from Lyndon's lawyer until shortly after Lyndon died in January of 1973. Then the payments immediately ceased to flow.

Reading her book a couple of days after we met, I learned that she was a longtime friend of Clint Murchison and had been at that infamous party in his home on November 21, 1963.

Bingo! I pulled out the card she had given me and immediately got Madeleine on the phone and began grilling her. I already could tell that she would pull no punches, but how much did she remember? She had named so many more than the colonel had volunteered to remember, so I specifically recalled his two favorites for her.

I was almost yelling into the phone with excitement. "Do you remember George Bush and Henry Kissinger being there?" (She had already named Nixon in her book.) No, unfortunately, she didn't, but that didn't mean they weren't there. Bush and Kissinger were very obscure characters in 1963 and two who did not yet carry much public recognition. But there was no doubt now that the party took place and that Madeleine was there. She remembered many of the details as if it were last week.

Clint Murchison was the owner of the Dallas Cowboys of the National Football League, an oil-rich multi-millionaire and a longtime financial supporter of Lyndon Johnson. He had called Madeleine in the afternoon of the 21st to invite her to come along that evening. He did not mention that Lyndon would be dropping by later that night, after his flight into Fort Worth with President Kennedy's entourage. He had bade everyone good night, but instead of going to his Fort Worth hotel suite, the vice president had instead surreptitiously launched a hasty jaunt to Dallas and the Murchison residence—normally a 40-minute trek during that (mostly) two-lane era which reportedly took little more than half that time in the Secret Service-piloted limousine.

Madeleine said that LBJ liked going at high speed wherever he went in the limo—it stroked his "bigshot" ego—and that he not only liked to brag about how fast they went but whenever they did get stopped, "the cops always let us go when they see who is in the back seat, especially in Texas."

A STRANGE COALITION

As an eyewitness, Madeleine Brown tells us of what must have been one of the largest and most secret bi-partisan gatherings of governmental bigwigs ever to assemble in Texas. Everybody who was "anybody" (but not a Kennedyite), Democrat and Republican, was there.

When LBJ did arrive late, he strode to the bar, where Madeleine was seated, and chatted for a moment while the bartender poured for him his favorite libation. He was soon summoned to join the others, and the group moved with their cigars and drinks into the large library room and it was apparent to Madeleine that LBJ was the one they had been waiting for. The double doors were closed behind them.

She confirmed that others in the private circle included the two highest-ranking men in the FBI, J. Edgar Hoover and Clyde Tolson; oilmen and industrialists H.L. Hunt, George Brown and R.L. Thornton; ousted (by JFK) CIA Director Allen Dulles (brother of John Foster, the former secretary of state in the Eisenhower administration); and John J. McCloy, chairman of the Chase Manhattan Bank. This was a gathering of some of the most powerful men in the United States and we find it of interest that at least two, McCloy and Allen Dulles, were later handpicked by LBJ to sit on the Warren Commission in order to portray the fraudulent investigation conclusions to the American people.

Madeleine Brown drops another bombshell on us. During the hour or so duration of this mysterious meeting, as she sat nursing a drink at the bar in Murchison's den, another acquaintance of hers walked in with a prostitute in tow. It was none other than Jack Ruby.

Now please understand, Madeleine is not suggesting that Ruby was invited for the pow-wow with the big chiefs but was there only to drop off the woman. It was common knowledge among this group that Ruby was the pimp—the supplier of female favors whenever the Washington bigshots came to town. She knew Jack well and she says he sat with her and had one drink before leaving alone.

(I asked her about Ruby and how she knew him. She said that she had known him for 10 years or more at that time and even used to hang out at his Carousel Club in downtown Dallas and play cards with the girl strippers and bartenders during the late night hours. I asked her, with a tongue-in-cheek smile, "Did you ever dance there?" And she responded with a sly beam saying, "No, but I always wanted to!" At 75, she was no longer a youthful "looker" but she still had the remaining smile and delightful personality to reflect that she once was.)

It is obvious from Madeleine's recollections that Jack Ruby was far better known among the Washington big boys than was ever let on in the press over the years. Even White House correspondent (for Scripps-Howard) Seth Kantor remembered talking with Ruby at Parkland Hospital after the president was pronounced dead and so told the Warren Commission, although the panel discounted it and refused to believe it was true.[3] Such an admission simply placed too much light on the truth of Ruby's involvement—especially with his probable dropping of the famous "pristine" bullet found on the gurney at Parkland only a few minutes later.

The night before, when the Murchison boardroom meeting with the bigwigs adjourned, a visibly agitated Lyndon came over and stood next to Madeleine while he ordered another drink from the bartender. He then said something that rang in her ears as long as she lived (she died in June of 2002). We quote from her text (which she also told me personally):

> I knew how secretively Lyndon operated. Therefore, I said nothing . . . not even that I was happy to see him. Squeezing my hand so hard it felt crushed from the pressure, he spoke with a grating whisper—a quiet growl into my ear not a love message, but one I'll always remember: 'After tomorrow, those !@No. $% Kennedys will never embarrass me again—that's no threat, that's a promise.'

Lyndon left immediately to return to Fort Worth. She had hoped to meet him for a brief love tryst at the Dallas hotel the next afternoon, but those plans were thwarted when Johnson suddenly had other things to tend to as the new president of the United States.

Was Johnson part of a conspiracy to murder his boss? Madeleine always believed it. The preceding excerpt from her life certainly suggests prior knowledge on his part, at the very least. He had the motive to cooperate—being elevated to the highest position of power in the world is no small reward—and was an overly active participant in the cover-up.

However, let us not jump to conclusions. While motive No. 4 cannot be totally eliminated, it also cannot stand on its own. While the vice president certainly would have been an essential player, he did not have the ability to head up such a complex operation on his own, even though he had orchestrated, or at least ordered, a few other murders in Texas in the past.[4] Yet surely the real architects knew that once he became president, he would be a main cog in the JFK cover-up and he certainly was that. We will discuss more of the charlatan's performances here, particularly those following his ascension to the throne.

Meanwhile, remember that the evil deed took place on Johnson's turf, the one territory that he could control; it was a Johnson man, Dallas Mayor Earl Cabell, who had officially diverted the parade route that week to swing awkwardly through Dealey Plaza and into the trap (the mayor's brother was Gen. Charles Cabell,[5] a longtime CIA operative). It was Johnson who held up the flight of *Air Force One* until the body could be un-lawfully spirited away and loaded aboard; it was Johnson who tele-phoned the doctors at Parkland Hospital two days later, while they were trying to save Oswald, begging for a deathbed confession; and it was John-son who handpicked the Warren Commission. But he, too, took his se-crets to his grave in 1973.

Madeleine Brown tells of her next rendezvous with her lover at the Driskoll Hotel in Austin, which is even more revealing. It was a New Year's Eve party on December 31, 1963. Sipping bubbly champagne on the featherbed, she burst forth with what had obsessed her for the past six weeks. Again, we revert to her words:

> "Lyndon, you know that a lot of people believe you had something to do with President Kennedy's assassination."
>
> He shot up out the bed and began pacing and waving his arms, screaming like a madman. I was scared.
>
> "That's BS, Madeleine Brown!" he yelled. "Don't tell me you be-lieve that crap."
>
> "Of course not," I answered meekly, trying to cool his temper.
>
> "It was Texas oil and those [expletives deleted] renegade intelli-gence [expletives deleted] in Washington."
>
> "What are you talking about?" I asked, my eyes bulging.
>
> "Hell, that [expletives deleted] Irish mafia Kennedy—with advice from the invisible government—came out for suicidal cuts in the oil depletion allowance. More than 280 million dollars per year! He stopped a half-dozen mergers under the Anti-Trust Act. In 1962's snag, the market dropped 100 and thirty-seven billion [expletive deleted] dollars. Steel fell 50 percent and he had the impertinence to talk about `rollback' of prices or worse, a freeze.
>
> "This was war, Madeleine, to some rich, fat cats in Texas you and I both know. He campaigned on an increased defense budget. Then he made plans to close 52 bases in 25 states, plus 25 overseas bases and he was getting ready to quit in Southeast Asia. And for the first time in history, he had sent in one intelligence agency, the FBI, to dismember another agency, the CIA. America simply could not have this!"
>
> "Who were the Texas oil men, Lyndon? Who are we talking about?" I asked.
>
> He turned and looked me straight in the eyes with a cold glare, saying, "Behind every success there is a crime. Do you remember what

I told you years ago, Madeleine? You see nothing, you hear nothing, you say nothing." As he stormed off to the bathroom, he added, "I can see that I've already told you too much. Hell, I should have listened to my own advice."

Madeleine Duncan Brown had no doubt that Lyndon told her the truth. She believed that LBJ and the Texas oil cartel did what they felt they had to do to protect their own interests. Did he play a participatory part in the actual assassination? Probably not. But did he have prior knowledge and organize the cover-up? Without a doubt. And that's the way the system, at least behind the scenes, really works.

When those in charge decide someone needs to be killed, they don't necessarily give direct orders and certainly *never* do it themselves. This is the reason for the longtime marriage between CIA (as well as FBI) and the mob and this is the reason that real killers are never caught, such as those shooting Kennedy from behind the fence on the grassy knoll in Dealey Plaza. They are not caught because they are not sought.

Mobsters delight in accepting government contracts. Not only does it make for a good payday, but the risks are minimal—especially after the fact when law enforcement will be sent elsewhere on a wild goose chase.

Another common ploy throughout history has been to destroy with sexual innuendo both men and women in the public's eye. Women are whispered to be "witches" or "whores," and the targeted men become plastered with the absolutely indefensible label of "child molester."

(Remember infamous David Koresh of Waco notoriety? Everything they ever told us about him was a lie.)

When Tim McVeigh failed to achieve the exalted status of wearing the green beret of the U.S. Army Special Forces unit in 1991, he was offered a black op position that kept him on their payroll and "on a leash" in order to set him up for a later crime. That turned out to be the Oklahoma City bombing in 1995. Meanwhile, during those four years, he traveled the country with no visible means of support. It doesn't take a Sherlock Holmes to figure out whence that support came.

McVeigh went where he was told, such as the April 19, 1993 holocaust outside of Waco long enough to be photographed there and drew a government check for four years after allegedly leaving the Army. He did what he was told, such as building a crude ANFO bomb and placing it in a

Ryder truck. This little firecracker did not nearly carry the power to destroy the Alfred Murrah Building, let alone inflict the damage it did through the several city blocks surrounding it, but the pre-placed demolition charges *on the inside of the building* (at the third floor level, just above the children's nursery) timed to go off at the same time as the patsy's truck bomb, were devastating and the government then had its "right-wing, government-hating, militia kook" with whom to charge the crime.

John Hinckley, Arthur Bremer, Sirhan Sirhan, James Earl Ray and Harvey Oswald (to name but a few) were caught in the same trap and realized it far too late.

A sad footnote to the Madeleine Brown story revolves around her son Steven, who for years had been asking her about his real father. The last time Madeleine saw Lyndon alive was in 1969 and she had implored him to go public with the truth, but he had refused, valuing his reputation more than his blood son. Over the years Madeleine had managed to avoid the issue with Steven, but she felt it might be time to enlighten him now. She feared the thought of dying without telling him. When she finally moved forward, he was livid to learn the truth—something he had silently suspected for a long time.

In June of 1987, Steven Mark Brown filed a $10.5 million lawsuit against Lady Bird Johnson for his rightful share of his father's estate, believing that in a public forum the truth would come out. However, as do most, Steven underestimated the power of his enemies. After a short period of drastic harassment and intimidation, during which he refused to back off, Steven disappeared. Madeleine hired a private detective who found him three months later in a hospital bed at Bethesda Naval Hospital. Steven died of cancer at age 39 two years later and the suit was never settled. She always suspected he had been injected with the cancer but could never prove it.

Lady Bird, Lynda Bird and Lucy Baines saved 10 million bucks and their father's reputation—but the latter only for awhile.

The people who had the most to gain from the death of JFK were those who did not want the peace in the world that John Kennedy had pursued. The people who didn't want John Kennedy to be president were those who were making astronomical fortunes from war productions. Substantial criticism never had a voice. A handful of critics and researchers in this

Malcolm Wallace was born and educated in Texas. He graduated from the University of Texas and was quickly recruited by Lyndon Johnson and given a job at the Federal Department of Agriculture. He first came to the attention of authorities when he was arrested in 1951, tried and convicted of killing a professional golfer named John Douglas Kinser. At the time, Kinser was alleged to be having an affair with Lyndon Johnson's sister, Josefa. Josefa was an alcoholic and drug user. She had a reputation for being loose-lipped when she was "high" and disclosing confidential information about Lyndon. It was feared that she might have already disclosed some secrets about Johnson to Kinser. Shortly after Kinser was gunned down in his golf club, Wallace was arrested and found guilty of first degree murder. During his 10-day trial, Wallace was represented by LBJ's own lawyer. Although found guilty, Wallace received a five-year suspended sentence—ostensibly because Kinser was also having an affair with Wallace's wife. In a related matter, according to expert fingerprint analyst Nathan Darby, the one partial print found at the Texas Book Depository was an exact match on 14 points and demonstrated a correlation of 35 points between that print and a fingerprint taken from Malcolm Wallace. A match of 12 points is usually considered good enough to say definitively whose print it is.

SOURCE: viewzone2.com/lbj/

case have gotten a long way on their own, but if the press had just been honest about it and done its job, we could have learned a lot more. The fact of the assassination conspiracy is beyond doubt. Only the scope is in question. The following theatrics choreographed by the CIA for no less than a decade prior to the assassination should convince anyone of that certainty.

One of the clever pieces of subterfuge often utilized by the enemies of truth is the activation of two side stories (neither of which is true and they know it) that engage the public in a pointless argument that can never have a conclusion. Examples are *"Why did Sirhan kill RFK?"* while we now know that such a supposition was impossible or the still oft-mentioned *"Vince Foster suicide"* when we have known from almost the beginning that Foster was a murder victim in a case that may have taken place in his White House office.

Another is the oft-repeated question of whether or not Oswald "acted alone," when the facts proved long ago that Oswald never "acted" (in the murder) at all. Here is how the world was fooled and will continue to be.

ENDNOTES:

1 Murchison was an oil millionaire who owned the Dallas Cowboys football team at the time and was a longtime (liberal) backer of Lyndon Johnson. Hunt was even a richer oil tycoon, maybe the richest man in the country at the time, who was a strict conservative. Media trashing managed to implicate Hunt from the fringes while never getting near the real involvement of Murchison.

2 The evidence showed, over and over, that there were several assassination teams on the scene. This was purposefully set up to confuse not only witnesses but even each of the shooters on the question of exactly who fired the finishing shot.

3 It was another piece of subterfuge by the Warren Commission. Kantor had known Ruby in the mid '50s while working the Dallas news beat as the Carousel Club was a popular hangout for newsmen. Ruby knew Kantor well enough to call him by name when they stumbled on each other at Parkland.)

4 He has been accused in various publications over the years of complicity in at least six murders, even that of his own sister, and some of these cases carried very convincing evidence.

5 JFK had ousted Air Force Gen. Cabell from the CIA, along with Allen Dulles, following the bungling at the Bay of Pigs and their failure to brief him on the operation. Both men hated JFK for firing them.

*"Treason doth never prosper.
What's the reason? When it prospers,
none dare call it treason."*

—SIR JOHN HARRINGTON

This widely circulated photo, first published by *Time* and *Life* magazines in December 1963, served well to convince the public of Oswald's murderous character. However, photographic experts later proved it to be "Harvey's" head attached to the body of someone else.

THE TWO OSWALDS

O ne of the most revealing, yet little-known, aspects of the plot to kill President Kennedy was the existence of two (or more) Lee Harvey Oswalds, one of whom was the designated "patsy." Investigative reporters were aware of this fact early but had no idea exactly who the imposter(s) might have been. We now know that these two men looked enough alike to have been (almost) identical twins. Even a third Oswald, who looked nothing like the others, appeared at the Soviet Embassy in Mexico City in September of 1963, attempting to get a visa to Cuba in the name of Lee Harvey Oswald. CIA surveillance photos clearly showed this man to be someone else, both much older and much heavier than the other two, and was probably another piece of subterfuge thrown in to strengthen the supposition that Oswald had attempted to get a visa for Cuba.

Richard Popkin wrote a book in 1966 entitled *The Second Oswald*, in which he documents numerous occasions of a "duplicate" Oswald being in places where later evidence showed the real Oswald could not have been. The "second Oswald" would often draw attention to himself by creating a disturbance with outrageous behavior and make a conspicuous attempt to be remembered.

On November 9, 1963 and for several days following, when one Lee Oswald would have been at work or with his family, another one using that name appeared at a target range and often would make a pest of himself by shooting at targets of other patrons. And yet another fascinating incident took place on the same day.

Someone appeared at a Lincoln dealership in Dallas to test drive a new car. He drove at high speeds up and down Stemmons Freeway, dropped hints about receiving "lots of money" in a few weeks and told the credit manager that if he were not given credit, he would go back to Russia and buy a car. The most perplexing aspect of this episode is that the Lee Harvey Oswald the world was soon to learn about did not even drive. Indeed, it appears over and over throughout the weeks and months prior to Kennedy's murder that many persons unknown were setting up one Harvey Oswald to take the fall. That other Oswald, much of the time, might very well have been Lee.

"Harvey Oswald" cashed checks that Lee Oswald never had. Popkin's source is the voluminous Warren Report and it lists numerous incidents of Oswald, his wife Marina and two children of the identical age being in places where Marina later proved they could not have been at the time. Did the "other Oswald" have a double for Marina and the children as well? We also now know there were two "Marguerites" and that the one the world met later was not the mother of the Lee born in New Orleans.

Famed U-2 pilot, Francis Gary Powers, who was shot down over the Soviet Union on May 1, 1960, flew out of the Atsugi Base, where one of the Oswalds had been stationed. While it is likely that he and Powers knew each other, there is no record of their association. The military altered Oswald's service records to conceal the fact that he had been transferred out of his regular unit in 1958 and placed—with a new pay grade—in a different, unidentified unit in Taiwan.

Astute researcher and best-selling author Jim Marrs tells us that it is his belief that this was the time when Lee and his military records and his whole persona began to disappear. After some five years, since junior high school in New Orleans, the two Oswalds became one again and this time it was Harvey, not Lee, in the forefront.

The Merchants of Myth would like for us to swallow the story that the high school drop-out, loner and misfit Lee Harvey Oswald, who may have studied the Russian language for six weeks at Atsugi, while in the Marines (although the military brass denied even this), later went to the Soviet Union and denounced the United States of his own volition. He was then able to reverse his decision and return to the U.S., taking but two days acquiring a visa and going through no bureaucratic red tape in order to do so. When his life since age 17 is closely examined, it becomes obvious that this Oswald was getting inordinate and special attention and had unwittingly become a lackey-on-a-string being prepared for use somewhere else down the road, in the proper place at the proper time. A June 3, 1960, FBI memo signed by no less than J. Edgar Hoover himself shows that the director had knowledge of "a possibility that an imposter is using Oswald's birth certificate." What significance could this have had to the FBI more than three years before the assassination? Just how long *had* Oswald been a player?

He also was no dummy but rather a brilliant young man—or at least *one* of them was. When his future wife, Marina, met him in Minsk in 1960, his grasp of the Russian language was so perfect that she thought him to be a native. His quick placement in a job, his Russian contacts and the ability of this "American dissident" to get a new passport issued within two days for his return to the United States after defecting all indicate that he had been sent by some bureaucratic entity—most likely the CIA.

Oswald was demonized in the public's eye from the day of the assassination as a "Communist defector." Yet there is much to suggest that "Lee Oswald" (in this case, *both* of them) was recruited by the CIA before he was a Marine and the *duplicate* was sent to Russia either on a mission for the agency or to begin the charade of his "defection."

Although his bank account showed a balance of $203.00, he was able to make a $1,500 sojourn across Europe and into the Soviet Union. He went to Russia with the approval of the State Department and, by some fortuitous windfall, received his Soviet visa in Finland in only two days—another mystical trick, as this process usually requires two weeks or more, even for people who have no record of a treasonous past.

The forthcoming investigation will clear all this up for the reader—something that took 30 years for the author. Researcher John Armstrong of Tulsa, Oklahoma is the investigative hero of this story.

SOME CLARIFICATION

While it is ludicrous to even assume that Oswald was being groomed for the murder of John F. Kennedy in 1956 or even 1959, considering that Kennedy did not even take office until 1961, the whole scenario is indicative of the manner in which the shadow government works. Many military "stooges" are constantly being placed in various levels of society for future use even though the handlers have no definite plans for them at the time. (Reference Tim McVeigh above again.) It's called "sheep dipping," and, certainly, some are never used for anything at all.

Author John Armstrong did the most in-depth research on the Oswald subject that anyone can imagine and came up with some irrefutable proof of the existence of the two Oswalds as far back as 1953 in New Orleans. Apparently, there were even two "Marguerite Oswalds." Throughout his 1,000-page book, Armstrong disparagingly refers to Harvey's mother as "the short, dumpy, heavy-set, poorly dressed Marguerite Oswald the imposter," while always glowingly defining her counterpart as "the tall, lovely, nicely dressed, classy" mother of Lee.

Prior to discovering Armstrong's work a decade ago, I always referred to the two as: "the skinny and thin-haired Oswald, the one Jack Ruby shot on TV that Sunday morning" [Harvey] and "the better looking, more muscular and two inches taller Oswald [Lee].

Armstrong is the one who separated for clarity these two players by naming them "Harvey" and "Lee," which is a much better route out of this confusing maze. Lee was the Oswald who was born and grew up in New Orleans. "Harvey" was the imposter who grew up in NYC after immigrating as a child with his Russian parents. He spoke the Russian language in his home growing up, while learning English in the New York school system.

This tidbit alone solved my own 30-year mystery of how a 17-year-old high school dropout (with a "New Awlins" accent) could possibly go to a Marine language school for six weeks in Japan and come out speaking Russian so fluently that when he met his future wife two years later, after immigrating to Russia, she would believe him to be a native Russian.

It was ridiculous for anyone with even half an education on the case to believe that it could have been Lee who had immigrated to Russia. On the other hand, it took no stretch of the imagination to agree that it had to have been "Harvey."

Nothing and I mean absolutely *nothing* else made any sense of this fantastic scenario. There were at least two Oswalds all the time and sometimes there were others, such as at the Russian Embassy in Mexico City in October of 1963. But only a glance at the photo (of the heavier man old enough to be Oswald's father, claimed by the CIA to be Oswald) quickly discounts it as being neither Lee nor "Harvey."

While in Russia, "Harvey" Oswald declared that he was renouncing his U.S. citizenship and intended to give the Soviets all the secret information he had access to as a radar operator at Atsugi Marine Base.

Yet when he changed his mind two years later and decided to return to the U.S., he not only was *not* arrested for espionage but was granted a $435 loan by the State Department to aid with his return home with his wife and child.

Harvey Oswald was being handed special treatment and it all reeked of CIA influence. When he took his job at the Texas School Book Depository only five weeks prior to the assassination, the designated patsy was firmly in place.

But was this actually Lee or was it "Harvey Oswald?" Today the question is more pertinent than ever before. It now appears that New Orleans-born Oswald (Lee), the gregarious, fun-loving son of Marguerite, was deeply involved with the conspiracy but only from behind the scenes. The New York-born "Oswald" ("Harvey") was a quieter introverted intellectual who went to Russia with a perfect capture of the language, married Marina, returned to Texas, took a job at the School Book Depository, was framed for the murder of the president and was murdered by Jack Ruby, as we are about to see.

Most of this aforementioned information was known and written in several books during the first decade following the assassination and there most of the growth of information stopped for the next two decades.

But in the 1990s, John Armstrong of Tulsa, Oklahoma, with one of the most indefatigable pieces of research ever compiled, proved with irrefutable facts, figures and testimony from government documents *the absolute impossibility of the personage we knew as "Lee Harvey Oswald" being one solitary human being.*

JOHN ARMSTRONG'S REVELATIONS

Armstrong dug into these facts more than anyone else had ever attempted and his evidence is astounding. He shows that:

1) The killer of Officer J.D. Tippet dropped a wallet on the street at the scene. It conveniently held the identification cards of both Lee Harvey

Oswald and his AKA, "Alec Hidell," the name in which the alleged murder rifle of JFK—the Italian Mannlicher Carcano—had been ordered from the Chicago wholesale house. The problem was/is that when "Oswald" was arrested in the Texas Theater ("Harvey," downstairs, in a middle seat) only minutes after the Tippet murder, he also carried a wallet with both identical I.D. cards. This is from a (soon suppressed) Dallas Police Department written report.

2) Several witnesses, including the ticket seller, directed police to the balcony, where the first Oswald (who could have been at the Tippet murder scene and dropped the wallet) had run. Apparently, this Oswald and a couple of cops watched the arrest proceedings (of the "second Oswald") below them. The original police report said that Oswald was arrested in the *balcony* of the Texas Theater. Yet this was contrary to all the news testimony given on camera by several of the arresting officers. Even the seat in the middle of one of the downstairs rows was labeled and made a shrine as "the seat where Lee Harvey Oswald sat when arrested by Dallas Police on November 22, 1963." It is now a valuable collector's item. Did the officers who made out the report not get the message in time? Was it Lee who had run upstairs and could it have been he and Dallas police officers in the balcony watching the arrest of Harvey below?

While Lee had been out of the picture for some time at this point, we have to consider the story of Laura Kittrell, of the Texas Employment office following shortly. With knowledge of this scene, there remains little doubt that Lee was still in the deception picture only five weeks before the murder.

3) Comparison of some 70 photos of "Oswald" indicate that pictures of the two men were severed vertically through the middle of the face in order to manufacture a composite ID of both—utilizing the left side of one pasted to the right side of the other. Both men carried the same ID cards for years. Only with close inspection can one discern the chubbier half of the chin, the different ears and the slightly off-center hairline. The composite picture, first uncovered in the 1970s by Texas photo analyst Jack White, is a fake and a very good one.

After his arrest when "Oswald" ("Harvey") was shown the infamous pictures of himself at his backyard fence, wearing a holstered pistol and holding the Mannlicher/Carcano rifle and a Communist newspaper, his immediate response to the police was, "It's a fake! That's my head pasted on someone else's body." He knew he had never stood in any such pose, and it was Jack White, Robert Groden and other photographic experts who confirmed the photo doctoring years later.

At the Warren Commission hearings, Lee Oswald's real brother, Robert, was shown the picture of Lee handing out "Fair Play for Cuba" leaflets on Canal Street in New Orleans and asked to identify him. He could not. When shown a school days picture of "Lee" in New York, again he said it was not his younger brother. Armstrong displays more convincing evidence that the CIA had groomed the men since puberty, at a time when someone had discovered the similarity between the young New York native and Robert. However, when Robert saw the picture he said that not only was he closer to his younger brother's age but looked even more like him (Lee).

4) In one of the most interesting episodes revealing the two Oswalds in place in Dallas at the time of the murder, Armstrong cites the suppressed testimony of Laura Kittrell, who worked for the Texas Employment Commission and interviewed an Oswald before he began work at the Book Depository on October 15th. Only a week later, "Oswald" showed up for another interview, but Mrs. Kittrell realized it was not the same man she had interviewed before.

(Were the conspirators testing to see if these two could pass for the same person? Why else would they be so brazenly foolish to risk exposing their own ploy? Could it have been "Lee" who applied for the job, but "Harvey" who was to actually go to work at the School Book Depository? Apparently.)

"The two Oswalds were very, very similar but different people," she said. "They were much alike in size, shape and outline, generally, yet there was a marked difference between them in bearing and manner. [The first] ... was a trim, energetic, compact, well-knit person, who sat on the edge of his chair. [The second] ... was sprawled over his chair and was rather messy looking."

After the assassination, Mrs. Kittrell wrote and phoned the FBI, but she was not interviewed until a year later, *after* the Warren Commission volumes were published.

This leads one to wonder about the real Oswald's mother and brothers. *Had they met the imposter and failed to recognize him?* Apparently not, from the brothers' Warren Commission testimony later *and the "short, fat, dumpy, heavy-set Marguerite"* didn't have to. After all, let us not forget, she really was his ("Harvey's") mother.

PHYSICAL DISCREPANCIES

We must remember that Lee Oswald had seen little of his family since joining the Marines in 1956 and human beings can and do undergo great physical change in those years of late teens and early 20s. This may account for the innocent comments from his family members on this subject. Assured by the State Department and the FBI that the real Oswald was returning, conditioned by their own pleasure at the thought of welcoming him home, conditioned by letters and presents received from the young couple, conditioned by the deceptive photographs received from the Soviet Union and the excited welcoming of the pretty young wife and infant daughter who had both appeared in photographs and looked and were the same; brothers Robert and John Pic never thought at the time to question that the man with Marina might not be their son and brother. (We now know that this is explained by the aforementioned clue that Lee had already been "disappeared" from the scene and "Harvey" was now the player. He did not have to fool his real mother and the older brother Robert, we have learned, was CIA all the time and was never a threat to expose the plot. Half-brother John Pic, expressed his concern to the Warren Commission, but it was glossed over. Even considering his initial suspicions as displayed by his testimony in front of the Warren Commission, we have to imagine that he finally figured it out—perhaps with an assist later from Robert.)

However, they did notice considerable differences between the previous and current Lee Oswalds. Marguerite commented that he had lost some hair and he told her that it was caused by the cold Russian winters. (?) Robert testified that his brother Lee's complexion had changed from fair to ruddy. . . "and that he had picked up something of an accent." He, too, mentioned that Lee's hair ". . . used to be brown and curly, a full set of hair," and that he had "lost weight" and appeared "drawn."

John Pic, the older half-brother of Robert and Lee, had his first reunion with (whom they thought was) Lee at a family Thanksgiving dinner in November of 1962. When asked how Lee looked physically as compared with when he had seen him last, Pic replied, "I never would have recognized him, sir." Pic also mentioned the weight loss, the lack of the "bull neck" Lee had acquired in Marine training and the totally different hair. When Pic arrived before dinner, "Lee" (actually Harvey) introduced him to Marina as his "half-brother," and this angered Pic because in the past they had never referred to each other with this term, always calling each other "brother." Such a scene would never have taken place with Lee, the actual blood brother, but would certainly be likely for an actor such as Harvey, who was coached with the information to remember that Robert was his actual full brother while John Pic was not.

It should be emphasized that all of the Oswald family only *accepted* rather than *recognized* the new "Lee" who had returned.

If the Oswald family had been more suspicious at the time, they might have examined the head behind the left ear of the new "Lee," which should have but probably would *not* have exhibited the lifelong evidence of a mastoid operation at age six. Close-up pictures of the arrested Oswald at the Dallas Police Station clearly show that there was no such scar on the left side of his head.

The new Oswald was in place and the family members would never see their blood relative again. Whether or not Marina knew of the deception cannot be ascertained, although it must be assumed that she probably did not because there was no reason for her to know.

(After months of emotional battering by the FBI, Marina became a totally unreliable witness. She changed her story so many times that it became obvious that she had been frightened into saying whatever the FBI (Federal Bureau of Intimidation) wanted her to say. We have now learned that the "battering" may have been far more than just emotional. She has confided to her closest friends that for the months while she was kept in "protective custody," she endured constant sexual abuse by her guards. According to Madeleine Brown, Marina told her that this abuse continued "almost every night" for several months, while she was being held incommunicado in a remote motel. We never confirmed whether this accusation refers to the Dallas policemen or the FBI agents or some of each, both of whom were "protecting" her.)

However, the aftermath shows that after much soul-searching, she, Marguerite and Robert may have begun to figure it out. This would account for why "Uncle Robert" has never once visited Marina nor made himself known to her two daughters, June and Rachel, now nearing 50 years of age. He knows that they are not his nieces. It would also account for Marina's agreeing to the exhumation of the Oswald body at the Fort Worth Cemetery for examination in 1981. It was over two years later before authorities finally confirmed that the body was that of Lee Harvey Oswald (*Why did this take more than two years?*), but there are several mysterious discrepancies yet still outstanding.

For instance, one of the Oswalds lost a front tooth at age 15. *Life* Magazine published a candid snapshot of "Lee" from his 1954 school yearbook, clearly showing the empty space in his smile. However, the teeth photos from the autopsy and x-ray pictures from the 1981 exhumation showed no such tooth loss. Neither did the Marine dental records of the new ("Harvey") "Oswald." Considering what follows in the next paragraph, we may have to wonder if *Life* (a longtime co-conspirator) might have used a yearbook photo of "Harvey," who was also in school in New Orleans at the time.

Mortician Paul Groody was very concerned about the head on the body in the Oswald casket in 1981. When the casket was opened, the body was dressed in the same clothing that he remembered putting on Oswald in 1963. But the exhumed head bore no marks of the brain having been removed, as it had been for the 1963 autopsy. He suggests that the head of Oswald No. 2 ("Harvey") may have been replaced with the head of Oswald No. 1 ("Lee") at some time after the burial, thereby gruesomely attempting to solve any future tooth and scar problems for the conspirators and the historical record.

Groody also said that after Oswald's murder on Sunday, FBI agents came into the funeral home at five or so on Monday morning requesting that they be able to spend some time with the body—unobserved. Groody allowed it, but after they had left, he noted a blatant stain of black ink on Oswald's palm of his right hand. Only a few days later did the FBI release to the press that they had found a palm print traced to Lee Harvey Oswald on the butt of the murder weapon rifle. Wow! What great investigative work that was. And *after* one of the finest fingerprint analysts in

America, the FBI's own Sebastian LaTona, had already dusted the entire rifle and found nothing of value.

Macabre as this may sound, this really is not far-fetched. There was no way that either of these men could be allowed to live. "Harvey" was rubbed out within 48 hours after the JFK murder in order to provide the scapegoat for the American people. It was his body that was buried in the Fort Worth cemetery the next day. But he may not have harbored nearly the number of facts and the names of the players as did "Lee," who almost certainly was quietly taken care of a very short time later.[1] While we have no evidence of this, it is reasonable to assume that the switch in the coffin took place in the early days before the dirt had even dried and settled on the grave. The head of No. 2 and the body of No. 1 were then likely dropped into the Gulf of Mexico. Case closed. "Oswald did it," they said once more, "and he acted alone."

CONSIDER THE REWARDS

"Coincidentalist" scoffers are always quick to point out that any conspiracy of this size would be impossible to keep secret because too many people would know about it and eventually someone would come forward to spill the beans. However, the untimely deaths of so many witnesses and players during the first 18 months following the assassination must have had a lasting influence over the many others, perhaps much higher up, who did keep quiet.

Many of the middle-level players, who certainly had nothing to do with the original atrocity, were handsomely rewarded for their participation in the shielding of the facts from the people. A Michigan congressman by the name of Gerald Ford sat on the Warren Commission.[2] In 1973, he was appointed to the office of vice president, replacing Spiro Agnew, who had been forced to resign under fire. At the time, the behind-the-scenes wheels were already turning to impeach Richard Nixon over the Watergate fiasco.

So it could be said, with probable accuracy, that in exchange for his cooperation on the Warren Commission, Ford was gifted with a brief residency in the White House by Nixon's resignation on August 9, 1974. Way up into his 90s and almost to his dying day, with occasional news interviews on the subject, Ford continued to deceive the people regarding the guilt of Oswald and the efficacy of the Warren Commission. Almost everything Gerald Ford ever told us about it was a lie. The position of JFK's back wound was crucial to the ridiculous "magic bullet" theory, and Ford finally admitted to that conspiracy before he died.

In his last years, Gerald Ford confessed that he and the commission moved Kennedy's back wound, an act that cannot be objectively reconciled with an attitude of pursuing the truth.

On July 2, 1997, the Associated Press ran a story in which Gerald Ford admitted that he raised the back wound several inches in the Warren Commission to better substantiate the Specter foolishness and to further convict Lee Harvey Oswald as the lone assassin. Ford stated that he was only attempting to be "more precise" and that his change had "nothing to do with conspiracy theories." Ford thus admits to falsifying the *Warren Report*.

It was Adolf Hitler[3] who is credited with initiating this observation on furthering deception: "If you tell a lie long enough, pretty soon you will believe it and soon you will begin to think that everybody believes it." Gerald Ford repeated it enough over the years that he may have begun to believe it.

Every November 22nd, Americans could watch and listen to TV's Dan Rather babble on ad nauseam with his assassination falsehoods, lamenting about that dark day in history. But how many remember that he was the first newsman, a street reporter from Houston, to see the Zapruder film—on Friday night, only hours after the president's murder, immediately after the film was processed. Dan Rather was one of the first to see the evidence that Kennedy was shot at least twice from the front—first, as we all finally see from the film, when JFK grabs his throat and seconds later when he is rocked backwards by the devastating head shot. Yet Dan always continued to perpetuate the prevarication that Lee Oswald killed JFK with three shots from behind—from the nearly impossible position at the sixth-floor window of the School Book Depository building with a large tree and its expansive branches between him and the target.

It could be easily and readily surmised that Dan Rather had been richly rewarded for his continual participation in the cover-up. He occupied the No. 1 news chair at CBS for the last 20 years or so of his career—

a position worth several million bucks a year.

In 1978, the government's second official cover-up occurred with the House Select Committee on Assassinations lengthy "investigation." Some of the new pieces explored included that of the acoustical evidence recorded at the Dallas Police Station dispatcher's desk because the handset on one of the police motorcycles had been stuck open during the Dealey Plaza attack. (Some investigators, including Dallas County Deputy Roger Craig and others not involved in the cover-up, believed that this was done intentionally to clog up communications and prevent Dallas officers from converging on the scene, which indeed was the situation for some 12 minutes.) The HSCA's conclusion was that at least four shots had been fired that day and at least one came from the front. The HSCA said that it ". . .believes, on the basis of the evidence available to it, that President John F. Kennedy was probably assassinated as result of a conspiracy." Then it diluted its own findings by ignoring the facts that were presented and went on to say, "The Soviet government, Cuban government and the national syndicate of organized crime, the Secret Service, FBI and CIA were not involved." (*Who, besides John Wilkes Booth, is left to absolve?*)

Judge Jim Garrison's comments summed up the whitewash more succinctly than anyone: "The official position of the United States Government on the assassination now appears to be that Lee Harvey Oswald killed John F. Kennedy with three shots from the rear and one shot from the front!"

Pennsylvania Sen. Arlen Specter is a beneficiary of government chicanery. In any other case, his Rube Goldberg design of the "magic bullet" theory would have been laughed out of the hearing room. Instead, when the Warren Commission was suddenly confronted with more wounds than shots (that they would admit to) being fired, Specter, a young lawyer for the commission in 1964, came up with the answer. The only solution was for the Commission to portray *one* of the shots as having caused all the extra wounds—not two but five more!

Specter's diagram was perhaps the most absurd lie of the whole case.[4] In order to make all of the shots come from the rear, the "magic bullet," according to the ruse, entered Kennedy's back at a downward angle, turned upward for six inches and exited his throat; then it stopped in mid-flight and angled downward into Gov. John Connally's back, exited his right chest, pierced and shattered his right wrist, before making another 90 degree turn and finally coming to rest in the governor's left thigh. And the commission members bought it!

(Were these exalted leaders in government really this stupid? Of course not. They simply had no other choice. If the American people could be sold on the theory that one bullet from the rear did all this damage, then the shots from the front and sides could be ignored. Only one man would be blamed and there would be no conspiracy—the result that Lyndon Johnson had instructed the commission to find from the outset. History still records the "single assassin" and "magic bullet" theories as being "fact." Everything they ever told us was a lie.)

A discharged bullet was found on a gurney at Parkland Hospital that day and was later determined to be this "magic bullet." However, the swept-under-the-rug fact was that Governor Connally walked around for the rest of his life with more lead remaining in his body than was missing from this pristine bullet.

Arlen Specter was soon appointed to the position of U.S. attorney in Philadelphia and was eventually elected senator from Pennsylvania. He occupies that seat today.

Conspirators take care of their own—one way or another.

As New Orleans Judge Jim Garrison said in 1988: "Lee Oswald was totally, unequivocally and completely innocent of the assassination. The fact that history, or rather in the re-writing of history—and this information that has made a villain of this young man, who wanted nothing more than to be a fine Marine—is in some ways the greatest injustice of all."

But Jim Garrison never met John Armstrong. Too bad, because both were honest and indefatigable investigators. Around the same time that Judge Garrison was completing his final work on the JFK assassination, *On the Trail of the Assassins,* Armstrong was launching into a whole new unexplored venue.

When Richard Popkin published his aforementioned book *The Second Oswald,* outlining the multiple occasions when the "real" Oswald (did he mean the one born with the name or he who died with it?) could not have been there but had to have been elsewhere, not even Popkin could have imagined the real truth as detailed in a book Armstrong entitled *Harvey and Lee*. This is a "must read" for anyone seeking the truth about the JFK assassination. It will change the way anyone thinks or has thought about this case over the past near-50 years.

So did "Oswald" kill Kennedy? Of course not. Neither of them did it. Much valuable and astonishing research has been done to determine it was not "Oswald"—and this research was done by non-professionals as often as not over the years. What sometimes gets lost is the plot. You and I might disagree about the details such as the relative involvement of the Joint Chiefs of Staff in the Kennedy assassination, or whether the CIA's James Jesus Angleton was the prime mover or Lyndon Johnson, or the unmentioned in this manuscript, another shadowy CIA operative named Ed Lansdale; but in any such analysis there will be large areas of agreement on the basics.

For the general public, these are easy-to-understand and simple areas in the investigation where the facts are overwhelmingly with us and is both legitimate and important to question the government's investigation of the Kennedy assassination.

The media continually represent that our questions are at best unimportant and at worst ridiculous. As public citizens, we have the right to ask questions of our government, and doing so makes us defenders of the Constitution, not "conspiracy nuts." For Gerald Posner and Vincent Bugliosi and other hirelings who would say otherwise, we need only present the following statements for their perusal:

"I never believed that Oswald acted alone, although I can accept that he pulled the trigger."—Lyndon Johnson(!)

(Johnson also told Sen. Richard Russell that he did not believe in the single-bullet theory either and he knew damned well that Oswald had not pulled any trigger. It was just one more example of not only LBJ's disingenuousness but how everything they ever told us was a lie.)

"It was the greatest hoax that has ever been perpetuated. [meaning perpetrated]"—Richard Nixon, speaking of the Warren Commission. (Probably not as great as his own NASA hoax, but nevertheless, this is an illuminating testimony from an insider who would have known.)

"Hoover lied his eyes out to the [Warren] Commission—on Oswald, on Ruby, on their friends, the bullets, the gun, you name it."—Rep. Hale

Boggs, one of the seven Warren Commission members. Boggs later disappeared mysteriously.

"If I told you what I really know, it would be very dangerous to this country. Our whole political system could be disrupted."—J. Edgar Hoover, in response to the question, "Do you think Oswald did it?"

"Goddammit, Georgi . . . doesn't Premier Krushchev realize the president's position? Every step he takes to meet Premier Krushchev halfway costs my brother a lot of effort . . . . In a gust of blind hate, his enemies may go to any length, including killing him."—Bobby Kennedy to Soviet envoy Georgi Bolshakov. (Bobby later enlisted Walter Sheridan to conduct a private investigation into the assassination and planned to reopen the case if elected president.)

"I never believed that Lee Harvey Oswald assassinated President Kennedy without at least some encouragement from others .... I think someone else worked with him in the planning."—Sen. Richard Russell, one of the seven Warren Commission members. [Here, again, is another projection by one of the Commission members that Oswald had something to do with the murder.]

"We really blew it on the Kennedy assassination."—Dan Rather (This is utter subterfuge. Nobody knew better than Rather that it was not "blown" but contrived.)

Now the point is not that all these people make it a fact that Kennedy was assassinated in a conspiracy. But how can it be impertinent to ask questions, if all these people—who presumably have far more access than we will ever have—don't believe fundamental conclusions of the *Warren Report*? The matter is not settled and we must keep asking.

The medical and photographic record of the assassination does not support the government's position and the Zapruder film fails to support the government's designation of a lone shooter. More important than this discrepancy, however, is that however one looks at the film, *neither interpretation supports Lee Harvey Oswald as the lone assassin.*

The amazing Zapruder film, as everyone knows, shows the president moving violently backward upon the last shot striking his head. This movement supports the idea that the fatal headshot came from the front—specifically, the area around the grassy knoll.

Now Robert Groden, in his new book *JFK—Absolute Proof*, has some amazing new revelations in his study of the Zapruder film.

Author and video expert Groden sets up shop every weekend at the grassy knoll in Dealey Plaza to sell his wares and further educate the thousands of tourists that come to see history there.[5] Recently he was approached by a woman who was there at the moment JFK was shot and told Groden that there was an earlier shot—even before Kennedy was hit the first time in the throat—that missed horribly, bouncing off the street and missing the whole presidential limo by some 15 feet. She said she never heard it but she and several others saw it glance off the asphalt.

Bob Groden, having done more exhaustive film research on the case than anyone else in the world for the past 35 years, took the story with a grain of salt but decided to check out her claim. When he got around to it, he began to examine the Zapruder film frame by frame from the moment the car turned the corner back at the School Book Depository. Sure enough, there it was, the bullet striking the street and even visible on the Zapruder film a couple of hundred feet away.

The significance of this, of course, is that it places one more nail in the coffin of Arlen Specter's magic bullet theory. Specter, Vince Bugliosi, Gerald Posner and everyone else who ever wrote about the guilt of Oswald avoided as much exculpatory evidence as they possibly could while weaving a believable tale of his guilt. These people also avoid any debate with Bob Groden, Jim Marrs or anyone else with working knowledge of the case in order not to look foolish. The facts of the case totally destroy the position of anyone touting the government theory of Oswald being the assassin or even acting in concert with anyone else on the day of the shooting.

One of the anti-conspiracy advocates' favorite tricks is to paint Oswald as a loser. The poor slob was just a lonely guy who wanted to be famous and he could have been shooting at anyone. This was Norman Mailer's premise in writing *Oswald's Tale*. It underlies the idea that Oswald shot at Gen. Edwin Walker, who was a right-winger made to look crazy after his attempted intervention at the forced integration of the University of Mississippi in fall of 1962.

For a poor lonely slob, however, Harvey Oswald sure got around. He went to Russia claiming to be a defector, married the niece of a Russian KGB colonel and then came back. Despite being a Marine and former radar operator who threatened to give away secrets to the Soviets, he was never charged with anything and the CIA has always (unconvincingly) denied debriefing him upon his return. He was paid both by the Russians, the American military and given money by the State Department. Then he was allowed to bring his Soviet wife Marina back to the U.S. with him. All this took place during the height of the Cold War—an unlikely scenario for any of us mortals, to say the least.

During the Warren Commission hearings, reports were discussed that Oswald was an agent of both the FBI and CIA. For instance, Texas Attorney General Waggoner Carr and District Attorney Henry Wade told the Warren Commission that Oswald was an FBI informant who earned $200 a month and had an informant number of "179."

Dallas DA Wade told Carr that his source told him Oswald had a CIA employment number. In addition to that, the June 3, 1960 FBI memo features J. Edgar Hoover complaining that someone was using Oswald's identity and he, Hoover, was requesting information on Oswald from the State Department to clarify the situation. Hoover began: "There is a possibility that an imposter is using Oswald's birth certificate...." This is more than *three years* before the assassination, as we cited earlier. FBI employee William Walter later confirmed that, in 1963, he saw an informant file with Oswald's name on it. Hoover would later point out to Lyndon Johnson that the person in Mexico City neither looked nor sounded liked Oswald. Lee Harvey Oswald was an FBI informant known to J. Edgar Hoover and therefore cannot be declared to be an "unknown loser."

The mob boys didn't do it, at least not by themselves. Anything that diverts the responsibility for the hit on JFK away from the involvement of the CIA, the FBI, the Secret Service and anything else suggesting an inside job is subterfuge, pure and simple. This is defined in a dialog between the Jim Garrison character (played by Kevin Costner) and his investigator in the movie JFK. Yes, it is fiction contrived by Hollywood screen writers, but it is an accurate summing up of the facts. Speaking of the organized crime units of Chicago, New Orleans and Tampa, the New Orleans district attorney said:

"I don't doubt their involvement, Bill, but at a lower level. Could the mob change the parade route, Bill? Or eliminate the protection for the president? Could the mob send Oswald to Russia and get him back?

Could the mob get the FBI, the CIA and the Dallas Police to make a mess of the investigation? Could the mob get the Warren Commission appointed to cover it up? Could the mob wreck the autopsy? Could the mob influence the national media to go to sleep. . . . This was a military-style ambush from start to finish . . . a coup d'état with Lyndon Johnson waiting in the wings. . . ."

These questions remain just as good now as they were in 1991 when the movie was done or even in 1963 when the dirty deed was done.

The "mob-did-it" theories have been such a fertile area for the government that we, as researchers, have to put some limits on the idea. Anyone who proposes that the mob did it on their own or that the Cuban invasion somehow backfired on JFK, barring some new and stunning evidence, is simply not one of us. The mob position is too damaging and the evidence too scant.

When we look at the total facts involved, in order to say the mob is the prime mover in the assassination, we are forced to ignore the larger context of the Cuban invasion, Operation Northwoods, the Vietnam War, the reduction of the oil depletion allowance and the sheer vastness of the operation required to kill the president and cover up the piles of evidence contradicting the official story. In other words, we have to do a series of logical back-flips in order to leap over all the contrary evidence, rather than accepting what is staring at us right in the face. The "mob-did-it" theory is, now and forever, an offshoot and a diversion. Did the mob have some level of involvement? Maybe. Even likely. Were they running the show? Absolutely not. Only one faction had the power to knock out telephonic communications[6] in Washington D. C. from 1:30 to 2:30p.m. on 11/22/63, and anyone who hasn't figured out which one that is should either go back and re-read the previous hundred pages or just skip ahead to the next subject.

The investigative process is a scientific one at its best and that means weeding out the ideas that don't work as well as promoting the ones that do. While accepted knowledge proceeds by falsification of facts, real knowledge advances with exposure of these lies with factual truth. By falsifying certain notions and promoting those where the evidence is irrefutable, we present a more unified front to the world and help to streamline and organize our public relations. It may not be to everyone's taste and may not surface for the masses in our generation, but it has to be done, if we are to ultimately win over the generations to come.

In the aftermath of November, 1963, Waggoner Carr, the attorney general for the state of Texas, wrote in his supplement to the Texas Report on the Assassination of John F. Kennedy that: "So far as is known to me or my special counsel there are no untapped sources of information in the assembling of all material facts pertaining to the assassination of President Kennedy. There is no useful purpose, therefore, in the convening of a Court of Inquiry. Should it develop at any time in the future that further investigation into this matter by a court of inquiry is indicated, a court will be convened."

This was lawyer double-talk to say that the State of Texas was stepping aside, permitting the Warren Commission to "investigate" the murder of President Kennedy. Yet neither Texas, nor the Warren Commission, would address the crucial figure of George de Mohrenschildt, a CIA asset and the "friend" of Lee Harvey Oswald during his residence in Dallas and Fort Worth in 1962 and 1963. Nor did the Warren Commission uncover the long relationship between de Mohrenschildt and George H.W. Bush. This task was taken up, beginning in 1992, by author and historian Bruce Campbell Adamson. George H.W. Bush wrote Adamson that he had known de Mohrenschildt beginning in 1942. They also had been partners in the oil business during the next 20 years prior to the assassination.

At Andover, George H.W. Bush was the roommate of Edward Gordon Hooker, the stepson of George de Mohrenschildt's brother, Dimitri. Later Hooker became George de Mohrenschildt's business partner. It is Bruce Adamson's original research that has uncovered relationships that cast an entirely new light on the background leading up to the assassination of President Kennedy.[7]

Among the anomalies uncovered by Adamson is that de Mohrenschildt's brother, Dimitri von Mohrenschildt, corresponded with Director of Central Intelligence Allen Dulles in 1953. This was the same Allen Dulles who, in Chief Justice Warren's frequent absences, presided over the Warren Commission, playing a crucial role in the commission's distorted conclusions. Other CIA connections of George de Mohrenschildt include that his one-time father-in-law, Samuel Walter Washington, worked for the CIA, supervising 250 agents, 10 years before the death of

A photo shows Jack Ruby (lower right) just before he shot Harvey Oswald. Whether this particular Oswald had been killed by Ruby or not, he most assuredly would have been killed by someone before being given the chance to spill the beans on what he knew about the JFK murder.

President Kennedy.

Since 1992 Adamson has published 14 books focusing on de Mohrenschildt, a highly connected figure who from the 1940's on, participated in projects for the intelligence services. Later at the suggestion of the head of CIA's Dallas field office, de Mohrenschildt pursued his curious and close connection to Lee Harvey Oswald. Without investigating the matter, the Warren Commission Report had to conclude that de Mohrenschildt was, indeed, Oswald's closest friend prior to the JFK assassination. The commission dared go no further.

We remind the reader that de Mohrenschildt was "suicided" only days before he was to testify at the HSCA hearings in Washington.

Among those interviewed by Adamson was Leon Panetta, who is currently the CIA's director of central intelligence. With Adamson, Panetta pondered the connection between de Mohrenschildt and G.H.W. Bush.

For some of their correspondence, see letters http://ciajfk.com/Letters.html . Mr. Adamson also published an interesting set of correspondence between Vice President Lyndon Johnson and de Mohrenschildt, which occurred seven months before the Kennedy assassination.

Bruce Campbell Adamson continues to investigate a neglected part of our history, one that sheds considerable light on that great unsolved crime of the past century, the suppressed information about the murder of President Kennedy. The deluded section of our society that has been brainwashed by our deceptive MSM should pay attention to Mr. Adamson.

The Kennedy assassination in 1963 was an inside job and everything they ever told us about it was a lie. While the identities of the actual trigger men remains in doubt, there is no doubt that President Lyndon Baines Johnson and FBI Director J. Edgar Hoover were accessories after the fact.

The following article is reprinted as it appeared in an August 2007 issue of *American Free Press*. We post it here because we believe it fits into this segment of "Assassinations etc." After reading the indicting words of Gen. Wesley Clark, one has to believe that there was an assassination here and the lack of any investigative journalistic probe also qualifies this case to also fall under "news media cover-up." We leave any further conclusions to the reader.

ENDNOTES:

1 Jim Marrs, one of the greatest living experts on the case, says that if the conspirators were forced to rub out uncooperative Dallas detectives, blabbing eyewitnesses and obscure receivers of no more than hearsay (nearly a hundred over the next few years) then they certainly could not afford to let the real Oswald live very long either. "He must have been one of the first to go," says Marrs, "and there was no problem about anyone filing a missing persons report. After all, the world knew Lee Harvey Oswald was already dead."

2 Ford was a former All-American center on the Michigan championship football team of 1935. As a congressman, he was such a dullard that LBJ once remarked for the press that Ford had "played too many games without his helmet." There is only one reason for LBJ to have appointed Ford to the Warren Commission: he knew he was a "player" who could be controlled and counted on, and certainly with the later appointment to the vice presidency, he was well rewarded for his lies. Ford continually repeated the commission's fabrications for the public's deception until the day he died.

3 Maybe or maybe not. There have been so many lies told by the MSM about Hitler, it is very difficult to know anymore what is true about him. We do know that he was funded by the international banksters and that his real enemy and target for war was Russia's Communist regime. It is because of these historical facts that we

tend to suspect that the demonization of Adolf Hitler was more of a media creation than factual history. Even Gen. George Patton said, "We were fighting the wrong enemy," which might have further sealed his own fate. His murder shortly after the war but while he was still in Europe was officially passed off as "an accident."

4 No one knew it at the time, except maybe Specter and a few other commission members, but the autopsy doctors found a *fourth* bullet in Kennedy's body. This discovery, of course, completely destroyed not only Specter's ridiculous theory but the whole Warren Commission cover-up along with it. Lawyer, investigator, researcher and author Mark Lane uncovered this very valuable evidence through a Freedom of Information request years later. The MSM to this day makes no mention of it, and the "magic bullet" fantasy remains a bone of contention with debaters everywhere. In reality, it will never amount to anything more than the "official lie."

5 As we go to press, Groden has just been arrested for the 81st time, for selling his books and DVDs without a license. Yet every time he has gone to jail, made bail and attempted to satisfy the local constabulary by applying for a license, he is told that none exists. After eighty arrests, we have to conclude this to be nothing less than harassment. He is now accusing the Dallas fathers of another conspiracy: that of getting him and other truth-tellers off the street before the upcoming Super Bowl when all its fans come to town.

6 No one at AT&T could explain this beyond a dubious, "We were just inundated with so many calls." However, more Americans learned about the assassination after the first hour than during, yet no such jamming phone traffic occurred in D.C. the rest of the day.

7 Let us remember the interview and testimony of CIA pilot Russell Bowen reported earlier, who told us that both the "lying bastards"—Nixon and Bush—were with him at the infamous gathering the night before the assassination at the home of longtime LBJ financier Clint Murchison.

Cpl. Pat Tillman gave up a lucrative career in the National Football League to serve in the U.S. military—a deadly mistake.

THE MURDER OF CPL. PAT TILLMAN

F or years, speculation has swirled that Cpl. Pat Tillman was killed by friendly fire to silence his anti-war views. This strange case of Pat Tillman, the U.S. soldier who turned down a lucrative career in professional football following Sept. 11 to go fight terrorists, has taken an even more bizarre turn. New evidence released as a result of a lawsuit by Associated Press reveals that Tillman, who was killed in Afghanistan in 2004, was shot multiple times in the head at very close range in a manner more consistent with execution than a "friendly fire" mishap. The question now remains: Was this a case of "fragging"—or was it a planned execution ordered by higher-ups?

American Free Press first reported on the strange circumstances surrounding the death of Tillman in its weekly publication of Oct. 10, 2005. Since then, the mainstream media have picked up on the case, reporting a series of new details that have shed considerable light on the incident.

When Tillman volunteered for combat service eight months after the Sept. 11 attacks, it was a great public relations opportunity for the White House. He quickly became the poster child for America's fight against international terrorism. After all, he had turned down a $3.6 million a year career in professional football to go chase mythical radicals in the mountains of Afghanistan and Pakistan, who were purportedly to blame for 9-11. Who could be more patriotic than this, from the Bush administration's perspective, that is?

A year later, Tillman and his brother Kevin had graduated from the elite Army Ranger training and were ready for war. But Tillman's first deployment was not to Afghanistan. Instead, he was sent to Iraq, where he first began voicing opinions in opposition to the Bush administration.

When Tillman discovered that the invasion of Iraq was based on a mountain of lies and deceit and had nothing to do with defending America, he became infuriated and told a comrade: "You know, this war is so [bleeping] illegal." He had also quite vocally urged his entire platoon to vote against Bush in the 2004 election and was deployed to Afghanistan.

On April 24, 2004, Tillman was killed in Afghanistan while on patrol near the border with Pakistan. To this day, the details remain fuzzy.

The Army quickly announced that Tillman died a hero during an enemy attack, defending his fellow soldiers. Five weeks after Tillman died, the official story changed to "accidentally killed by friendly fire." Army investigators said that there had been a firefight and U.S. machine-gunners had mistakenly shot Tillman from somewhere between 33 and 270 yards away, as the reports varied drastically.

While the military code gives clear guidance for informing family members upon a soldier's death when cases are suspected of being a result of friendly fire, that procedure was not followed in the Tillman case. After his death, the Army not only gave conflicting and incorrect descriptions of the events to the press, but immediately after the incident, the family was told that Tillman was hit with enemy fire getting out of a vehicle and died an hour later at a field hospital. This now appears to be a total fabrication.

The facts were always vague and constantly changing, according to his mother, Mary, of San Jose, California, a courageous amateur sleuth who would not give up and who eventually dug up more facts than the professionals. She was already driven by her early recognition of the Army's obvious cover-up.

Mary Tillman did not know how to react when she learned from the Army coroner that he did not sign an initial casualty report that stated her son had been killed by enemy fire because he knew the enemy at that distance was not skilled enough to send three bullets that close together through a man's forehead.

So Mrs. Tillman wondered how she was to let go when so many lapses in judgment and procedure appeared to have occurred. She also questioned who was influencing the changing of the testimony of soldiers at the scene. Other oddities included, why would Tillman's uniform and body armor have been burned only three days after his death and why was the initial report missing?

Recently, Gen. Wesley Clark came forward to publicly confirm that there was never any evidence of "accidental friendly fire" being responsible for the death of Tillman and that Army medical examiners concluded Tillman was shot with a three-shot burst to the head from just 10 yards away. Clark concluded that "orders came from the very top" to murder the former NFL star because they feared he was about to become an anti-war political icon.

Sports Illustrated, in a lengthy September 2006 article, first brought to light this unspeakable possibility with interviews with Pat's brother Kevin and others who served with him. Here was portrayed a side of Tillman not widely known: a fiercely independent thinker who enlisted, fought and died in service to his country yet was critical of President Bush and opposed the war in Iraq. He was an avid reader whose interests ranged from history books to works of leftist Noam Chomsky, a favorite author of his.

Apparently a meeting between Tillman and Chomsky was planned for after Tillman's return to the United States. Kevin and Mrs. Tillman believe that this may have bothered the "powers that be." Would top brass want to execute Tillman in order to prevent their "poster child" from returning home and becoming an anti-war icon?

From the start, those at the very top in the military had engaged in a sophisticated conspiracy to create a phony "friendly fire" cover story, now greatly underplayed by the establishment press. They then awarded Tillman a Silver Star for valor. For what? Getting shot? Everybody knew that Tillman had done nothing at this point to have qualified for the nation's second highest award for combat valor. It was an obvious case of subterfuge by the cover-up artists and the Tillmans back home were not fooled by it.

But Army medical examiners were suspicious about the close proximity of the three bullet holes in Tillman's forehead and tried without success to get authorities to investigate whether the former NFL player's death amounted to a crime, according to Army documents.

Their report stated: "No evidence at all of enemy fire was found at the scene. No one was hit by enemy fire nor was any government equipment struck."

The doctors, whose names were redacted, said that the bullet holes were so close together that it looked as though the Army Ranger was cut down by an M-16 fired from a mere 10 yards or so away. If this is true, then there almost certainly were witnesses to the murder, but none has come forward at this date.

(*Please bear in mind that those speaking here are the U.S. Army's own medical examiners and not some dreaded "conspiracy theorist" opining without facts.*)

Still, the cover-up remained. Army attorneys even sent congratulatory emails to one another for keeping criminal investigators at bay while the military conducted its own internal investigation that resulted in administrative wrist-slapping and non-criminal punishments.

The officer who led the first investigation testified that when he was given responsibility for the probe the morning after Tillman's death, he was informed that the cause was "potential fratricide"— obviously meaning murder. Why this was not followed up on is the big mystery.

Despite all of the damning evidence, the question remains, who killed Pat Tillman and why? As time goes by, say the Tillman family, this will become increasingly difficult to answer.

As of 2010, the Tillman family still has received no satisfaction.

"I will promise you this, that if we have not gotten our troops out by the time I am president, it is the first thing I will do. I will get our troops home. We will bring an end to this war. You can take that to the bank."

—BARACK OBAMA
October 27, 2007

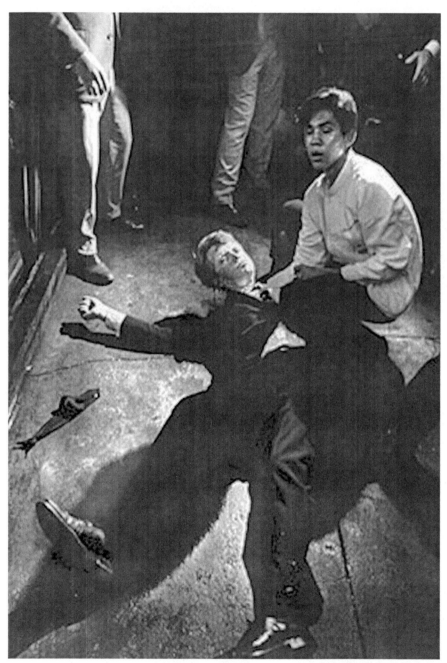

Above, Robert F. Kennedy lies on the floor; one of the kitchen employees kneels at his side. Note the clip-on necktie below RFK's outstretched right hand. The significance of this will be explained in the following chapter.

WHO KILLED ROBERT F. KENNEDY?

EVIDENCE SHOWS SHOTS CAME FROM THE REAR

T he facts of the murder of Sen. Robert Kennedy, who surely would have been president, show there was a official cover-up. This cover-up was even more thorough than the sloppy one shading the truth behind the assassination of his brother nearly five years earlier. The documented evidence in the first Kennedy murder was buried for 75 years, although much has surfaced through private investigation during the past forty-five. But the biggest secrets of the RFK murder lie locked in the most secure vault of all—a man's mind.

Discovering the second (and third and fourth etc.) gunman in Dealey Plaza was not difficult with the large number of witnesses and pictures. But in the kitchen pantry area of Los Angeles' Ambassador Hotel, where Sen. Kennedy was shot, there were few pictures available (after police confiscation) and with everyone's attention focused on Sirhan and the melee, only a few witnesses were able to come forward and say that they saw another gunman. Five are much easier to discredit than 50 or more.

The power structure almost did away with Sirhan Bishara Sirhan forever by gaining a death penalty verdict at his 1969 trial. However, before he could be executed, the State of California rescinded the death penalty for all sitting on death row and Sirhan was spared.

He serves a life sentence today and has never been able to remember what happened on the night of June 4, 1968. This is fact. It is not the likely story of one attempting to disclaim any involvement by saying "I cannot remember." It is the most *unlikely* one. Sirhan said to his psychiatric examiners: "This is not like me. I know I did it, but I don't know why. Can you help me understand? Why did I do it?"

It was election night and the final tallies were in from the crucial California presidential primary. The best known brand name in American politics was a late comer to the presidential campaign but had already emerged as the frontrunner. At just after midnight at the Ambassador Hotel in downtown Los Angeles, Sen. Robert F. Kennedy had completed a short victory speech with ". . . and now it's on to Chicago [scene of the August Democratic Convention] and let's win there!"

He began to move forward through the crowd toward the front door and a press conference in the Colonial Room when his Press Secretary Frank Mankiewicz turned him around and sent him through the kitchen pantry. Mankiewicz claimed later that he did this because it was a more direct and less hampered route.

Not only were these the days before Secret Service protection was afforded to presidential candidates but Kennedy himself had requested that no Los Angeles Police officers should be near him—or so LAPD claimed in a statement that was never substantiated. Indeed, he was courting the black vote and did not want to be associated with the stigma of the already infamous head-bashers. The reputation of the LAPD had preceded them long before the 1992 riots.

As the senator pushed through the throng in the kitchen's passageway, a brown-skinned man of obvious Middle Eastern descent was pushing a steel food cart on wheels toward the advancing crowd.

When they were close enough, he screamed an epithet and began to fire an Iver Johnson .22 revolver. He fired six of eight shots, but a later ballistics investigation showed that none hit Kennedy.

All six went wildly into bystanders, the walls and ceiling, before Sirhan was subdued by world-class athletes Rafer Johnson and Roosevelt Grier and "The Paper Lion," George Plimpton.

Yet Kennedy was wounded three times, all from the back. Twenty-four hours later, another Kennedy was dead by assassination.

All of the other wounded survived. For a day and a half Sirhan refused to identify himself.

His name was not learned until his brother came forward after seeing his picture on television.

CASE OFFICIALLY CLOSED

While LAPD was busy burying the truth, they were also assuring the public that they would not repeat the "mistakes of Dallas" and there would be no lingering doubts, once the investigation was complete. But special agent of the FBI William Bailey would soon be calling it "the biggest blunder in the history of criminal investigations." News reporters were frustrated by LAPD spokesmen who kept saying, "This is a solved case," but could never show why and how. In April of 1969, immediately following Sirhan's inevitable conviction, LAPD burned more than 2,400 photos of the crime scene. These were actually thrown in the incinerator for permanent disposal. The ballistics evidence, presented below, was ignored. The official explanation was and is that Sirhan acted alone. Another "lone nut." It was always expected to be accepted as truth but never quite made it.

CASE UNOFFICIALLY REOPENED

Retired Agent Bailey's assertion became clear when a total of 11 (some claimed 13, but two were questionable) bullet holes were found to be in the walls and people. It was obvious to the most obstinate conspiracy debunker that at least one more gun in addition to Sirhan's eight-shot revolver (which he fired only six times) had been fired in the melee.

New York Rep. Allard Lowenstein first went public with this information in 1974, in a vain attempt to get the case reexamined. He was later shot to death in his NYC law office by another "lone nut" that was described in the news as "a disgruntled client." Lowenstein had been thwarted in his efforts but had never backed off of his desire to see justice done.

Following his autopsy of Kennedy, it also became obvious to Dr. Thomas Noguchi, the L.A. County Coroner and world-renowned pathologist, that Sirhan had not killed RFK. The death shot was a bullet of undetermined caliber behind the ear—a wound that included powder burns and one that was fired from "one to three inches away." No witness could place Sirhan closer than "three to four feet" from Kennedy (and in front) at any time. Even if Kennedy had turned his head, as some had falsely claimed, the Sirhan gun was never close enough to produce powder burns.

Then who killed Robert Kennedy? The question was never asked because it had always been assumed that Sirhan had done it. The only question at the time was, "why?"

MOST LIKELY SUSPECT

Dan Moldea, the author of *The Killing of Robert Kennedy* (1995), has offered a comprehensive study of the assassination. In it he also performs an intensive examination of both the suppressed evidence implicating and the information exonerating the security guard who had been walking next to Kennedy at the moment of attack. Moldea seems to be swayed toward the guard's innocence, but the reader is not necessarily so convinced.[1] The guard seems to have altered his story at some place every time he was interviewed. He also requested not to be called to the witness stand and the prosecutors mysteriously honored that request. Somehow, the author seems to have a change of heart from the beginning of his book to the end.

Early in 1968, Thane Eugene (Gene) Cesar, 26, had applied for the position of security guard at Ace Guard Service because he was desperate to earn extra money and the $3 an hour was enticing. (Please remember from earlier chapters that this was equal to 16 or more times the $3 figure in today's phony dollars. Three bucks an hour may not excite a rentacop now, but $48 would.) In recent months he had worked part time on occasion. But it was not until late in the afternoon of June 4th that Gene received a call from Ace Guard to report to the Ambassador Hotel for duty. He says that he was called late because another guard was not able to show up at the last minute and that he was not there as a Kennedy bodyguard but for "crowd control." At 11:15 p.m. he was assigned to check credentials at the doorway of Colonial Room (where the press conference was to be held) and was to clear the way for the Kennedy entourage en route. As the crowd entered through the kitchen pantry swinging doors, he took up his duty and followed closely behind and to the right of Sen. Kennedy.

Seconds later when the shooting broke out, Cesar hit the floor and admitted drawing his weapon. Although two witnesses, one a newsman, said they saw the security guard fire, Gene says that he did not do so. He successfully passed a polygraph test organized by Dan Moldea in 1994. An LAPD polygraph was set up for him in 1968 but was canceled for unknown reasons by authorities the day before it was to take place.

However, as Moldea also points out, Cesar was standing directly behind Kennedy when Sirhan began firing and, according to his own statements, was in a position to shoot Kennedy at a point-blank range behind the right ear. There was no one else seen with a gun.

A total of five witnesses saw him draw the gun, and Cesar gave contradictory statements to police about exactly when he drew the weapon. (He also had been on guard duty in the pantry an hour earlier when Sirhan reportedly slipped into the area.)

The trajectory of the shots from the back, which went through Kennedy's coat as well as into his head, were perfectly aligned with where Cesar said he was on the floor. If he did not fire, then he should have been right next to whoever did shoot and witnessed the activity. He was never asked and never volunteered that information during the polygraph.

Cesar admitted owning a .22 caliber handgun but insisted that he did not carry it—even as a backup weapon—that night and that he had sold it in February. However, the sales slip showed that he had not actually sold it until three months after the murder. It was never tested by LAPD for ballistics and it subsequently disappeared. The buyer later reported it as stolen.

Gene Cesar somehow lost his clip-on necktie during the confusion. In the famous photo of a dying RFK sprawled on the pantry floor, a stray clip-on tie lies just a foot from Kennedy's clutched right hand. Did he momentarily grapple with Cesar when he saw the drawn gun aimed at him, pulling the necktie off in the scuffle? Could Cesar have then crouched down behind and to the right of Kennedy and pumped several shots into his back at point-blank range while Sirhan fired wildly into the crowd behind the senator, drawing all the attention of the witnesses in the pantry?

The evidence suggests but does not prove that the only armed man seen by witnesses close enough to Kennedy to fire and provoke powder burns was Cesar. Did he quickly shoot the senator point blank behind the ear while they both were still standing, then fall to the floor and fire three more times?

Kennedy was hit four times with shots that were impossible for Sirhan to have fired. Two entered his head (back and right side), one in his right armpit and the fourth went harmlessly upwards through the tufted shoulder of his suit coat from right to left, also leaving powder burns and (the last two) lodging in the ceiling, indicating that they were fired from below. All seem to implicate Cesar or, at the very least, someone who would have been close enough for Cesar to have witnessed.

MK-ULTRA?

Former *Time* correspondent Robert Blair Kaiser, who had worked for Sirhan's defense team as an investigator and knew the case better than anyone else, posed the possibility in his book, *RFK Must Die*, that Sirhan was "programmed to kill Bob Kennedy and was programmed to forget the fact of his programming."

Dr. Eduard Simpson, who examined Sirhan in prison for 20 weeks in a row, called it the "psychiatric blunder of the century." He believed that even the incriminating notes found in Sirhan's home ("RFK must die!" etc) were a forgery. Indeed, the handwritings are different.

Former FBI agent-turned-investigative reporter William Turner and his co-author Jonn Christian believe that Sirhan was a Manchurian Candidate assassin, "the robot of another," firing at Kennedy as a result of a posthypnotic suggestion. Simpson and other doctors who examined Sirhan said that he was easily hypnotizable and unusually susceptible to post-hypnotic suggestion. Sirhan's memory has always been totally blank for a two-plus hour period after 10:00 p.m. that night. He remembers nothing about it and only the evidence presented against him had convinced him of his own guilt.

Sirhan's attorneys did not challenge the prosecution with any of the exonerating evidence presented here but rather agreed with the prosecution of their client's guilt and attempted to show a "diminished mental state" in hopes of avoiding the death penalty. They failed.

Then we are faced with the Orwellian question (dwelling on the fringes of conspiratorial paranoia) of whether or not Cesar *also* was some-how under some kind of mind control. He certainly appears to *believe* that he is telling the truth, which is all it takes to pass a polygraph. But if "they" got to him, how and when did they do it?

THE POLKA DOT DRESS WOMAN

In addition to the discrepancies of too many bullets and Kennedy being hit from behind in the back, there was another important piece of evidence pointing toward conspiracy. There were at least five witnesses who saw a woman in a polka dot dress fleeing the assassination scene and gleefully shouting, "We shot him! We shot him!"

A Kennedy campaign worker named Sandra Serrano was sitting on a stairway and asked of the mystery woman whom she meant that they had shot. "Senator Kennedy," the woman replied and continued to hurry out with a young Mexican/American man. Serrano was too far away from the assassination scene to have heard the shots and was not aware of the chaos in the kitchen at the time.

A couple identified in the police report only as "the Bernsteins," who were interviewed briefly by a patrolman, told the same story. But the Bernsteins were outside the hotel, about 100 feet down a staircase from Serrano's position when they had a brief exchange with the same woman who was still exuberantly screaming, "We shot him! We shot him!" They also inquired, "Who was shot?" and received the same reply. The Bernsteins have never been heard from again.

Sirhan has always maintained that the last thing he remembers that night is drinking coffee with a young woman. Serrano and another witness, hotel waiter Vincent DiPierro, reported seeing Sirhan in the company of the woman in the polka dot dress before the shooting. Was it the same woman? Nobody could ever be certain.

However, the whole incident seemed to be a thorn in the side of the cover-up corps and one that needed to be handled. The LAPD responded to their statements by sending Enrique "Hank" Hernandez to administer polygraph examinations designed not to ascertain the truth but to browbeat them into recanting. The following is from the official transcript of the preliminaries of the Serrano polygraph that was concealed for 20 years:

HERNANDEZ: I think you owe it to Senator Kennedy, the late Senator Kennedy, to come forth, be a woman about this. If he and you don't know and I don't know whether he's a witness in this room right now watching what we're doing in here. Don't shame his death by keeping this thing up. I have compassion for you. I want to know why you did what you did. This is a very serious thing.

SERRANO: I seen those people!

HERNANDEZ: No, no, no, no, Sandy. Remember what I told you about that. You can't say something when you didn't see it.

SERRANO: Well, I don't feel I'm doing anything wrong. . . .I remember seeing the girl.

HERNANDEZ: No, I'm talking about what you have told here about seeing a person tell you, "We have shot Kennedy," and that's wrong.

SERRANO: That's what she said.

HERNANDEZ: No, it isn't, Sandy.

SERRANO: No! That's what she said.

HERNANDEZ: Look it! Look it! I love this man!

SERRANO: So do I.

HERNANDEZ: And you're shaming him!

SERRANO: Don't shout at me.

HERNANDEZ: Well, I'm trying not to shout, but this is a very emotional thing for me, too. If you love the man, the least you owe him is the courtesy of letting him rest in peace.

This flavor of interrogation of Sandy Serrano went on for over an hour. When Hernandez finally administered the polygraph test, he concluded that the badly shaken Serrano had lied about the entire matter. Under Hernandez's relentless and often abusive pressure, both Serrano and Di-Pierro did finally back down.

Many months later, LAPD produced Valerie Schulte, a young Kennedy groupie who had witnessed the murder in the pantry, as being the girl in the polka dot dress. It was another weak imitation of truth. Schulte was a blonde wearing a dark dress with white polka dots that night. Serrano saw just the opposite: "She was a Caucasian. She had on a white dress with polka dots. She was light skinned, *dark* hair. She had on black shoes and she had a funny nose."

Pictures of Schulte clearly show that she was an attractive blonde who also lacked "a funny nose."

Not only that but Schulte was on crutches that night at the Ambassador, which certainly would be the most outstanding feature of identifying her by anybody.

Nevertheless, it was one more case of "That's our story and we're sticking to it." Serrano's eyewitness report was discounted forever.

CONVINCING EVIDENCE OF COVER-UP

Because the (autopsy) evidence also shows that Sirhan could not have been in back of Kennedy or close enough (one to three inches) to shoot him and create powder burns behind the ear, someone else actually murdered the senator.

With political assassinations, it has been a longtime standard operating procedure to establish the diversion of another shooter in order to take the spotlight off of the real culprits.

In Dallas in 1963, someone fired diversionary shots from the sixth floor window of the Texas School Book Depository, but the evidence proved it was not Lee Oswald (*either* of them).

When James Earl Ray-handler "Raoul/Paul" emerged from the bathroom of the cheap hotel across the street from the Martin Luther King, Jr. murder scene, with the rifle in hand that Ray had purchased in Birmingham only days before, the testimony of three eyewitnesses showed that it was not Ray in the bathroom.

On another note, when the alleged "ANFO" (ammonium nitrate/fuel oil) bomb went off in Oklahoma City, it was preceded by a few seconds by an enormous explosion inside the Alfred E. Murrah Building. The truck bomb, whatever it was (and there are grave doubts as to whether any ANFO was even at the scene), was a diversionary tactic to place the spotlight on another patsy, Tim McVeigh, and away from the implosion *inside* the Murrah Building. A report published (Oct. 2009) in the pages of AMERICAN FREE PRESS discussed the FBI's release of heavily edited—yet still incriminating—OKC surveillance tapes from the vicinity of the Murrah Building, this after 14 years of publicly lying about their very existence. More government perfidy and obfuscation we'll discuss in Volume Two.

SIRHAN SIRHAN

Sirhan was a participant in the RFK murder, probably unwittingly, as were Oswald, Ray and McVeigh in some of the other federal government cover-ups.

In 1973, investigative journalist Ted Charach produced the best evidence of the cover-up in Los Angeles with what is now a long-forgotten documentary film. Charach interviewed William W. Harper, a 68-year old Pasadena-based criminalist and firearms expert, whose testimony in hundreds of cases had been relied upon by both prosecutors and defense attorneys since the 1930s. In late 1970, Sirhan's defense attorneys enlisted Harper's aid to examine the bullets, trajectory and other physical evidence entered at trial. Had Harper been called to examine and testify the previous year at the 1969 trial, his findings would have blown the case wide open.

His astounding evidence showed, with blow-ups of the microscopic ballistic printouts, that the bullets removed from Kennedy's body were not fired from the same gun that wounded the other five victims. Harper said without reservation that there was no way (because of the rear trajectory) that Sirhan could have inflicted any of the shots that hit Kennedy anyway. He left no doubt that two guns had been fired with near-simultaneous timing in the room that night.

Charach also proves with an interview with the district attorney that a second .22 pistol was fired in the room that night and that it was introduced into evidence at trial by the prosecution, no less. *LAPD criminologist DeWayne Wolfer testified under oath that he had personally test-fired the weapon—an Iver Johnson .22 revolver with the serial number H-18602—and had found it to be the weapon that had fired the bullets that had been removed from Kennedy's neck and several other victims.*

However, the serial number on Sirhan's Iver Johnson weapon was H-53725 and not one member of the defense team caught it! In a complaint to the attorney general later, Wolfer was accused of ". . . suffering from a great inferiority complex for which he compensates by giving the police exactly what they need for a conviction. He casts objectivity to the winds and violates every basic tenet of forensic science and proof by becoming a crusading advocate. This is rationalized as being entirely legitimate since the accused is guilty anyway. . . ."

However, what Wolfer had actually done was totally exonerate Sirhan of the murder once and for all and it strains one's credulity to imagine that not one on the high-powered legal team had the perception to check these serial numbers as they were being recited or read from the witness stand. They almost certainly would have been hoping for a discrepancy of only one digit—even if was just a mistake in reading by the witness—in order to belittle the testimony and disparage that witness. The only other answer is that the defense team was in on the fix and this was not the only example.

When confronted with the discrepancy, District Attorney Joseph P. Busch, Jr. went behind closed doors for five months (after saying that he would look at the problem and have an answer in two weeks) before emerging at a press conference to say that Wolfer had made a clerical error. He had mistakenly officially listed (twice) the tested bullets as being fired from the wrong weapon, Busch claimed.

Further, when the serial number on the second weapon was checked at the Criminal Division of Investigation and Identification in Sacramento, the records showed that it had "been destroyed by LAPD in July of 1968" (prior to the trial). Later that date was changed in the Sacramento records to show "July of 1969," again because of a "clerical error." (Just how stupid are these clerks? Can they not even type? Or is it not more likely that this is one more cover-up and subterfuge by those in charge of those typists?)

According to LAPD's property card, the Iver Johnson pistol H-18602 had been originally booked as evidence for an earlier robbery case on March 18, 1967, more than a year before the murder of Robert Kennedy and it had already been test-fired four days later by LAPD in connection with that prior investigation.

Busch, fast-talking and deceptive, claimed that LAPD had purposely gone to their gun bin and chosen a similar weapon (yeah, right) to use in tests at the Ambassador because it would have taken a court order to obtain the Sirhan gun. *In such a high-profile investigation, what's so hard about that?* asked the reporters privately.

Dr. Thomas Noguchi said that the bullet fragments removed from Kennedy's head were too mutilated not only to test but to determine the precise caliber. Yes, it could have been a .38 but not one of the other guns in the room that night was tested to see if they had been fired, including the .38 service revolver security guard Cesar admitted drawing.

KNXT-TV newsman Don Schulman not only confirmed that Cesar pulled his weapon but that he fired it. Schulman was pilloried by the judiciary and the press for years but has always stuck by his story. He also found his testimony to be altered by LAPD to reflect that he had not seen what he knows he saw.

Three years later, KNXT ignored its own previous story and announced to its viewers that not only had Schulman never made such a report from the scene in 1968 but that he had not even been in the kitchen area at the time of the shooting.

AND THERE IS MORE

Herbert McDonald, director of the Laboratory of Forensic Science in New York, was world renowned for his ballistics testing and investigation of high-profile cases. He studied the evidence of the Sirhan case and came to this succinct conclusion: "The revolver taken from Sirhan, considering all of the physical factors, could not have been the one that fired the projectile removed from Robert Kennedy."

The high-ranking criminologist with all his years of experience testifies under oath that the weapon tested that killed RFK is serial-numbered H-18602 and yet the recorded number of the weapon carried by Sirhan Sirhan is H-53725. Should not this phony charade be over? Yes, indeed, except for the obvious fact that we don't have an honest trial here but another sham. I have asked many, very experienced defense attorneys if such a thing could have gotten past them in the heat of a trial, and every one said to one degree or another, "No way! We would have had the actual serial numbers right in front of us at the defense table." All concluded that no experienced trial defense attorney could have missed it and that Grant Cooper had to have been paid off to lose the case. Nothing else made sense. "No trial attorney in his rookie case could have been so blind, let alone a high-profile professional such as Cooper," said one. "He didn't blow the case, he sold it out. No doubt." That's what your author thought, too, and that's why he took it to a "higher court." The dodging and dancing by Busch that follows here made this conclusion ever clearer.

Amateur photographer Scott Enyart, 15, was at the Ambassador with friends that night, more to be around the excitement than anything else, but his story of teenage shenanigans ended up becoming one more chapter in the book of "cover-up" written by authorities.

When one of his young buddies swiped several "Press" badges, Scott and they began to move where the action really was. He snapped a 36-shot roll of film, mostly of Bobby and Ethel at the podium during the speech. However, his last 10 photos were taken in the pantry at the Ambassador kitchen during the murderous melee. Scott trailed the entourage by only 15 feet and held the camera high over his head, aiming at the senator. However, the young photographer would never learn exactly what his last 10 pictures might have memorialized.

Immediately after the shooting, Scott was accosted, interrogated, held for a lengthy time by six LAPD cops and ordered to surrender his film "as evidence." When he tried to retrieve it a year later, they had never heard of him. Finally, through the efforts of his father's lawyer, he was able to get 26 of his pictures returned. The 10 from the assassination scene had disappeared and no negatives were returned. In 1988, Enyart was informed that his pictures were likely among the group of 2,400 destroyed by LAPD immediately after the trial.

LAPD was stumbling all over itself. When Ted Charach and William Harper had clearly illustrated the plausibility of the second gun, District Attorney Joe Busch defended the physical integrity of their investigation but continued to perpetuate the confusion by barring access to the evidence, thus denying Charach and Harper a chance to vindicate their claims.

However, the publicity they had raised did lead to a Los Angeles County Grand Jury inquiry in August of 1971. Charach and Harper and others testified in an attempt to prove that the evidence presented at Sirhan's trial was tampered with after the trial. Deputy District Attorney John Howard, who had interrogated Sirhan two hours after the crime and stayed with the case all along, opened up with this stunning testimony: "The gun was an eight-shot revolver and there were six [empty] casings inside, which indicated that there had been six bullets fired. So we had both the live bullets from the gun and the six casings, as I recall.

This, of course was an outright admission that more than one gun had been fired. But when they were confronted with it, Howard and Busch passed it off as "just another mistake." It is not known whether or not they, along with Dewayne Wolfer, now have cushy jobs working for the FBI, but we do know that John Howard was soon promoted to Chief Deputy District Attorney.

At trial time, chief defense attorney Grant Cooper forfeited many times the opportunity for full disclosure and meaningful cross-examination by stipulating to vague facts and agreeing to just about anything short of the gas chamber for his client. For example (the trial transcript shows), talking about the fatal, fragmented bullet while Wolfer was on the witness stand, Cooper declared, "We will stipulate that these fragments did come from Senator Kennedy. We will further stipulate they came from the gun."

Moments later, Wolfer testified about one of the same bullets: "Because of the damage, I cannot say that it was fired from the same gun, that is Sirhan's gun," which publicly displayed how foolish Cooper's stipulation had been. Throughout the trial, it appeared that the burden of proof was on the defense rather than the prosecution.

But was it really foolish or had Cooper been forewarned—even paid— by the powers behind the scene to lose this case? Grant Cooper had been one of the most renowned criminal attorneys in California, yet his bumbling of these elementary issues could have been spotted by a sophomore law student.

Whatever was the truth of the matter, by design or actual ignorance, thanks to the deficient defense, the state of California did not have to prove the crux of its case. As a result, Sirhan did not get a fair trial.

Later in the trial proceedings, even Sirhan smelled the proverbial rat and stood up to say that he was firing his attorneys and demanding competent counsel. The trial judge ordered him to sit down, that he was not allowed to speak and threatened to bind and gag him if he did not comply. His request for new counsel was ignored.

Sirhan's attitude over the past decade has changed from resigned to his own guilt to pursuit of the truth. At every parole hearing he ever had— up until the one in 1999—he has apologized to the board with great remorse and always saying he still does not know why he did it. However, in 1999, undoubtedly after reading some of the evidence presented above, he pleaded for his release on the grounds that he had been "framed," but his parole was denied one more time.

WHAT REALLY HAPPENED?

Because LAPD and the infamous FBI (Federal Bureau of Intimidation in action again) have suppressed so much evidence for so long and in so many cases, the following scenario can only be submitted and accepted as speculation. However, it appears that Sirhan B. Sirhan was somehow pre-established as a diversionary patsy and that drugs and hypnotism aided in the setup. The evidence shows that even if he fired the .22 handgun all eight times, it would not equal the holes in bodies, walls and ceiling. (Doors and ceiling panels mysteriously disappeared before and after trial.)

Not only do we have apparent *duplicity* on the part of the defense but a strong case could be made for *complicity* by LAPD prior to and after the fact.

A gun that had been under the control of LAPD over the previous year was documented twice by their expert as being the murder weapon. Perhaps it actually was. Then it was pulled out again for the tests in order to cement the frame of Sirhan. If this were the case, Dewayne Wolfer's "clerical error" then could have been that he wrote the *correct* serial number on the evidence envelope rather than the one he meant to—that number from Sirhan's revolver.

The behavior of the cops at the scene, with the illegal confiscation of film and the failure to confiscate all the guns on the scene for test-firing, indicates the potential for prior knowledge, as well.

A NEVER-MENTIONED MOTIVE

The question always looms in an assassination case, what was the motive? And the answer always seems to be from multiple choice. The Kennedys had been at war with the Mafia and the Teamsters, to mention only a couple of their numerous fronts. And not only did Bobby Kennedy make more political enemies in a much shorter career than did his brother Jack, he had an arrogant, abrasive way about him that provoked much more personal dislike. While the president's personality was warm and magnetic, Bobby's public image was far more likeable than his private one.

Longtime mob lawyer Frank Ragano brought the point home to this writer during a luncheon interview in Tampa three years before he died. As an attorney for Santos Trafficante, Carlos Marcello and Sam Giancana at various times, Ragano was the natural choice for Jimmy Hoffa to hire in the early '60s to aid with the problems he was having with then-Attorney General Bobby Kennedy. Hoffa harbored an enmity for Kennedy that was expanding daily. One morning in the attorney general's Washington office in 1962, it was inflating by the mili-second.

Hoffa and Ragano had a 10:00 appointment with Kennedy to discuss a plea bargain. Kennedy was late. At 10:15, the secretary told them that she didn't know where her boss was but was sure that he would arrive shortly. At 10:30, as the two men sat cooling their heels, Ragano noticed Hoffa becoming more and more agitated as the big clock on the wall ticked away their morning. They had another appointment soon and had hoped to dispose of this one in short measure. Finally at almost 11, Kennedy walked in with his Chihuahua on a leash, removed his overcoat and began to hang it on the clothes tree in the corner by the entrance.

"I'm sorry I am late, gentlemen," he said, "but I was walking my dog."

Hoffa went ballistic and sprang to his feet. "You !@#$%, selfish, arrogant %$#@!," Hoffa screamed and went for the throat. "You keep me waiting for an hour while you walk your !@#$% dog?" He choked Kennedy down to the floor and fell on top of him, as Ragano and the secretary watched in horror. She yelled for help and Ragano, after he regained his composure and realized he was about to witness a murder, jumped in the pile in a futile attempt to pull the union leader off of the greatly overmatched highest-ranking legal officer in the nation.

"I am convinced that Jimmy would have strangled him to death right there in his office, if one of the assistant AGs had not run out to help me pull him off," Ragano said. "He went absolutely berserk and I could not stop him alone. Hoffa was strong. Bobby had about 30 seconds to live. Imagine *those* newspaper headlines!"

Needless to say, Frank Ragano did not pursue Hoffa's plea bargain delusions any further, but perhaps the point about Bobby Kennedy's aloof personality is made. Even his brother's widow Jackie, with whom Bobby had a brief affair in 1966, was quoted as saying about his ego: "I sometimes wish that Bobby, because he is so wonderful, had been an amoeba and then he could have mated with himself."

The first thing a detective looks for in a murder investigation is "Who benefits?" Who gets the life insurance? Who gets the estate? Who gets the company? Who has the most to gain? These are all subsections under the column of "motive."

While Jimmy Hoffa and other Bobby-haters certainly had the means to complete the operation, even from inside the prison gates, the greatest beneficiary to the death of Bobby Kennedy was Richard Nixon.

In November of that year, Nixon beat the second-best Democratic candidate, Hubert Humphrey by the second narrowest margin in history. Even the Republican diehards concede that he would not have made it against Bobby Kennedy. The handwriting was on the wall; Bobby Kennedy was about to become the next president. In five more months, Nixon was going to lose for the second time to a Kennedy.

Take that motive for whatever it is worth, but before making a final decision, consider what happened four years later.

Nixon's character became evident at the end of his tenure ("Your president is not a crook") as he lied his way deeper and deeper into the trap. But the election events of 1972 reflected those of 1968 more than anyone wanted to realize.

In 1968, George Wallace had garnered 10 million votes and was the prime reason Humphrey was able to keep it so close. Most Wallace votes would have gone to Nixon. In 1972, Wallace was threatening in the primaries to double that. It was beginning to appear that Governor Wallace would be the single derailer of the Nixon train.

If Gov. Wallace, the third party candidate, were to grab 20 million votes, it could throw the election into the House of Representatives, as it would prevent any candidate from having a majority. As it turned out, Nixon swamped the Democratic nominee George McGovern that November, carrying 49 states out of 50. But Wallace was no longer in the race. With Wallace still in and dividing the vote, the Democratic-controlled House of Representatives might have handed the presidency to

Democratic Sen. George McGovern. The dismal prospects may have been greater than the Nixon camp was willing to face.

On May 15, 1972, the Alabama governor was shot by Arthur Bremer (and others unknown, as we are about to see), following a campaign speech in a Laurel, Maryland shopping center parking lot. The attempted murder was as suspicious as the Robert Kennedy case four years earlier.

Bremer carried a five-shot, Smith & Wesson .38 revolver. Wallace was hit four times in the chest and abdomen. However, three other people were seriously wounded: a Secret Service agent was hit in the neck, a female campaign worker in the leg and Wallace's personal bodyguard, an Alabama Highway Patrol captain, was shot through the abdomen. Once again, it fit the pattern of a much larger conspiracy by the simple fact that from a five-shot weapon seven bullets cannot fire.[2]

Also once again, Richard Nixon was the greatest beneficiary of the power move. With Wallace no longer around to swallow up a large percentage of the conservative vote, Nixon won in a breezy landslide.

Was the power structure in 1968, that Unseen Hand, worried about a second "Camelot" arriving with the election of RFK? In any case, Nixon was never implicated. In both of the two high-profile crimes, no one else was either—except the two patsies, Sirhan and Bremer.

ENDNOTE:

[1] Moldea's book is not unlike Gerald Posner's deceptive *Case Closed* (which ignores all of the exculpatory evidence and fingers Oswald alone in the JFK murder), or the book by two New York newsmen, Michel and Herbeck (who claimed to have spent 75 hours on the phone with Tim McVeigh before having him confessing to the impossible in the OKC bombing).

2 Check the microfiche at your local library for the 5/16/72 issue of *The NY Times* to see all these facts. Are we to believe that no newsman of the era was smart enough to count to seven? Or is it more likely that any mention of this was cut by his editor before it saw the light of day? Everything they ever told us was a lie.

*"The fact that an opinion
has been widely held is
no evidence whatsoever that
it is not utterly absurd."*

—BERTRAND RUSSELL

FACE IT AMERICA:
9-11 WAS AN INSIDE JOB
ALL EVIDENCE—NO THEORIES

SPECIAL THANKS TO THE TRUTHTELLERS AT WWW.911TRUTHSEEKERS.ORG

O n September 11, 2001, thousands of innocent people were destroyed by the ruthless actions that resulted in the total wipeout of three skyscrapers at the World Trade Center in New York City, as well as other related events at the Pentagon in Washington and in Shanksville, Pennsylvania.

Americans were immediately instructed that it was "Muslim terrorists" (for which we had been pre-programmed) that had perpetrated this surprise attack upon our nation and an official story quickly evolved as to how the events of this fateful day had allegedly unfolded.

However, astute observers immediately recognized that the formal storyline of 9-11 was thoroughly inconsistent with the readily observable facts at hand. Sadly and shamefully, it became increasingly evident that rogue elements within our own federal government had engendered this false flag operation for diabolical purposes that included the creation of bogus justification for two foreign wars as well as an escalation of the domestic political attack upon our liberties at home under the guise of the misnamed Patriot Act legislation.

Apologists for the flagrantly errant official portrayal of what supposedly took place on 9-11 have sought to employ all manners of illicit tactics in an effort to silence and/or discredit (or even prosecute) anyone daring to expose the truth of treason and criminal activity at the highest echelons of power. One of their most reprehensible tactics has been to allege that the mere questioning of officialdom's story was somehow an insult to the survivors of those murdered on 9-11.

(Would the whistle-blowing on a crooked small town cop who was a serial rapist and killer be a disservice to the mayor and fellow towns-people? No, but what steps might the mayor take toward cover-up of the crimes if he had been secretly involved himself?)

On the other hand, those of us on the side of truth believe precisely the opposite: that it would be a disservice to the naïve of our time as well as the historians of the future to go along with the lies and allow the actual culprits to continue to duck responsibility for their heinous offenses. There is no other way to avenge the innocent blood shed on 9/11/01.

There is no evidence whatsoever that the official 9-11 story spun by George Bush, Dick Cheney and the ultra-cooperative MSM has any truth inserted anywhere; and on the other hand there is a preponderance of evidence that none of the cover story is true and that the crimes were planned and carried out by powerful people on the inside controlling every move. We are going to present you with that powerful evidence on the next few pages. If you cannot see it the obvious picture by then, we can only conclude that you are victim and carrier of "Red, White & Blue Fever."

Oh, you want cachet? How's this for starters?

John Farmer is currently the dean of Rutgers University's School of Law. He is the former attorney general of New Jersey and during that tenure, as senior counsel to the Kean Commission, was responsible for the drafting of the original 9-11 Investigative Report. No can know better than he what he reports right here.

This is from his recent book, *The Ground Truth*: "What do we know? We know the conjecture about 9-11 still stands but for certain, we know we were lied to, not in a minor way, but systematically as part of a plot covering up government involvement at nearly every level, perhaps gross negligence, perhaps something with darker intent."

Are we willing to live with another lie to go with the Warren Report, Iran Contra and so many others? Has the sacrifice of thousands more

Americans, killed, wounded or irreparably damaged by a war knowingly built on the same lies from the same liars who misled the 9-11 Commission pushed us beyond willingness to confront the truth?

On December 4, 2001, President Bush looked foolish (again) by exposing himself as another liar for the establishment at what was billed as a town hall meeting in Orlando, Florida. During the meeting he answered uncensored questions asked from the floor by local people, a chore at which he had never earned high grades and one he never attempted again. (Following this meeting, it was decided that all questions, even those from the news media, would have to be pre-screened before being exposed for public consumption.)

A White House briefing was published with a transcript of the meeting. The newsworthy part of the transcript is Bush's exchange with Jordan, who was a third grade student (about 8 years old), asking the president how he felt on 9-11 when he heard the tragic news.

Below is an excerpt from that transcript with the exchange between Bush and Jordan. The excerpt is unaltered from the full transcript except for my commentary debunking the Bush comments:

> From a young mother of two: Mr. President, I want to say they haven't won. I got in my car today and I'm in the same building with you, speaking to you. They have not won.
> President Bush: Thank you very much.
> Young mother: And would you say hello to my son, Jordan and my daughter, Patricia?
> President Bush: Jordan and who?
> Young mother: Patricia.
> President Bush: Hi, Patricia. How are you?
> How old is Patricia?
> Young mother: Five and Jordan's in third grade. And Jordan has the question, if I could give him the microphone.
> President Bush: You bet. That's—your mother's relaying the mike to you, Jordan.
> Jordan: One thing, Mr. President, is that you have no idea how much you've done for this country. And another thing is that—how did you feel when you heard about the terrorist attack?
> President Bush: Well—(applause)—thank you, Jordan. Well, Jordan, you're not going to believe where—what state I was in when I

heard about the terrorist attack. I was in Florida. And my chief of staff, Andy Card—well, actually I was in a classroom, talking about a reading program that works. And it—I was sitting outside the—the classroom, waiting to go in and I saw an airplane hit the tower of a— of a—you know, the TV was obviously on and I—I used to fly myself and I said, "Well, there's one terrible pilot." And I said it must have been a horrible accident.

Please ponder some known facts. First, at 9 a.m. on September 11, when Bush was at the Booker School, there was no TV footage of the first plane hitting the World Trade Center for the very good reason that the TV news people didn't know it was going to happen.

Peter Jennings told the world on ABC-TV News after the second plane hit the World Trade Center, that is, after the time when Bush claims he saw TV footage of the first crash: JENNINGS: ". . . No, nobody who saw—watching "Good Morning America" today, for example, saw, at least those of us working on television, saw a first plane crash into the building. Much of the country watching television this morning will have seen the second plane crash into the other tower and we have, as you can see from a distance there, until we get our cameras on the ground producing material which we can put on the air, a pretty limited view."

Video footage did surface later. But at 9:00 a.m. on September 11, 2001 Mr. Bush could not have seen the first plane hitting the World Trade Center on TV. Period. (Some have speculated that Bush and his White House entourage in Florida may have had some sort of closed circuit apparatus from which he did view the first crash, then forgot that he wasn't supposed to have seen it, but this has never been proved one way or the other.) We concede that this does not prove Mr. Bush was consciously lying . . . yet.

It is theoretically possible that Mr. Bush's memory played a trick on him. There might have been a TV in the hallway of the school and it might have been tuned to the news and Bush might therefore have heard about the WTC crash and seen footage of the first building burning and later he might have thought he remembered seeing footage of the plane hitting the building. Theoretically, this might be the case.

However, based on the testimony of Gwen Tose Rigell, principal of the Booker School, where Bush was that morning, this was absolutely not the case.

When MSNBC reporter Ashleigh Banfield interviewed her, Principal Rigell said, "I actually heard the first plane had hit from the president and he said that a plane had hit the World Trade Center and that it was a commercial plane. He said 'but we're going to go on,' and in my mind I had created this picture of a plane knocking off some bricks on the corner of the World Trade Center."

Obviously, if there had been a TV in the school's hallway tuned to news of the World Trade Center burning, everyone would have flocked around it, Rigell would have seen it too and the reading of the goat stories probably would have been canceled. She certainly would not have formed the false impression "in [her] mind," as she and everyone else in the school would have known the attack was very serious.

In that case Principal Rigell would not have told MSNBC, "I actually heard the first plane had hit from the president," and she would not have said, "I had created this picture of a plane knocking off some bricks in the corner of the World Trade Center," meaning it was a minor incident. Instead she would have said something like, "I watched the horrifying news on television standing next to the president of the United States."

So Bush lied and now we have to wonder if Jordan and his mother were unwitting White House "plants" ("Well, Ma'am, why don't you have your little boy ask the president how he felt on 9-11?"), but the president, in typical fashion, got his answer all screwed up by mixing lies with facts. The question asked by the little boy afforded Bush the opportunity to lie about what he did at the Booker School, attempting to use the child as a disarming prop, but he blew it.

> BUSH: But I was whisked off there; I didn't have much time to think about it. And I was sitting in the classroom and Andy Card, my chief of staff, who is sitting over here, walked in and said: "A second plane has hit the tower. America's under attack."
>
> And Jordan, I wasn't sure what to think at first. You know, I grew up in a—a period of time where the idea of America being under attack never entered my mind, just like your [parents'] minds, probably.

And I started thinking hard, in that very brief period of time, about what it meant to be under attack. I knew that when I got all the facts, if we were under attack, there would be hell to pay for attacking America. [Applause, cheers. Great way to get it, too.]

I tried to get as many facts as I could, Jordan, to make sure I knew, as I was making decisions, there were—that I knew exactly what I was basing my decisions on. I've got a fabulous team. A president can't possibly be president without a good team. Starts with having a great wife, by the way. [Applause. Another shallow way of achieving it.]

And so I got on the phone from *Air Force One* asking to find out the facts. You've got to understand, Jordan, during this period of time, there were all kinds of rumors floating around. Some of them were erroneous. Obviously, we—for example, there was a news report saying that the State Department had been attacked. I needed to know what the facts were. But I knew I needed to act. I knew that if the nation's under attack, the role of the commander-in-chief is to respond forcefully to prevent other attacks from happening. And so I talked to the secretary of defense and one of the first acts I did was put our military on alert.

This is 100% double-talk. First, consider Bush's assertion that "I was whisked off there; I didn't have much time to think about it." What does he mean? Isn't he the president of the United States? Duh. If he can't think about it, what does he expect the rest of the country to do?

What does he mean, "I was whisked off"? Who whisked him? Is Bush saying he doesn't control his own locomotion? Is he telling us he was "forced" to sit in a classroom laughing and even cheering as kids practiced reading a story about goats—because that is where he went and what he did—instead of conferring with his military command, which is the positive obligation of the commander in chief during a national emergency? Why did the "whiskers"—presumably the Secret Service—wait a half an hour to go into their "whisking" action?

According to the MSNBC article on Bush's visit to the Booker School, quoted above, Bush wasn't whisked anywhere. Quite the contrary, it was he who informed the school Principal, Ms. Rigell, that despite the crash, he would continue as planned and sit in on the reading class. As noted earlier, the Booker Principal, Ms. Rigell, said, according to MSNBC:

"I actually heard the first plane had hit from the president and he said that a plane had hit the World Trade Center and that it was a commercial plane,' says Rigell. 'He said. 'But we're going to go on.' . . ."

"We're going to go on" means, "I will be observing the reading class." Note that he was not asking permission, nor was he being told what to do. There was no "whisking."

Bush says "I was whisked off" because he wants to create the impression that he was moved around by his overly efficient staff and Secret Service Agents too quickly to have time to absorb what he had, supposedly, just seen on TV. Of course, if Bush had actually seen TV footage of the World Trade Center crash he would have heard what everyone else watching the TV was hearing after 9 a.m.—that this was a terrorist attack—the biggest terrorist attack in U.S. history.

And while we're noting, note also that Bush claims he "first" learned of the attack just before he went into the classroom. But according to the article on MSNBC:

"'The limousine stops and the president comes out,' says [Booker School Principal] Rigell. 'He walks toward me. I'm standing here in a lineup; there are about five people. He walks over and says he has to make a phone call and he'll be right back.'"

[MSNBC comments:] "That phone call was to National Security Advisor Condoleezza Rice. It was the first inkling the president would get about what was to unfold."

So if Bush first heard about the World Trade Center crash from the TV, what was he talking to Condoleezza about? And if he spoke to Ms. Rice, why didn't she tell him that the FAA knew it was a "hijacked plane" that hit the World Trade Center?

Let us return to Bush's claim that he was "whisked" into the reading class at the Booker. He describes a similar inability to control his movements in recounting his supposed response after Andrew Card came into the classroom and whispered something in his ear. This was about 9:06 a.m.

We are told that Card whispered that the second World Trade Center tower had been hit and "America is under attack," but of course we don't know that that is what Card really said. We really only know that he whispered something, because we saw him do it on the video replay.

Anyway, Bush told the meeting in Florida that he had the following reaction: "I started thinking hard, in that very brief period of time, about what it meant to be under attack. I knew that when I got all the facts, if we were under attack, there would be hell to pay for attacking America."

Now really, what is this man saying? "I started thinking hard . . . about what it meant to be under attack"? This guy is the commander-in-chief of the U.S. armed forces and planes are flying into buildings and he is having an existential moment? Why doesn't he get up and get out of there and do his job? And if indeed Card did tell him that a second hijacked plane—because the Federal Aviation Administration knew these planes were hijacked—had hit the World Trade Center, how could the drunkest dolt in a New York sleaze bar doubt that "America is under attack," let alone the president of the United States?

In this quote Bush is attempting to accomplish three somewhat contradictory things.

One thing is to picture himself as only having learned the full truth at 9:06, when Card whispered something in his ear. The goal here is to explain away his failure to do his job before 9:06.

Second, he is also trying to get us to sympathize with him—make us feel that he was, like most of us, stunned by the news. So how can we blame him if, like us, he didn't immediately know what to do? That's why his script writers gave him the following lines: "The idea of America being under attack never entered my mind, just like your daddy and mother's mind, probably. . . ."

Previously Bush said that he saw a TV news report on the first plane hitting the World Trade Center. And yet the possibility that "America was under attack" never crossed his mind? Is he comatose?

Then comes the line, "I started thinking hard, in that very brief period of time, about what it meant to be under attack." So, never having conceived the possibility of his country being attacked, he was stunned, just like Jordan's mother and daddy, who, he suggests, are also as dumb as a post.

The problem with Bush's "you-were-stunned, I-was stunned" line of defense is that the Secret Service had open lines to the FAA starting at around 8:45 AM, according to Vice President Cheney.

Now, the FAA knew that Flight 11 had been hijacked at 8:20, or so they say. And it was Flight 11 that hit the World Trade Center, or so they say. One would assume that the FAA imparted this information to the Secret

Service when they took the emergency measure of setting up open lines. Therefore the Secret Service knew that "America is under attack" around 8:45, well before Mr. Bush and his staff, including the Secret Service, arrived at the Booker School. And this was about 21 minutes before Card whispered whatever he whispered in Mr. Bush's ear.

And while the Secret Service does not talk to Jordan's "daddy and mother", presumably they do talk to President Bush—after all, they are in his constant company.

Bush is also trying to accomplish a third thing here, which is to give people the impression that he's tough and competent, that he quickly recovered, rolled up his sleeves and did his job. The idea is, we Americans may be remarkably obtuse, but once we get riled, we get mean.

So he says that he remained frozen with shock for only a "very brief period of time"—and then he vowed revenge ("there would be hell to pay") and got down to the hard work of gathering those all-important but elusive facts because, "the role of the commander-in-chief is to respond forcefully to prevent other attacks from happening." (Oh, now he finally remembers!) And therefore he "got on the phone from *Air Force One* asking to find out the facts." In order, you understand, to prevent other attacks from happening.

Here Bush fails to mention one thing: he couldn't have been "on the phone from *Air Force One*" until around 10:00 a.m. Eastern time because that's approximately when *Air Force One* taxied down the runway to depart Sarasota-Brandenton Int'l Airport. This was almost an hour after Card whispered in Bush's ear, which was also almost an hour after the FAA took the very extreme measure of closing the air corridor between Cleveland and New York.

And which was an hour and 15 minutes after the Secret Service went on emergency open lines with the Federal Aviation Administration (according to VP Cheney).

Not to mention that it was one hour and 40 minutes after the FAA says they knew Flight 11 had been hijacked out of Boston.

There is a video of Bush's visit to the Booker School. It shows that even after Card whispered in his ear, Bush laughed and even cheered the kids having a reading lesson.

Certainly the largest, most blatant and outrageous conspiratorial undertaking since the assassination of JFK has to be the hoax of 9-11. During near 40-year time span separating the two, many other government-sponsored operations took place, but none could match the credulity-stretching acceptance that this one did. After a year or so of screaming the facts refuting the official story, many of us writers were agreeing that, with a cooperative news media and the convincing deceiving power of television, the rascals could make the world public believe darn near anything.

Now stop and think for a moment: did you ever *really* believe that 19 untrained and inexperienced Arabs with no history of terrorist activity—all of whom were known to the INS, FBI and the CIA and could be instantly identified as potential Arab terrorists—actually managed to hijack four large airliners and fly three of them into critical targets? Most Americans didn't really ever totally swallow that ridiculous fabrication, but because of the power of the TV and other controlled news, we could not reject it either and be allowed to formulate another scenario. But even that was less rapacious to the average mind than what happened next.

One of the most outrageous lies in the mind-bending department was the lie that the "intense heat" where the planes had crashed caused the collapse of the WTC towers 1 & 2. Who of higher intelligence than a seventh grader could fall for this kind of conspiratorial and distorted news reporting?

Well, the answer to that is: 100% of the carriers of "Red, White & Blue Fever," some of whom are eventually cured, but not many. Those who are finally cured tend to at least border on suicidal tendencies and almost always end up in some degree of depression ranging from mild to serious. The shock is simply too great to withstand and cast away without care. It is mentally devastating. It is worse than the death of a loved one. It is the death of lifelong-held dream and belief.

Let us review in detail for a moment, errr . . . several moments or . . . let's make that an hour or so. . . . Go pour a glass of wine.

1. Where is the plane that crashed into the Pentagon? It never showed up. Where are the wings, the tail, the two 9-foot Rolls Royce steel engines, the fuselage etc? How does a 757 with a wingspan of 125 feet fit into a 16-by-20-foot initial impact hole the size of your living room? Why were only five photos of "something" hitting the Pentagon released that certainly didn't look like a 757? Why did the FBI confiscate all other videos and

photos of the Pentagon crash? Why didn't any of the Pentagon's five an-
tiaircraft batteries shoot the plane down? One large piece of evidence that
was found was covered in blue tarp and hauled away into obscurity! They
did find a three-foot engine, which is coincidentally the same size as the
Global Hawk's engine. Also, many eyewitnesses saw a "plane that appeared to hold eight to 12 people" hit the building.

2. Why the apparent "stand down" by the FAA, NORAD and NMCC
on 9-11? NORAD had routinely intercepted planes 67 times earlier that
year within 20 minutes each time and *never* had a failure like they did on
9-11, nor after 9-11. On June 1, 2001, new instructions issued by the chairman of the Joint Chiefs of Staff reassigned aircraft interception authority
to Donald Rumsfeld, contradicting normal procedures. When either radar
and cockpit contact is blocked, when transponders are turned off, or when
planes deviate from their flight plan, standard military procedure is to
scramble fighter jets immediately in order to regain contact with the pilot.
According to Richard Myers (then chairman of the JCS) and NORAD
spokesman Mike Snyder, NORAD did *nothing* (for more than 90 minutes)
until *after* the Pentagon was hit! When someone finally initiated some action, F-16s were scrambled not from Andrews AFB only 12 miles away
but from Langley Air Force Base 120 miles from the Pentagon. (What a
brilliant military strategy for a counter attack!)

To top off this peculiar event, the F-16's conveniently traveled at 400
mph, well under their 1500 mph capacity and of course they didn't make
it in time to the Pentagon. Because this was a clear violation of standard
operating procedures, we should have seen and heard of the reprimands,
but there were none (also see #24). When those in charge of protecting the
people are actually the ones committing the crime, it is always the "perfect
crime," because it always goes uninvestigated.

Two months prior to 9-11, the FAA, FEMA, NORAD, DOD and the
White House were engaged in at least 35 drills including a series of elaborate war games, anti-terror drills and hijack field training exercises (FTX).
They had five drills on the very morning of 9-11; Operation Northern Vigilance, Biowarfare Exercise Triopod II, Operation Vigilant Guardian, Operation Northern Guardian and Operation Vigilant Warrior. One drill
covering New York City involved hijacked planes used as missiles to attack
prominent buildings! MASCAL, a mock terrorist exercise, was held in the

conference room of the secretary of defense on October 24-26, 2000. This exercise required emergency response teams, members of the defense protective services and U.S. government officials to conduct emergency simulations in preparation for possible attacks on the Pentagon headquarters at the hands of incoming passenger planes. (It seems they didn't learn much, doesn't it?)

3. Heat from burning jet fuel was reportedly the sole cause of the WTC collapses. What a ludicrous, ridiculous theory, but even many of America's engineers bought it. Consider this:

A. Steel melts at 2,750°F.

B. The steel in the towers was certified by Underwriters Laboratories Inc. to withstand 2000°F for 6 hours!

C. Jet fuel produces a maximum temperature of 1,800°F in a special combustion chamber. These theories that claim the steel melted from the jet fuel fire simply violate the laws of physics. Also, steel frame buildings have *never* collapsed due to fires. (Witness the hotel fires in Los Angeles, Las Vegas and Madrid that burned for days in recent history.) Steel frame buildings cannot collapse at free-fall speed, symmetrically, straight down into a relatively small pile of rubble due to fire. That's a fact. Further, one of the high-ranking NYC fire chiefs wrote an article for the December 2001 issue of one of the industry's leading magazines pointing out that in all the years of recorded firefighting, there has *never* been the first incident of a skyscraper falling because of the heat from within. He went on to highlight the famous cases in recent years in Los Angeles, Nevada and Spain, where the high-rise hotels had burned *for days without collapse*, yet we are supposed to believe not one, not two but three skyscrapers collapsed from this very problem in a matter of minutes. (Did you even know about the third one? Most Americans didn't, because of the suppressed news coverage, but we will come to it shortly.)

WTC maintenance workers confirm massive explosions in the sub-basement area that closely coincided with the aircraft impacts on the upper floors. FDNY rescuers also confirm coordinated explosions "like demolition charges" in the North Tower, as they escaped. The MSM conveniently failed to show these witnesses. According to civil engineering professor Hyman Brown, the WTC's construction manager, WTC 1 and 2 were designed to survive an impact and resulting fires from a collision by the largest commercial aircraft at the time, a Boeing 707, carrying 23,000 gallons of fuel. He also stated the towers "could have easily withstood multiple airplane crashes."

Another feature that would be expected only if explosives were used to slice the steel columns would be molten steel and its massive existence at the WTC site was indeed reported by several witnesses, including the two main figures involved in the clean up, Peter Tully, president of Tully Construction and Mark Loizeaux, president of Controlled Demolition, Inc. Tully said that he saw pools of "literally molten steel" at the site. Loizeaux said that several weeks after 9-11, when the rubble was being removed, "hot spots of molten steel" were found "at the bottoms of the elevator shafts of the main towers, down seven basement levels."

Hot spots were recorded up to 1377°F five days *after* 9-11! To top off this peculiar event, the steel structures and columns were quickly removed from the site (before any examination and to the objection of fire safety officials, firefighters and victims' families) and shipped to China and India to be recycled. (The real cause of the collapses was a highly sophisticated controlled demolition, obvious to anyone who has ever seen one.)

4. How did WTC 7 collapse when no plane hit it? The collapse of Building 7 was later admitted to be a demolition by owner Larry Silverstein on a PBS interview in Sept. 2002. In a phone call with the FDNY chief regarding Building 7, he said "We've had such terrible loss of life; maybe the smartest thing to do is pull it. And they made that decision to pull it and we watched the building collapse," referring to the demolition of building 7. Silverstein later claimed "pull it" meant to evacuate firefighters, but since there were no firefighters in the building at that late date, nobody bought it. "Pull it" is industry lingo telling someone to "hit the demolition button."

Also, the FDNY is not equipped or trained to "pull" any building in a controlled demolition as Silverstein stated. Nor can any building be prepared for such a well-designed demolition in the few minutes after Silverstein asked to "pull it". It takes days, even weeks for a large one, to prepare a building to "pull it." Are we to believe that the Salomon Brothers Building (WTC-7) was prepped during the day of September 11th, *after* the initial attacks at 8:45 and 9:02 a.m.? Silverstein's whole quickly contrived cover story was "Bravo Sierra." (For you non-pilots who haven't checked the earlier footnote yet, that's the aeronautical alphabet connoting "B.S." Everything they ever told us was B.S. Oh, I said that, didn't I!)

Coincidentally, Silverstein assumed a 99-year lease on the WTC towers on July 24th, just six weeks before September 11, 2001. After the attacks, Silverstein boldly asserted he was entitled to twice the insurance policy value because "The two hijacked airliners that struck the 110-story twin towers Sept. 11 were separate 'occurrences' for insurance purposes," entitling him to collect twice on $3.6 billion collective worth of the policies, or $7.2 billion. Now is it likely that maybe we can figure out why he wanted Building 7 to collapse? Is it not much more prudent to pay the scoundrel off than let the cat out of the bag? The official FEMA report on WTC 7 concludes "The specifics of the fires in WTC 7 and how they caused the building to collapse remain unknown at this time." (Oh, yes. You guys are brilliant investigators.)

5. Many do *not* believe that the U.S. government is capable or quite so ruthless as to murder Americans to justify a war in Iraq. Whether you are one of these or not, it would expand your education to read about "Operation Northwoods," which shows the plans that Lyman Lemnitzer and the Joint Chiefs of Staff drew up in 1962 and approved for what may be the most corrupt plan ever created by the U.S. government up to that date.

They proposed launching a secret and bloody war of terrorism against their own country in order to trick the American public into supporting an ill-conceived war they intended to launch against Cuba. The plan called for innocent people to be shot on American streets; a commercial plane full of college students to be shot down (hmmm, do you mean like TWA 800 in 1996?); a wave of violent terrorism to be launched in Washington, D.C., Miami and elsewhere. They also contemplated causing U.S. military casualties, writing: "We could blow up a U.S. ship in Guantanamo Bay and blame Cuba," and "casualty lists in U.S. newspapers would cause a helpful wave of national indignation."

People would be framed for bombings they did not commit; planes would be hijacked. Using phony evidence, all of it would be blamed on Castro, thus giving Lemnitzer and his cabal the excuse as well as the public and international backing they needed to launch their war. Does this sound familiar in recent times?

6. Why the strange pattern of debris from the Flight 93 crash in Penn-

sylvania? Where is the plane? Where are the bodies? Wally Miller, Sumerset County coroner, stated, "I stopped being coroner after about 20 minutes because there were no bodies there."

Cleveland, Ohio Mayor Michael White reported: "A Boeing 767 out of Boston made an emergency landing Tuesday at Cleveland-Hopkins International Airport due to concerns that it may [might] have a bomb aboard. The plane had been moved to a secure area of the airport and was evacuated."

United verified the plane as Flight 93, but was deeply concerned about another jetliner in the vicinity, Flight 175.

The government claims the plane exploded on impact (sometime later outside Shanksville, Pennsylvania), yet a one-ton section of the engine was found over a mile away and other light debris was found scattered over eight miles away. Several witnesses heard "a loud bang" just before the plane began to drop and others saw a small military type plane flying around shortly before UA93 "crashed."

Was Flight 93 shot down with a missile? Many thought so at the moment, the evidence and witness testimony seemed to confirm it and nothing has surfaced in nearly a decade to refute these assumptions.

Secretary of Defense Paul Wolfowitz said, "The Air Force was tracking the hijacked plane that crashed in Pennsylvania and had been in position to bring it down if necessary."

The official theory says Flight 93 crashed at 10:03, but seismic analysis shows 10:06. Is that why there are three minutes missing from the Cockpit Voice Recorders (CVR) and the FBI is still hiding the analysis of the Flight Data Recorder (FDR) and the air traffic control tape from that flight?

How did passengers on Flight 93 make cell phone calls while in flight? Regular cell phones don't work on commercial airliners flying at normal altitudes, contrary to the TV movies and books claiming Todd Beamer called his family prior to saying the heroic, "Let's Roll!" Sorry about the bubble and its bursting, but we don't think it ever happened.

Yes, believe it or not, these calls were likely staged. On February 1, 1999, a new voice morphing technology was introduced to Gen. Carl Steiner (former commander-in-chief, U.S. Special Operations Command) at the Los Alamos National Laboratory in New Mexico. By taking a 10-minute digital recording of Steiner's voice, scientist George Papcun was able to clone his speech patterns and develop an accurate facsimile so exact it even fooled Steiner himself. He was so impressed, he asked for a copy of the tape.

7. The invasion of Iraq was actually planned back in 1992 (during Bush I) by Cheney, Wolfowitz, Rumsfeld, Perle and Lewis Libby in their "Defense Planning Guidance." They later audaciously proposed a basic blueprint for U.S. world domination in PNAC's "Rebuilding America's Defenses." PNAC's Sept. 2000 Statement of Principles—which states "the process of transformation, even if it brings revolutionary change, is likely to be a long one, absent some catastrophic and catalyzing event, like a new Pearl Harbor"—would consequently advance their policies, i.e. justify wars and "regime changes". When they got back into power in 2001 they had an opportunity to enact their plan. The problem was that they needed a catalyst, an event that would justify these invasions. The preliminary plans were put into action during the first week of the new Bush Administration in January 2001, when the "Patriot Act" was first put on paper. Shortly after that, Secretary of State Condoleezza Rice and others said, "We need a new Pearl Harbor."

Their operational plans were then drawn up in June 2001 and 9-11 was treated as a Pearl Harbor pretext. Their original basis for war was to unseat the Taliban. They were claiming that the primary reason for these hostilities would be the Taliban's unwillingness to cooperate with UN inspectors, a pretext that would have not gone over well. They received a better pretext for attacking with the 9-11 attacks. Of course what they really wanted was to aggressively expand U.S. (globalist) influence throughout the region and eventually secure a pipeline through Afghanistan for the benefit of UNOCAL and other big globalist oil companies.

Another "smoking gun" is the Downing Street memo, which contains an overview of a secret July 23, 2002 meeting where British intelligence officials visited Washington informing Prime Minister Tony Blair that war was nearly inevitable with Iraq.

8. Usually in high crimes, investigators follow the money trail to find the perpetrator. Not in this case of never-ending coincidences and anomalies, however. On September 10, Pakistan's Inter-Services Intelligence (ISI) agent Ahmed Omar Saeed Sheikh made a wire transfer of $100,000 to Mohamed Atta's bank account in Florida at the instruction of Gen. Mah-

moud Ahmad, the Director of the ISI. "Money man" Gen. Ahmad was in Washington on 9-11, arriving on Sept. 4. He first met with CIA Director George Tenet until Sept. 9 and then met with officials in the Pentagon, the NSC and the State Department on Sept. 13. The chairmen of the House and Senate Intelligence committees Porter Goss and Bob Graham had breakfast with Gen. Ahmad on Capitol Hill the very morning of Sept. 11! (Can you say conflict of interest?!) Due to pressure from the Bush administration, General Ahmad was subsequently forced to resign on October 8, 2001, effectively blocking any further investigation into the matter. (How convenient!)

9. Whatever happened to the anthrax sent by terrorists? The letters contained a specific type of high quality mil-spec weaponized anthrax made only by a U.S. military lab at USAMRIID Fort Detrick, Maryland. When the FBI discovered that the end of the hunt for the sender of the anthrax letters was not Dr. Ayaad Assaad the Egyptian, but Dr. Philip Zack, who is Jewish, both the FBI and the media stopped making any public comments on the case! The targets of the anthrax attacks were the senators who opposed the Patriot Act. (Coincidentally, since Nov. 2001, over 80 microbiologists have died under suspicious circumstances, most specializing in vaccines and bio-weapons research—very suspicious.) And why was Dick Cheney's staff ordered to take the antibiotic Cipro weeks before the first anthrax attacks began?

10. Why did the Bush administration endorse a forgery about Iraq's nuclear program? On September 24, 2002, George Tenet, Director of Central Intelligence, stated to the Senate Foreign Relations Committee that the CIA. had recently received "intelligence" showing that, between 1999 and 2001, Iraq had attempted to buy 500 tons of uranium oxide from Niger. Bush even mentioned this in his State of the Union Message, on January 28, 2003. However, on March 7, 2003, Mohamed ElBaradei, the director general of the International Atomic Energy Agency, in Vienna, told the UN Security Council that the documents involving the Niger-Iraq uranium sale were fakes. One senior IAEA official went further. He told us, "These documents are so bad that I cannot imagine that they came from a serious intelligence agency. It depresses me, given the low quality of the documents, that it was not stopped. At the level it reached, I would have expected more checking." Another official said that the IAEA has not been

able to determine who actually prepared the documents. "It could be someone who intercepted faxes in Israel. We don't know. Somebody got old letterheads and signatures and cut and pasted."

11. Where are the flight recorders ("black boxes")? The FBI says the recorders for flights 77 and 93 were found, but claims they were "too damaged to provide any record. As for the WTC planes, two N.Y. City firefighters, Mike Bellone and Nicholas De Masi, claimed that they had found three of these four boxes, but federal agents took them and told the two men not to mention having found them. Another source from the NTSB also says these boxes "were in fact recovered and were analyzed by the NTSB, but you'd have to get the official word from the FBI as to where they are." (Nice cover-up again, FBI. Everything you have ever told us about this case, Oklahoma City, Waco, TWA 800, Vince Foster and a hundred others was just another lie.)

12. Did you know that the 9-11 Commission Executive Director Phillip Zelikow had incestuous conflicts of interest with the Bush administration? Shortly after 9-11 he was on the President's Foreign Intelligence Advisory Board up until he became executive director. He also co-authored a book with Condoleezza Rice about their experiences in the first Bush White House. Chairman Thomas Kean was director of oil giant Amerada Hess; had business ties to Saudi Khalid bin Mahfouz; co-chairman of Homeland Security Project; and CFR member. This commission stank worse than the Warren Commission of 40 years earlier. Furthermore, an official investigation of the attacks cannot be taken seriously when it took 14 months to authorize it, was then underfunded and obstructed, was then staffed only by government insiders who failed to ask hundreds of questions posed by victims' families and excluded important information provided by whistleblowers. The few documents it was given had to be filtered through the White House for approval, it based its whole premise on proving the "official theory," and allowed the FAA timeline to be changed.

13. Why was the budget for the 9-11 Commission investigation initially just $3 million (later raised to $15 million)? Compare that to the commission budgets for the Space Shuttle *Columbia* crash and Clinton's Whitewater scandal, which were both given $50 million!

And why did the Bush Administration wait 411 days to form the 9-11 investigation commission? Compare that to just six days for the *Titanic*, seven days for the JFK assassination (phony as that was), seven days for the *Challenger* tragedy and nine days for Pearl Harbor. And to top this off, the commission only released 25% of the 11,000 documents requested! (Talk about dragging one's feet!)

14. How did Bush see the first plane crash into the building on live TV when it wasn't shown anywhere until September 12? (Our guess is he saw it on his closed circuit live camera feed that was already set up to view their operation.)

15. Why did put option purchases on United Airlines and American Airlines stock rise above six times the normal levels in the days preceding 9-11? Abundant evidence shows that a number of transactions in financial markets indicated specific (and criminal, let us not forget again) fore-knowledge of the 9-11 attacks. Between September 6 and 7, the Chicago Board Options Exchange saw purchases of 4,744 put options (predicting a lower future price) on UA, but only 396 call options (predicting a higher future price). On September 10, 4,516 put options on AA were bought, compared to only 748 call options. On September 10, the volume of trading in AMR put option contracts increased to 60 times the daily average and almost five times the total of all $30 put options traded before September 10.

In the case of at least one of these trades—which has left a $2.5 million prize unclaimed—the firm used to place the "put options" on United Airlines stock was, until 1998, managed by A.B. "Buzzy" Krongard who is now executive director of the CIA. (You can't purchase stock, futures, mutual funds or put options without providing your identity! The FBI, CIA and SEC know who made these purchases. Why aren't they telling anyone else!?)

16. Why were the bin Laden and Saud families (142 people total) permitted by the FBI and the White House to fly out of the U.S. on private jets on September 13 when all other private flights were still grounded by the FAA? In June of 2004, Tampa Bay International airport verified that this flight indeed took place. And why did Bush stop all investigations into the bin Laden family before 9-11? The FBI documents "199-I" (indicating a national security case) show that the FBI was pulled off the trail of Abdullah and Omar bin Laden in 1996—and reopened Sept. 19, 2001, eight days after 9-11.

17. How did they find Mohammed Atta's and Satam al-Sugami's passport, which magically survived, unscathed, the plane crash, explosion, fire, over 200,000 tons of steel and 425,000 cubic yards of concrete totaling 1.2 million tons of rubble? Yet they can't locate the flight recorders from either plane? And who "found" them and at what time did they "find" these? This is the real outrageous conspiracy theory. (I have an idea, why doesn't Boeing design a new data recorder manufactured from the same indestructible material used to produce magical Saudi passports?)

18. Why are none of the hijackers' names on the official UA and AA airline passenger lists? In fact, there are no Arabic names whatsoever! And how are nine (of 19) hijackers still alive and well? The Egyptian lawyer Muhammad Atta, father of engineer Muhammad al-Ameer Atta, denied his son's involvement in these operations. In a statement to the London-based *al-Sharq al-Awsat* daily, Muhammad explained that his son phoned him after the attacks and did not talk about the 9-11 incidents. He expressed his conviction that his son's identity was stolen and believes the Israeli Mossad murdered him a day later.

19. You may ask how and when the bombs were planted in the towers. There were plenty of opportunities to plant bombs with low risk of detection. Here are a few examples:

• Ben Fountain, a 42-year-old-financial analyst who worked in the South Tower, said the weeks before 9-11 there were numerous unanswered and unusual drill exercises where sections of both the twin towers and WTC 7 were evacuated for "security reasons".

• Bomb-sniffing dogs were inexplicably removed from the twin towers five days before 9-11

• Scott Forbes, working for Fiduciary Trust in the 97th floor of the South Tower, reported that there was a 36 hour "power down" in the upper half of the South Tower on September 8–9 to complete a "cabling upgrade" (this would have been on the weekend prior to 9-11) where, security systems consequently were shut down and many workers ran around busily doing things unobserved. They were informed by Port Authority three weeks prior to this.

Yet another coincidence, a Bush-linked company, Stratesec, handled security for three clients that figured prominently in the attack:—United Airlines; Dulles International Airport where AA FL 77 was hijacked; and the World Trade Center itself. The president's brother, Marvin P. Bush and his cousin, Wirt D. Walker III, were principals in Stratesec, with Walker acting as CEO from 1999 until January 2002 and Marvin reportedly in New York on 9-11.

20. Why were General Richard Myers of the Joint Chief of Staff and Sen. Max Cleland in a meeting on September 11, until after the Pentagon was struck, completely unaware of the attacks? Why did Gen. Montague Winfield, the director of the NMCC or "war room" located in the Pentagon, request on September 10 that someone stand in for him in the "war room" on September 11, between 8:30 a.m. and 10:30 a.m.?

21. On Wednesday September 12, 2001, Tom Kenney, a spokesman for FEMA's "National Urban Search and Rescue Team" during an interview on national TV with CBS news anchor Dan Rather, let slip a frightening truth. Mr. Kenney told Dan Rather, "We were one of the first teams that was deployed to support the City of New York in this disaster. We arrived on late Monday night, September 10th and went right into action on Tuesday morning" (September 11). This was validated by former NY mayor, Rudy Giuliani when he testified to the 9-11 Commission during the May 18-19, 2004 hearings in NY that FEMA was in fact there the day before for a Project "Tripod II" terror drill that was scheduled for 9-12! (What a coincidence!) Yet FEMA denies all of this!

22. Mayor Giuliani in an interview with Peter Jennings on ABC News stated: "We were operating out of there [the Emergency Command Center on the 23rd floor of WTC-7] when we were told that the World Trade Center was gonna collapse and it did collapse before we could get out of the building." What a remarkable statement. There was no publicly available reason to believe that the towers were going to collapse. After all, steel-frame high-rise buildings had never before collapsed because of fire. Yet Giuliani's statement suggests that he somehow knew—he says he was told by someone—that the towers were going to collapse. (Who told him the towers were about to collapse? How could anyone have known this in advance unless it was a planned demolition? Were they warning only "their own"?)

23. On October 26, 2001 George Bush signed the misnamed USA PATRIOT Act, which was proposed just five days after 9-11 and just six weeks later this bill was passed. It is *impossible* for a bill to be conceived, written,

debated and passed this quickly. In actuality, this bill had been written during the early days of the Bush administration the previous January and the bill needed this disaster to justify its passage. In addition, testimony by Rep. Ron Paul revealed that most members of Congress were compelled to vote for the bill without even reading it. This was a vote to eliminate the Constitutional Bill of Rights, which has defined American freedom for 200 years and it was accomplished when legislators voted for the bill without even reading it.

24. Initially the military reported on 9-11 that no fighters were sent up to intercept the hijacked planes until after the Pentagon was hit. Later the same week, the military put out a second story, saying that it had sent up fighters but because the FAA had been late in notifying it about the hijackings, the fighters arrived too late. The 9-11 Commission also reported a third version that the FAA gave the military insufficient warning of the first hijacked airline and no warning of the other hijackings until after they had crashed. (Why did the military change its story two times?)

25. Why was the District of Columbia Air National Guard website mission statement significantly changed immediately after 9-11? The DCANG mission BEFORE 9-11 read: "To provide combat units in the highest possible state of readiness. We will support the Air Force and other DOD agencies. We will provide operational support to our local communities whenever possible." The DCANG mission statement AFTER 9-11 reads: "Capital Guardians, patriotic Americans, supporting and defending the United States of America and the nation's capital when directed by the president in order *to ensure the survival and success of liberty.*" The post-9-11 mission now has to be directed by the president in order to do anything. (What a peculiar and coincidental change!?)

26. Did you know that the U.S. financed, armed and trained al Qaeda? After Russian troops invaded Afghanistan in 1979, the CIA financed (with billions of dollars), armed and trained bin Laden and thousands of other Mujahideen rebels. (Reagan called them "freedom fighters") The name "al Qaeda" as an organization was first used in early 2001, when the U.S. government decided to prosecute Bin Laden in his absence (for the Aug '98 bombings of U.S. embassies in Kenya and Tanzania that killed 224 people) *and had to use anti-Mafia laws that required the existence of a named criminal organization.*

27. What about the president's odd behavior at the elementary school? After hearing about the second plane attack, President Bush sat down with a classroom of second graders and began a 20-minute pre-planned photo op. Bush's behavior is made even more astounding by the fact that his Secret Service would have had to assume that he was one of the intended targets. One Secret Service agent, seeing the television coverage of the crash of the second airliner into the WTC, reportedly said: "We're out of here." He was obviously overruled. Why wasn't the president immediately "whisked" out (as he later falsely claimed he was) and protected? The terrorists could have targeted the president, along with the 200+ people at the school. The Secret Service breached all standard procedures and allowed President Bush to remain at a highly publicized location for 25 minutes after it was known that the nation was supposedly under attack.

28. Did you know that there is a remarkable "signature" of the 9-11 attacks? They occurred exactly 11 years to the day after President George Bush Senior gave a major address to Congress entitled, "Toward a New World Order." That address was on September 11, 1990. Precisely 11 years to the day later, American Airlines Flight 11 started the attacks of 9-11-2001 when it slammed into the north tower of the World Trade Center. The towers, of course, symbolized a huge 11 over the skies of New York. The Pentagon was modeled after the satanic symbol of the pentagram. Another fact about the Pentagon is that its ground-breaking ceremony and beginning of construction, took place on September 11th 1941. Of course, 911 has been the emergency phone number in the U.S. since the '70s. What better way to start an era of a perpetual war and a perpetual state of emergency, than using a date that was already numerically etched into the minds of people as a number associated with "emergency"? Numerology and symbolism are very important to the occult, to which many of our leaders belong. And their main goal is a "New World Order," with them in charge. Occultists believe the number "11" is important to the coming Antichrist.

These are just a few of the hundreds of unanswered questions that the Bush administration didn't want us to know. With but a simple study of the facts, any open-minded person will see that the official incompetence theory is the real "outrageous theory."

What's it all for? Power and money. The truth of 9-11 is difficult for most people to swallow because it takes them down roads they don't want to go. We are not paving the road to tyranny here, just exposing what has been done by very powerful people. When we research 9-11 facts, we find more of the hand of intelligence involved at every single step of this elaborate cover-up. This truth needs to be exposed before their next attack is aimed at furthering their agenda.

Knowing the truth allows us to make sense of the chaos America is going through such as the lies we've been told about the Saddam-9-11 connection and WMD's, illegal torturing and murders at Guantanamo and Abu Ghraib, the never-ending Iraq War soon to move to Iran and Syria, the NSA secretly spying on Americans (and getting away with it), the phony bird and swine flu pandemics, RFID chips that are to be implanted in people's arms for our own "protection," the Security and Prosperity Partnership of North America (North American Union) that will take away America's borders and turn the dollars into ameros and merge us all into a globalist society under one-world rule. You will also realize why PATRIOT Acts I and II were rushed through Congress without being read and how these laws actually take away rights rather than protect anything other than government "snoopervision."

"[T]he people can always be brought to the bidding of the leaders. That is easy. All you have to do is tell them they are being attacked and denounce the pacifists for lack of patriotism and for exposing the country to danger. It works the same in every country."—Hermann Goering, Hitler's Reich Marshal, at the Nuremberg Trials after World War II.

The attack on America on September 11, 2001 was an inside job. Face it, America, and go to the next step of understanding who your real enemy actually is.

Those who cannot believe the facts need to cure themselves of an ailment we have referred to as "Red, White & Blue Fever." Psychologists call it "Cognitive Dissonance." Cognitive Dissonance is the inability to proceed with clear thinking due to previous information clogging the credulity pipeline.

We coined it "Red, White & Blue Fever" a few months after 9-11, after we discovered so many people simply could not believe the irrefutable facts of their government's involvement.

No one seems to know whence this malady first came, but we can tell you that George M. Cohan (*Yankee Doodle Dandy*), Irving Berlin (*God Bless America*), John Wayne and the WWII movies were some of the first carriers. Another early spreader was James Stewart and *The FBI Story* in 1955 and TV's Efram Zimbalist Jr. with the FBI years-long series of the 1960s. In the '70s and '80s, it was more TV and movies featuring our "heroes" from the Korean and Vietnam conflicts who were unable to solve anything, yet were able to fraudulently coat themselves in the same patriotism that inspired the nation to win in 1942-45. In the '90s it was that skinny-shouldered imbecilic Lee Greenwood with his ridiculous *I'm Proud to Be an American* [". . . where at least I know I'm free"] that is still heard blasting from today's propaganda radio from the car flashing the bumper stickers that remind us to "Support Our Troops."

Now while I know that the previous paragraph will not offend anyone free of the malady, we still must address ourselves to those readers who have not shaken that fever yet. This is the reason for this long discussion of most utterly absurd "conspiracy theory" of all—that official story released by the U.S. government.

Do you remember that clumsy bozo posing-as-a-Christian ("The Constitution is a goddamned piece of paper") president who managed to fool enough people in the 2000 election to persuade the Supreme Court justices to appoint him as CEO of the American corporation, George II? He was the one who said that "they" hate us because of our freedoms! The only Americans stupider than he were the idiots who believed him and said, "Yeah, yeah, let's kill all the Arabs."

(And here is the point where all the dumbed-down, Bush-enamored, TV news worshipping, government school graduates will part from me. But they must be forgiven when we consider that their only source of news has been the controlled mainstream media and that they are only parroting lies that they believe to be true. However, we must ask ourselves and them just who is more dangerous: the liar or the people who believe the lies?)

So America sent troops into Afghanistan. Had there ever been a peep about Afghanistan attacking us on 9-11 or any other time? No, and there also was no peep about the oil-pumping pipeline running through there that needed to be captured by Bush/Cheney Inc. for control of the oil. This took about a year or so and then it was on to Iraq.

When Matthew Hoh, a senior Foreign Service officer and former Marine captain, resigned his post in Afghanistan, his action reverberated as far as the White House, not only because of his superb credentials but also because of his view that the presence of U.S. troops is fueling the insurgency.

"They are only fighting because we are there," he said.

Did anyone ever accuse any Iraqis of instigating or participating in the 9-11 attacks in New York and/or Washington, D.C.? Not that we ever saw reported anywhere, but suddenly American troops were slaughtering innocent women and children in Iraq—all under the auspices of "protecting our freedoms."

Did you ever lose any sleep worrying about Saddam Hussein attacking your home town or any other in America? I didn't. Yet the overseas reports (unpublished in America) claim that over 1 million innocents have been murdered by the American insurgents in order to "protect your freedoms." Did you really sleepily buy that? And just what would you be doing about it, should the situation be reversed and a foreign army was shooting and bombing your hometown every day and night?

Because of the news blackout, we were not allowed to know (without our own private research) that Osama bin Laden had been a CIA operative for 20 years prior to the 9-11 attacks for which he was so conveniently blamed. He not only was friendly with the whole Bush clan but had actually been in the oil business with George I. (See *The Unauthorized Biography of George Bush* by Webster Tarpley.)

We can best explain this with the wonderful little tongue-in-cheek satire originally composed by Matt Kjeldsen that follows. Forty-seven years ago we were "amazed" how the elusive and magical Lee Harvey Oswald could have (A) been in the second-floor lunchroom at the TSBD, composed and unconcerned, when only 90 seconds earlier he had been on the sixth floor shooting the president of the United States three times from the rear; (B) been stupid enough to shoot a policeman and not only empty his gun of shells on the street to offer traceable evidence back to himself but also drop his wallet containing picture I.D. of himself on the street; and (C) manage to pull the communication plug on Washington DC for the first hour (1:30 to 2:30 EST) following the JFK assassination, thereby shutting down the complete telephone system in the district.

Yes, that Lee Harvey Oswald was one (actually two, which we have already shown you) remarkable dude. So was Osama bin Laden, if we are to believe the legends.

[Note: Bin Laden was a CIA operative until shortly after Sept. 11, 2001, when he realized he was being used as a scapegoat and had been double-crossed by his masters. The oil business associations between the Bush family and the bin Laden family have been tracked back to 1980 as a certainty and likely a few years before that. Before proceeding to the tongue-in-cheek fun-making of the ridiculous official story, the reader should understand that fact of collusion.]

FAIRYTALE MAGIC OF THE BIN LADEN LEGEND

This is a shorter, rewritten version of various verifiable pieces of information compiled for Internet publication over the past several years. All of the facts are documented and can be seen in factual detail by performing a simple computer Internet search for "9-11 Truth" or anything similar. This is meant to poke fun at the foolish and ridiculous "coincidence theorists" who enjoy disparaging truth with the foolhardy blanket of "conspiracy" whenever it doesn't fit their fabrications. The bottom line again was/is: everything they ever told us was a lie.

Most people hate and fear Osama bin Laden the boogeyman [the legend]. He is accused of being a mass murderer and an enemy of free people. That being said, let us give the man credit for what he can do: the man is an amazing magician. He is, undeniably, far more talented than David Copperfield and all of the illusionists of today and any day. Once one buys into the official story, one has to agree that Osama's sleight-of- hand, his mind control performances and his supernatural theatrics far surpass those of anyone.

Bin Laden is a known recluse and his video and audio appearances have been few and far between. This adds to the mystique. We must assume that there is a lot of pressure on his shoulders to top the 9-11 performance. Clearly, it was a masterpiece performance. Let's revisit the 9-11 scenario and dissect it for the myriad of smaller illusions that became the master illusion and solidified Osama bin Laden's name [legend] into the annals of magic. The facts that follow can be verified and the assertion that bin Laden is the best illusionist of all time will either be confirmed or the big government lie will be exposed.

Let's talk about the little stuff first. His assistants were able to board four different planes without being recorded on security cameras and without appearing on any of the passenger lists. None of his assistants had the ability to fly a jet airliner. Most were already working with the CIA and yet they agreed to the stunt. And finally, none of their bodies or DNA has ever been found. From Afghanistan, bin Laden was able to fool the cameras and four ticket agents, drive planes precisely into targets and then make his assistants disappear without a trace. This is classic David Copperfield stuff, but this performance was just beginning. You won't believe what happened next. Oh, yes you will, I forgot. You saw it all on TV, didn't you?

Then, with his mind-bending magic, Osama was able to sidestep, confuse and defeat NORAD, the most sophisticated air defense system on Earth, and, therewith, prevent every single person in charge of defending the United States from doing his job and even performing his default options.

Once again, from a cave in Afghanistan, bin Laden was able to schedule his performance on the exact same day that several war games and several terror drills were all running. It is for this reason that we must assume that he is a master clairvoyant as well as a magician.

Most of our fighter jets were in Alaska and northern Canada as a part of Operation Northern Vigilance. Put this site in your browser and have a look: http://en.wikipedia.org/wiki/War_games_in_progress_on_September_11,_2001

Global Guardian was running in conjunction with Vigilant Guardian. In essence, this is a massive nuclear air defense drill that puts blips all over radar screens and involves the United States Strategic Command in conjunction with Air Force Space Command and NORAD. But there is one drill he emulated, that really speaks to his genius. *A National Reconnaissance Office drill was being run exactly in conjunction with Osama's real life performance that simulated a plane flying into a building.* Excepting some sort of mental clairvoyant advantage, he could not have known this, but just how coincidental with precision timing can you get?

In addition to that, FEMA was running a bio-terrorism drill in New York City that morning in conjunction with Mayor Giuliani's running Tripod 2—an emergency management drill where he and all of his staff were well clear of their state of the art command center in WTC 7. It is indeed amazing that bin Laden could have known about all of these opportunities to use as distractions for his audience.

Bin Laden had to know that the default protocol for aircraft that veer from their flight paths is a [required] scramble and interception by U.S. air defense. At that point, the aircraft either corrects its course or is escorted to landing; or is shot down. 67 aircraft had been escorted to landing in 2001 through September 10th. Yet, on September 11th, in a performance that lasted for an hour and a half, four airliners all veered off course, not one interceptor was scrambled in time and three of the four reached their targets, precisely and accurately.

[Red Alert: if all this is not evidence of an "inside job," what more do you need? Oh, that? Okay, coming up.]

But frankly, the even more mystifying feat was the long-distance mind control over Vice President Dick Cheney performed by Osama from his cave halfway around the world. Was he manipulating a microwave beam from a satellite in space directly into Cheney's head in the White House hideaway?

Cheney watched from the White House as the last radar blip came toward Washington, D.C. He wasn't evacuated from the White House. He never ordered the blip intercepted. He never ordered the blip shot down. He never ordered the Pentagon to use its ground to air defense system. He never stood up and shouted, "Why isn't our air defense system following protocol?" This is sworn testimony by Transportation Secretary Norman Mineta before the 9-11 Commission. Nothing short of mind control could have triggered this collaboration with the enemy (a treasonous offense) by no less than the Vice President of the United States. To minimize damage and loss of life, bin Laden directed the plane into the only part of the Pentagon building to be recently reinforced to sustain such a hit [and where the exposers of the neo-cons were working].

Not being satisfied with the simple display of accuracy and the Keystone Cop confusion caused by his trans-Pacific Jedi mind tricks, Bin Laden went for the inexplicable and the supernatural monster finale. Osama the Magnificent was then able to effect the collapse into dust of not just one, not only two, but three skyscrapers, as if they were destroyed by carefully placed, incendiary devices. By not supplying an energy source for the free fall speed disintegrations of three skyscrapers, Osama bin Laden literally suspended the laws of physics right before our eyes! Keep in mind that only two of the buildings were hit by planes. The third fell as an encore seven hours later. There was some damage to a corner and 2 fires, but it pretty much looked like an intact, 47-story building that crimped and fell in six seconds. All that remained of three skyscrapers was severed steel, dust, flying paper and molten metal fires that burned at over 2,000 degrees for two more months in the sub-floors.

End of show. Or, was it?

Only after coming to terms with the absolute horror of this magic show did we realize that Osama bin Laden, from a cave in Afghanistan and on dialysis, had made the Pentagon jet airliner disappear as well. However, the aluminum jet airliner that hit the Pentagon pierced three rings of heavily enforced concrete and yet left no holes for the wings or tail section. Little pieces were picked up by government men, carted away under a tarp and never seen again. Apparently, he was able to make wings disappear; titanium engines disappear and the entire fuselage disappear! He's also still using mind control on government officials, because to this day they have refused to let us see the 84 surveillance tapes from the Pentagon and from the surrounding businesses that the FBI stole for him just minutes after the show. It must be a magicians' code thing.

Osama performed the same basic trick with the Flight 93 crash in Pennsylvania, except he added a little touch of art to it. The fuselage, tail section and the titanium engines all vaporized just as at the Pentagon, but he made debris bounce back eight miles from a plane that was flown straight down into the ground. It is these added touches that make him so masterful, so brilliant. Terrorist, magician and artist all rolled into one.

But don't stop at this point, dear reader, to praise his superb expertise quite yet. You must not miss the pure genius of this masterpiece. It turns out that once again, just when the audience thought there could not possibly be any more, the true climax is revealed. As if toying with us, Osama in December finally releases a video taking credit for the performance. But, the video was a fake, with a right handed actor playing the role of left handed Bin Laden. It was a hoax, but why?

The U.S. then vowed to hunt him down and smoke him out of his hole. But, just like the steel from the World Trade Center, nearly all of the black boxes and an actual investigation, bin Laden vanished into thin air. In September, he was the most "wanted" man on Earth, but six months later, Bush told reporters that he wasn't even interested where Osama might be.

In what turns out to be more mind control, bin Laden had U.S. intelligence draft the Patriot Act in secret before 9-11. Through the unread passage of this bill by a mind-controlled Congress, American citizens lost many of their rights formerly protected by the Constitution. And with continued mind control, the Congress and the president have passed law after law gutting the Constitution. Now all of the freedoms that Osama bin Laden hated us for have been erased by our own government and we've spent a trillion+ dollars brutally attacking a nation that had nothing to do with Osama bin Laden's grand illusion.

Along with the planes, the buildings, his assistants, the U.S. air defense system and any curiosity from our representatives and the press as to how he pulled it off, Osama made something else disappear as well. The final curtain opens back up to reveal an American stage now empty. Before Osama bin Laden's masterpiece of illusion we now call 9-11, that stage was filled with freedoms.

Now I ask you, how magical is that?

[Tongue now removed from cheek, we can only conclude that Cheney is the legendary Osama! If you have been at least temporarily relieved of your Red, White & Blue Fever, you have to concur.]

Except for the value of the oil pipeline, can anyone suggest why the 9-11 fake attack would have been used as an excuse to invade Afghanistan, of all places? In our investigation, we have not uncovered a single piece of paper—either here in the United States or in the treasure trove of information that has turned up in Afghanistan and elsewhere—that mentioned any aspect of the Sept. 11 plot. Only the MSM's mention of Osama bin Laden, supposedly hiding in a cave in Afghanistan, planted the ridiculous scene in the innocent minds of the American people that Afghanistan needs to be attacked "because that's where the evil SOB is hiding."

But even most of them know that the "evil SOB" was not only a CIA asset for two plus decades but a close friend and business partner of George Herbert Walker Bush in the international oil business for that long or longer.

Even bin Laden himself said much the same as Lee Harvey Oswald (#2) said nearly 50 years earlier upon being fingered in the conspiracy: "I am a patsy." Osama bin Laden was just as convenient a set-up as with the case of "Harvey," and he probably discovered too late how he had been used.

On the other hand, considering that his large family from the Boston area and elsewhere was allowed to fly out on September 12th, when all other flights were grounded, showing the protection granted by the U.S. government, indicates that Osama bin Laden might have been part of the overall planning all along and knew that he would be protected.

We can't prove it yet, but the odds are at even money and rising that Osama is not only already dead but has been in exactly that state of inactivity for many years.

However, his ghost remains very handy for the chief deceivers to pull out of the closet whenever it is needed.

Meanwhile, George Bush apparently gave up hunting the ghost only six months after the 9-11 hoax. On September 13, 2001, he said, "The most important thing is for us to find Osama bin Laden. It is our No. 1 priority and we will not rest until we find him."

He couldn't be much more emphatic than that, could he? But six months later to the day, on March 13, 2002, after obviously forgetting what he had said, he lackadaisically told another press conference (following a question on the same subject):"I don't know where he is. I have no idea and really don't care. It's not that important. It's not a priority."

With the mission of fooling the American and world public already accomplished, one can readily see how the "#1 one priority" became no priority at all in only six months.

George Bush II was a fraud who fooled the good people of America.

SOME SIGNIFICANT TIDBITS

• The company that Todd Beamer's dad worked for had a $4 million contract at the renovated section of the Pentagon that Flight 77 supposedly hit.

• There are no records of the famous "phone call" Todd supposedly made and experts have shown how it probably was contrived through electronically engineered voice-manipulation called "morphing."

• The planes from which Barbara Olson supposedly made her "collect call" to her husband had credit card slots on every seat. You needed a credit card to get access to the phone system. "Collect calls" were not an available service.

• Her husband, Solicitor General of the U.S. Ted Olson, gave three different versions of what supposedly happened that day—each time wrapping himself in new lies.

• All commercial aircraft are equipped with remote control anti-hi jacking devices tested in April. When the Germans learned of this device on craft they had purchased from the U.S., they removed the American computers and replaced them with their own.

• Were the 9-11 pictures pulled from TV and other "news" programs because people were starting to see the pictures did not match the government's official stories?

• As anyone not totally mesmerized by the bewitching words and pictures crafted by Dan Rather, Tom Brokaw, Peter Jennings et al. could figure out, it was not a 757 that hit the Pentagon. Even their own reporters (and Pentagon employees) on the early scene said it was "a bomb" and "an explosion." But even without those sources, logic should take a front seat here.

• Go to any search engine, Google or others, type in "757" and get the same quick education I did. A fully loaded 757 can weigh over 250,000 pounds. It can carry over 11,000 gallons of fuel. This amounts to over 90,000 pounds of fuel alone.

• A 757 fuselage stands 29 feet tall and is 18 feet wide, yet the initial and single hole in the Pentagon before the collapse, was only about 12 feet in diameter. Each engine, mounted about 15 feet away from the body on the wings, weighs over 35,000 pounds. Yet this airplane was packed into that little hole? Whom are they kidding? This is a bigger joke than the Moon walk.

• Seasoned pilots say that if a plane had actually flown into that area that low, it would have had to have hit and scorch the ground before hitting the Pentagon. Yet the lawn is clean of any such tracks.

• Immediately after the explosion, a group of people (strangely, all in business suits) was seen and videotaped going across the lawn picking up pieces of wreckage and putting it in garbage bags. Since when could the wreckage of a 60-ton airplane fit in a few garbage bags? The most visible and recognizable piece was obviously from the wreckage of an American Airlines plane but later proved to be impossible to have come from the alleged plane claimed to have hit the Pentagon. That wreckage pickup, lots of carbon fiber and other subterfuge, has never been seen again.

• No LANDING GEAR, NO LUGGAGE, NO SEATS and NO BODIES were ever found at the Pentagon scene. (Sorry about that yelling, but everything they ever told us about it was a lie and when one lies to me, I get upset.)

• A 757 has a wing span of almost 125 ft. Yet there was no wing damage to the building and no wing debris at the lawn and garden scene.

• Much of the fuel is carried in the wings, yet there was a little fire outside the single hole in the Pentagon but very little and unmistakably, without question, not enough to account for nearly 5,000 gallons of fuel exploding at the scene. Everything they ever told us was a lie.

• Now do the same search with the "767," which is significantly bigger than a 757. It can weigh over 300,000 pounds.

• A look at pictures of the alleged "plane" crashing into the World Trade Center shows only one story of the buildings being damaged and penetrated, not to mention that the planes not only insert themselves completely inside but actually exit partially at the other side, which challenges the Pentagon story. However, our point here is not penetration but overall coverage. The tail of a Boeing 767 is over 40 feet tall.

• A 767 would cover more than three floors of those buildings and with the tail's elevation, an easy four. A 767 would not have gone completely into those buildings. It could not fit between the floors as what allegedly hit them was made to appear to do. An aluminum fuselage crushes upon impact like a beer can underfoot.

While some of the plane would have penetrated the building to the center, the vertical foundation of steel erection would have undoubtedly stopped its forward progress. Certainly, much wing and tail debris, unable to penetrate the structure, would have fallen to the street, but as everyone witnessed, none did. (Let us remember from the demolition videos shown to us a hundred times by MSM via TV that plenty of debris *did* fall to the street prior to collapse when the buildings were imploded in the next hour.)

• If a plane even hit the WTC, it was not a commercial airliner, but much more likely an unmarked military aircraft with a bomb underneath, as proposed with video evidence in Dave von Kleist's documentary, *In Plane Sight*. The video, derived from nothing less than the MSM network news presentations, clearly shows an ignition of light and explosion at the split second the plane enters the edifice. Yup, it was in plain sight.

• The single engine found in the street after the WTC's crashes was not that from a 767, it was proven to be too small and was another deceiving fabrication planted by someone or some agency wishing to perpetuate the myth. The unanswered questions would fill 10 times the pages of the report from the phony 9-11 Commission.

MORE MAGIC FROM OSAMA BIN LADEN:

• Through mind control (as one wag suggests), bin Laden oversees the largest destruction of evidence from a crime scene in history as all of the steel beams from the WTC are cut up, shipped overseas and then melted down.

• First time in history three steel framed buildings collapse from fire.

• First time in history jet airliners vaporize and the NTSB doesn't investigate and doesn't have/put the parts in a hangar to piece together. Mind control of 9-11 Commission patriots—he leads them to leave the hundreds of police, fire fighters and victims, all witnesses, who claimed there were secondary explosions at the WTC and at the Pentagon, out of their final report—ditto for the witnesses who did not see a 757 hit the Pentagon Mind control of all politicians and media personnel—none of them questions even one aspect of the performance, and in fact, they will belittle and disparage any who do. In 2007, Scripps News said it was 34% who now believed the whole plan was an inside job.

SOURCE: http://www.scrippsnews.com/911poll

• In destroying WTC 7, bin Laden wiped out between 300-500 securities fraud cases being investigated and housed there. Stock options were made days prior to 9-11 on United, American and Boeing, betting on the fall of stock. Did Osama make a killing on these or had he just told others so they could make the killing?

SOURCE: http://PatriotsQuestion911.com/ list of military/government experts who question 9-11. "Why isn't bin Laden wanted by the FBI for the 9-11 murders?"

• "Al Qaeda is nothing more than an extension of the operandi linked to U.S. intelligence that was allowed, by script, to remove itself as a rogue breakaway entity of the U.S. government; allowed to de-compartmentalize from oversight and was run instead by rogue black ops specialists for scripted activity outside of the U.S. government, with its funding being orchestrated through the Pakistani secret police, [itself] an entity of the U.S. government. . . ."

—THOMAS HENEGHAN, heroic American, intelligence expert, federal whistleblower

Secondly, here is a list of facts nobody has ever disputed! If you think 9-11 was a "terrorist" attack, *think again on your own this time*, then explain these facts with the inconsistency of the "official stories."

None of the congressmen we contacted could refute any of these facts, so instead, they refused to even give us the courtesy of a reply. Much as with the so-called "9-11 Investigation," their attitude was/is, "If we can't explain away the facts, we'll just ignore the whole thing."

The 47-story Salomon Brothers structure, known as Building 7 in the WTC complex, collapsed late that afternoon. No planes hit it, the fires inside were very minor, yet it just took a nosedive at 5:23 p.m. The incident is not mentioned in the 9-11 Commission Report released in 2004.

It would be nice if someone would explain how it was that the 800 page Patriot Act was already written, printed and ready to be sent to Congress immediately after 9-11, when, before the event, there would have been no chance of its passage. Another coincidence?

As anyone with normal intelligence should be able to figure out, 9-11 was a faked attack that could not have happened without the Air Force standing down that day. A big problem for Americans, especially those suffering from Red, White & Blue Fever, is that their normal intelligence is muddled by deceptive TV pictures and stories from a news media cooperating with every government cover story.

A few months earlier a test was run of the technology used to fake the "attack."

April 23, 2001: A Global Hawk plane flies 22 hours from the U.S. to Australia without pilot or passengers. Says a Global Hawk manager, "The aircraft essentially flies itself, right from takeoff, right through to landing and even taxiing off the runway."

—[ITN, 4/24/01] (see 1998 and September 25, 2001)

(Hmmm, so contrary to the *NY Times* report saying that ". . . someday in the future we will be able to fly remote controlled planes across the waters." It had already been accomplished five months prior to 9-11.)

Remember the world class golfer Payne Stewart and when his plane went off course the year before 9-11? It took a total of 24 minutes to get two F-16s on him immediately and they stayed on him until he got to Missouri, then two more took over, and they stayed with him until he crashed in South Dakota. This was a single, privately owned aircraft mysteriously off course because of what proved to be an equipment malfunction and it took 24 minutes.

Yet for an hour and a half after two commercial airliners, *known to have been hi-jacked,* flew into the World Trade Center, nothing is done about two more zooming around the northeastern United States. NORAD—the North American Aerospace Command, the most sophisticated and sensitive defensive system on the planet—remains grounded.

Only one of three things is supposed to be necessary to trigger two F-16s being scrambled: 1.) Planes going off course; 2.) Loss of transponder contact; and 3.) Loss of radio contact.

On September 11, 2001, all three of these red flags waved at NORAD four different times within an hour and not one F-16 was ordered to take off. It became obvious that the orders were just the opposite. They were ordered not to take off. Yet 67 times during 2001, before September 11th, wayward aircraft were intercepted and escorted.

One of the wayward planes (Flight 93) was a third of the way across the country and turned back, yet no F-16's were scrambled.

Each one of these four planes flew over major military bases and into the most heavily defended airspace in America, and no F-16 was scrambled until it was far too late.

FEMA spokesman Tom Kenney stated on the Dan Rather show right after 9-11 that FEMA arrived in New York *Monday* night (September 10th) ready to spring into action Tuesday morning. Who called them in on Monday, the ghost of Jeanne Dixon?

ALL KINDS of FEMA and FBI "suits" were in the streets just minutes after the first "crash" "springing" into action. How did they know where to be and when? In a normal investigation, the first people the police look at are those who benefit from the crime. That certainly wasn't Arabs or Muslims in this case.

What about the men seen celebrating and videotaping the crashes from the top of that Israeli "moving systems" building as they occurred? They were Israelis. They were arrested and jailed but were allowed to silently slip out of the country a few months later. The federal judge responsible for their release at the time was Michael Mukasey, later appointed attorney general by George Bush.

There is only one logical explanation for their display of obvious foreknowledge of what was going to happen as it happened or why they were celebrating with such obvious joy—along with the owner of that "business" who fled back to Israel before he could be questioned. Yup, another Israeli.

Let us remember that Afghanistan and Iraq were attacked and hundreds of thousands of innocent people murdered on proven false "evidence."

Saudi Arabian TV and news agencies reported six (later discovered to be nine) of the men still alive who were supposed to have been on those planes. They were working in the Mideast right after their names were released by the FBI. These men were interviewed by several foreign news services after 9-11 but these interviews were never shown in the American "news"—not even by the "balanced" news of Fox.

A total of 233 passengers on four transcontinental jets, each about 25% filled? Never happens. No mail was reported lost.

No videotapes of the 233 passengers boarding any of the magic jets. Airport "security" at those airports was provided by another company out of Amsterdam.

In an April 19, 2002 speech delivered to the Commonwealth Club in San Francisco, FBI director Robert Mueller said that the purported hijackers, in his words, "left no paper trail." But then he seemingly contradicted himself by asserting, "Tickets, regardless of how or where purchased, would leave a paper trail."

But maybe he didn't contradict himself. Upon reflection we have to wonder if he was confirming that these passengers were actually mythical and never bought tickets at all. Even the mayor of Cleveland, Ohio was quoted in a next day's news story confirming that the famous United Airlines Flight 93 actually landed at his city's airport before reversing its course and heading back east to its eventual hole in western Pennsylvania. Did it stop, perhaps, at one of Ohio's Air Force bases to unload passengers, switch to a military aircraft and begin a remote-controlled piloting? Or were there never any passengers on board after the Cleveland landing?

So the question here to ponder is just who are the "evildoers." At this point, we would hope that you have figured out the answer to that.

And there is more from other publications:

"WMR has received another confirmation (bringing the total number to three) that United Flight 93, hijacked on the morning of September 11, 2001, was shot down over rural Pennsylvania by U.S. Air Force jets scrambled from Andrews Air Force Base in Maryland. There are also reports that one F-16 scrambled from Langley Air Force Base in Virginia returned to base minus one air-to-air missile but the National Security Agency CRITIC report specified the interceptors that downed United 93 took off from Andrews.

The third confirmation is from a National Security Agency (NSA) source also, as were the first two. In fact, a number of personnel who were on watch at the Meade Operations Center (MOC), which is a floor below the NSA's National Security Operations Center (NSOC), were aware that United 93 was brought down by an Air Force air-to-air missile. Personnel within **both** the MOC and NSOC had reported the doomed aircraft was shot down.

The 9-11 Commission, which is now known to have been influenced by Bush adviser Karl Rove and its Executive Director Phil Zelikow, never interviewed the on-duty signals intelligence personnel who were aware that United 93 was brought down by Air Force jets. The coverstory is that passengers on board the plane struggled with hijackers and flew the plane directly into the ground near Shanksville, Pennsylvania. Investigators have stressed that the eight-mile debris field left by the doomed aircraft proves the government's story is a hoax.

One exhausted researcher wrote: "I am 9-11 worn out. Never have I seen so much evidence of a crime being ignored. Not at Oklahoma City, not with the murder of Vince Foster. I can do no more. Take it or leave it, scoffer, I can do no more."

I, Pat Shannan, agree and continue to remind the world that we can lead the mule to knowledge, but we can't make him think.

Indeed. We know that there are those carriers of the Red, White & Blue Fever who will never have the eyes to see nor the ears to hear. Too bad. 9-11 is the crime of all centuries and it was committed by those who were supposed to be protecting us. Everything they ever told us about it was a lie, and I am reminded at this moment of the fears of Jim Garrison 40 years ago, after realizing that the federal government could be his enemy when necessary. He said, *"Huey Long once said, 'Fascism will come to America in the name of anti-fascism.' I'm afraid, based on my own long experience, that fascism will come to America in the name of national security."*

So are we.

CONCLUSION

I t has become evident, after a whole adult lifetime of observing
these and other cases, where cover-up has been the order of the day
rather than investigation and evidence-gathering, that the FBI has
embarked on a different mission from its original one of crime
solving. In nearly every major case of recent years, the FBI's motives have
almost immediately been shown to be that of "protector of the government" rather than "preserver of the truth."

One of the best examples of this back-handed activity has been the
harsh treatment of those who have attempted to expose the unlawful occupation of the White House by Barry Soetoro, aka Barack Obama.

After watching a dozen or more lawsuits challenging the natural
birth of the sitting president be quashed by the courts, Lt. Cmdr. (ret.)
Walt Fitzpatrick III, of Monroe County, Tennessee, took it a step further
by filing a criminal complaint in Knoxville's federal court charging
Obama with fraud and treason.

But instead of proceeding lawfully by at least initiating an investigation, U.S. Attorney for the Eastern District of Tennessee Russell Dedrick
phoned the Secret Service in Washington to report that Fitzpatrick "may
be a threat to the president."

After months of finding no satisfaction at the federal level, Fitzpatrick
tried to get his local grand jury to take a look at the case, but not only
was he not allowed an audience but found more corruption in the fact
that the "court appointed" foreman, Gary Pettway, had been sitting for
more than twenty consecutive years, in violation of a Tennessee law that
restricts anyone from sitting more than one year. So Fitzpatrick filed a
criminal complaint against Pettway and the Tennessee officials who had

been perpetuating this fraud on the people of Monroe County, Tennessee. After all, a court-appointed grand jury foreman is tantamount to a rubber stamp indictment of anyone "they" wish to indict.

But Fitzpatrick was frustrated again because the police chief and sheriff told him that they could not arrest Pettway without a warrant from the court, and he had already found out that no court was going to issue that order against itself.

So with no cooperation from law enforcement, Fitzpatrick attempted to affect a citizen's arrest upon Pettway at the courthouse but ended up getting himself bounced into jail for five days while "they" could figure out some charges to file on him.

Meanwhile, Darren Huff, Chaplain of the newly founded Georgia Militia near Atlanta, wanted to show support of Fitzpatrick and the law, so he and a few others drove to Madisonville, Tennessee a few weeks later for Fitzpatrick's arraignment.

Huff's black pickup truck, easily identified by the large gold letters and insignia of the "Oath Keepers" painted on its doors, was stopped by five patrol cars from state, county and city law enforcement outside of Madisonville. He was detained for 90 minutes while the police attempted to have him surrender his legal firearms—one rifle and one pistol. Huff refused to do so but did agree to lock both in his tool box in the truck until after the hearing. The police released him to proceed to the courthouse. There were no incidents. Huff had never planned any "incidents."

Ten days later, the federal court in Knoxville indicted Huff on five counts, eventually reduced to two grasping-at-straws charges of "crossing a state line with firearms with the intent to incite a riot" and the even more trumped-up "selling firearms without a license." Huff has never done anything of the sort, but if a hand-picked federal jury can be made to believe that he did, he could get five years on this count alone.

As this book goes to press, Fitzpatrick and Huff are facing indictments on multiple charges at both the federal and state levels in Tennessee. These are the lengths to which the judiciary will stretch in order to protect a lie and preserve what has replaced "of the people, by the people, and for the people" in this once-great nation.

Meanwhile, its tactics are growing more vicious by the month.

Also currently, an Idaho lawyer sits in jail awaiting a trial on charges of "murder for hire." The FBI claims it has the voice recordings of Edgar J. Steele, obtained by a Confidential Informant, plotting the murder of his wife and mother-in-law. Steele's family and friends believe these to be contrived by hi-tech fabrication..

However, after a month in jail, Steele finally heard one of those recordings and became terrified. He told friends on a jailhouse visit that he heard himself say some of the most "bone-chilling" threats anyone could imagine, but that he never said anything like that to anyone.

His friends and family suspect that he has been framed, and the evidence is reflecting just that. Steele made himself a target of the system by defending—often *pro bono*—White separatists and those accused of "hate crimes" as well as his outspoken distaste for the system that created such statutes that prosecute crimes without victims.

Indeed, with the modern technology of computer "voice-morphing" at its finger tips, this may be the FBI's latest version of evidence tampering and crime creation – an infraction that ever since the days of J. Edgar Hoover has never been beneath this or any government agency that can operate with impunity.

And of course, the cooperative news media are constantly throwing its darts, referring to Fitzpatrick as a "hatriot" (i.e., "hate-triot") and Steele, predictably, as "anti-Semitic."

The federal judiciary boasts a 97% conviction rate, but what is not generally known is that probably 97% (my arbitrary guess) of those 97% are achieved through plea bargains. By threatening a defendant with 15 years in prison for convictions on the aggregate counts if he goes to trial versus a year or two for pleading guilty without the headache and expense of a trial, it usually does not take long for the defendant to accept the discounted rate.

It also does not take long for honest men such as Fitzpatrick, Huff and Steele to develop an enmity for such a system and all of those who operate it. They begin to realize that everything they have ever been told was a lie.

—Pat Shannan
September 2010

Everything They*
Ever Told Me Was a Lie
VOLUME ONE

Investigative journalist, author and radio show host Pat Shannan has been in pursuit of the truth for nearly half a century. Intrigued by the deception and on-going cover-up of the JFK assassination, he began to notice a similar pattern in the 1968 murders of Martin Luther King and Robert F. Kennedy. Then he found altered and intentionally fabricated FBI official reports regarding these and other cases and began to notice the cooperative news media ignoring blatant and pertinent facts as well.

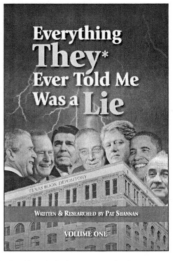

The films of Ronald Reagan exiting the Washington Hilton clearly show Secret Service Agent Tim McCarthy being shot by someone other than John Hinckley, Jr. And what are the odds that the greatest potential beneficiary of Reagan's demise would be the close friend and business associate of John Hinckley, Sr.? Why did the wounded Reagan arrive at the hospital 15 minutes after Jim Brady, when his limo left the scene five minutes before Brady's ambulance?

How could Arthur Bremer fire seven shots from a five-shot revolver the day he nearly killed Gov. George Wallace and three innocent bystanders in 1972? Why was Pat Tillman murdered in Afghanistan in 2004?

Shannan has long maintained that the hidden power behind the expansion of the central government has been the unconstitutional use of legal tender that is produced at will, and herein proves his case. He also shows that government plots survive because of little or no investigation, and only through the aid of a cooperative news media can such ridiculous conspiracy theories as the 9-11 official story not only survive but thrive.

Shannan submitted so much suppressed information from so many historic cases that we have divided it into two books, the second of which we are eagerly compiling for a Volume II publication in the very near future.

Order copies of *Everything They* Ever Told Me Was a Lie*—Volume I (softcover, 280 pages, #EAL, $30 plus $3 S&H inside the U.S.) from AMERICAN FREE PRESS, 645 Pennsylvania Avenue SE, #100, Washington, D.C. 20003. To charge call toll free 1-888-699-6397 and use Visa, MasterCard, AmEx or Discover. Outside the U.S. please email juliafost@gmail.com for best S&H rates to your nation. Interested in more than one copy at a discount? Email Julia at the email address listed above.

FRONTMAN

OBAMA'S DARKEST SECRETS REVEALED

I n 2008, Barack Obama became the face of hope and change. Yet lurking behind the scenes is a host of personages who long ago selected this man to forward their global agenda. *Frontman* reveals the actual powers behind his throne: Bilderberg plotters, Zionist handlers, global financiers and Marxist activists.

Critics have called Obama an empty suit, but in actuality, the suit is filled by a cabal of men and women whose primary goal is to radically transform the United States. To cover their tracks, an air of secrecy has enveloped Obama's past, including his birth records, college transcripts and employment history.

While other books merely scratch the surface, *Frontman* tears away the deceptive smoke and mirrors that have been used to propel him into the Oval Office. By far the most comprehensive expose to date, President Barack Obama can no longer hide behind a façade that had been carefully created and orchestrated over the past few decades by people who are still pulling his strings. The title says it all: America's commander-in-chief is merely a figurehead for much more powerful people and forces.

Now, at long last, one of the most brutally honest portraits ever presented shows how our nation is being controlled by unseen hands that are leading us perilously close to disaster.

FRONTMAN: Softcover, 112 pages, #O, $20. Available from AMERICAN FREE PRESS, 645 Pennsylvania Avenue SE, #100, Washington, D.C. 20003. Add $3 S&H inside the U.S. Call 1-888-699-6397 toll free to charge. Outside U.S. add $12 S&H for 1-4 copies.

9/11

WHAT REALLY HAPPENED

The official story of the Sept. 11, 2001 attacks on the United States is well known to most Americans. According to the U.S. government and the mainstream media, a group of 19 members of al Qaeda, a Muslim group led by Osama bin Laden, hijacked four U.S. airliners. Three were flown into buildings (the World Trade Center North and South towers and the Pentagon), and one crashed in Pennsylvania after a heroic effort by the passengers to regain control of the plane. That's the federal story.

But what facts are there to support this official scenario? As there was no debris from any airliner found at the Pentagon or at Shanksville, there is little to back up the claims there. And although most people will admit planes hit the World Trade Center towers, it is the strange collapse of those buildings and another massive skyscraper nearby that still confounds researchers and 9/11 skeptics.

In *9/11: What Really Happened*, Ed Whitney (author of *The Controllers: The Secret Rulers of the World*) explains what did and did not happen and presents a much more plausible scenario. In the end, Whitney convinces readers that the truth, in the case of 9/11, has been carefully kept from the U.S. public for nefarious reasons. Unlike other books, this one gives you what most likely happened.

Softcover, booklet, saddle-stitched, 61 pages, $10. Bulk prices: 1-9 copies are $10 each; 10-49 copies are $7.50 each. 50 or more are reduced to just $5 each. Add $2 per booklet for S&H in the U.S.; $12 S&H outside U.S.

Order from AMERICAN FREE PRESS, 645 Pennsylvania Avenue SE, #100, Washington, D.C. 20003. Call toll free 1-888-699-NEWS to charge.

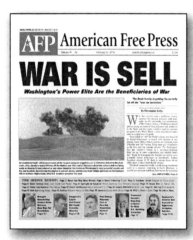

DEBUNKING 9-11
100 Unanswered Questions About Sept. 11

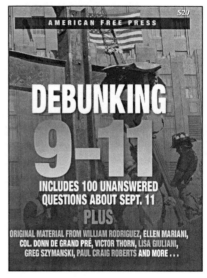

SUBSCRIBE TO *AMERICAN FREE PRESS* NEWSPAPER AND GET FREE GIFTS!

AMERICAN FREE PRESS ORDERING COUPON

Item#	Description/Title	Qty	Cost Ea.	Total
			SUBTOTAL	
S&H: $3 inside U.S. per book. Outside U.S. $12 for one book				
Send a 1-year subscription to AFP for $59 plus 1 free book*				
Send a 2-year subscription to AFP for $99 plus 2 free books**				
			TOTAL	

*NOTE ABOUT FREE GIFTS: For a one-year subscription to *American Free Press* newspaper ($59), we'll send you one free copy of AFP's *CITIZENS HANDBOOK*. **For a two-year subscription we'll send you AFP's *CITIZENS HANDBOOK* PLUS *9/11: WHAT REALLY HAPPENED*—$16 in free publications (domestic USA only).

PAYMENT   ❏ CHECK/MO   ❏ VISA   ❏ MC   ❏ AMEX   ❏ DISCOVER

Card # _____

Expiration Date _____ Signature _____

PSB810

CUSTOMER INFORMATION:

NAME _____

ADDRESS _____

CIty/STATE/ZIP _____

RETURN WITH PAYMENT TO: AMERICAN FREE PRESS, 645 Pennsylvania Avenue SE, Suite 100, Washington, D.C. 20003. Call 1-888-699-NEWS (6397) toll free to charge a subscription or books to Visa or MasterCard.

AFP Citizens Handbook
With Rulebook for Jurors

Back by popular demand in a new, larger format, the *AFP Citizens Handbook* is loaded with vital information for every American—from elementary school kids to seniors.

Besides the full texts of the Declaration of Independence, Constitution and Bill of Rights, the *AFP Citizens Handbook* also dedicates a key portion to our rights as jurors. This 9-page section has been requested again and again by readers and supporters who find this information invaluable when called for jury duty. This

special 2009 edition also includes George Washington's Farewell Address and Patrick Henry's reconstructed "Give Me Liberty" speech.

The *AFP Citizens Handbook* (softcover, 57 pages, #CHB, $6 with full color cover) is available from AMERICAN FREE PRESS, 645 Pennsylvania Avenue SE, Suite 100, Washington, D.C. 20003. Call AFP toll free at 1-888-699-NEWS to charge copies to Visa or MasterCard. Add $1 S&H per booklet.

BULK DISCOUNT PRICING:
1 copy is $6
2-5 copies are $5 each
6-9 copies are $4 each
10-49 copies are $3.50 each
50-99 copies are just $3 each
100 or more $2.50 each

SUBSCRIBE TO *AMERICAN FREE PRESS* NEWSPAPER AND GET FREE GIFTS!

AMERICAN FREE PRESS ORDERING COUPON

Item#	Description/Title	Qty	Cost Ea.	Total
	SUBTOTAL			
S&H: $5 inside U.S. for one book. Outside U.S. $11 for one book				
Send a 1-year subscription to AFP for $59 plus 1 free book*				
Send a 2-year subscription to AFP for $99 plus 2 free books**				
	TOTAL			

*NOTE ABOUT FREE GIFTS: For a one-year subscription to *American Free Press* newspaper ($59), we'll send you one free copy of AFP's *CITIZENS HANDBOOK*. **For a two-year subscription we'll send you AFP's *CITIZENS HANDBOOK* PLUS *9/11: WHAT REALLY HAPPENED*—$16 in free publications (domestic USA only).

PAYMENT ❏ CHECK/MO ❏ VISA ❏ MC ❏ AMEX ❏ DISCOVER

Card # _____

Expiration Date _____ Signature _____

PSB810

CUSTOMER INFORMATION:

NAME _____

ADDRESS _____

CIty/STATE/ZIP _____

RETURN WITH PAYMENT TO: AMERICAN FREE PRESS, 645 Pennsylvania Avenue SE, Suite 100, Washington, D.C. 20003. Call 1-888-699-NEWS (6397) toll free to charge a subscription or books to Visa or MasterCard.

The Great Escape of John Wilkes Booth
And the Conspiracy of Silence Surrounding the Most Infamous Act in U.S. History

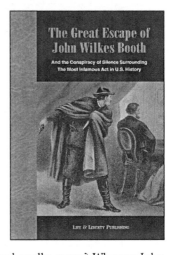

The conventional wisdom is that the assassin of President Abraham Lincoln—John Wilkes Booth—was shot in the neck and killed in a barn on the Garrett farm in Virginia just 12 days after the murder. But truth is always stranger than fiction. In this booklet longtime investigative author Pat Shannan and others detail a wealth of evidence showing how Booth actually escaped, lived a long life and who the man in the barn really was. Once you read this booklet, you'll never look at the Lincoln assassination—or American history—in the same way ever again. Who was in on the high-level plot to kill Lincoln? Who was Lafayette Baker and what did his cryptic poem, written in the margin of a military manual, really mean? Who was John Stevenson and was his deathbed confession real or fiction? What happened to Booth's accomplices? Who were the Knights of the Golden Circle and how did they fit into the plot? Were members of Lincoln's own cabinet in on the assassination scheme? What about John Wilkes Booth's last will and testament? Who was Izola D'Arcy Booth and what inside secrets did she hold? What happened to Booth's diaries? Booth's gold? How could the body of "Booth" been so easily misidentified? How could all of this been kept secret for so long—and why? Much more. Softcover booklet, 76 pages, *$10*. Available from LIFE & LIBERTY PUBLISHING, P.O. Box 2770, Stafford, VA 22555. Add $2 S&H per booklet. Check or money order drawn on U.S. banks only. Call 1-888-698-8706.